RUSSIA-UKRAINE WAR

The Conflict and its Global Impact

RUSSIA-UKRAINE WAR

THE CONFLICT AND ITS GLOBAL IMPACT

AJAY SINGH

PENTAGON PRESS LLP

First published in 2023 by

PENTAGON PRESS LLP
206, Peacock Lane, Shahpur Jat
New Delhi-110049, India
Contact: 011-64706243

Typeset in Adobe Garamond, 11.5 Point
Printed by Aegean Offset Printers, Greater Noida, U.P.

ISBN: 978-93-90095-71-1 (HB)

www.pentagonpress.in

Mars ... The God of War;
May his shadow never fall upon this Earth

CONTENTS

Major Characters

UKRAINE

Volodymyr Zelensky

The 44-year-old President of Ukraine was a former comedian and actor (one of his most famous roles was of a simple man who is catapulted into the position of president and then changes his country by 'being good'). His inspiring leadership helped Ukraine stand firm in the war. When the USA offered a helicopter to fly him out of Kyiv, his reply, "I need ammunition, not a ride" became a wartime classic. His insistence on standing firm and recapturing "every inch of occupied territory" helped build morale and won the Western nations over completely to his side.

Olena Zelensky

The First Lady of Ukraine, she stood by her husband, using social media and personal appearances to boost Ukrainian morale and the country's image.

General Valerii Zaluzhnyi

Commander-in-Chief of the Ukrainian Armed Forces. He used his meagre resources to defend a 1,800-kilometre long front and fight a delaying battle for months. He also skilfully coordinated the Ukrainian counter-offensive that recaptured vital territory in a matter of weeks and orchestrated a reversal to the war.

Oleksiy Reznikov

The Minister of Defence since November 2021, he helped get Western arms and equipment and funnel it to the troops, while coordinating the war effort. He is also credited with mobilizing reservists at short notice to build up the Ukrainian forces.

Roman Hrybov

The Ukrainian soldier on Snake Island who defied a Russian warship by telling it to "go f*** yourself". Was later awarded the Hero of Ukraine medal.

'The Ghost of Kyiv'

A MiG 29 fighter pilot who was credited with shooting down six Russian fighter jets in a single day and then went on to get 40 more kills. It was later proved to be fictitious.

RUSSIA

Vladimir Putin

The former KGB spy, who considered the break-up of the Soviet Union to be "The greatest geopolitical catastrophe of the 20th century". He has been President of Russia since 2012 (served as Prime Minister 2008–2012) and his vision of taking Russia to the glory of erstwhile USSR drove him to the war. However the reverses have weakened his position—both internally and internationally—and made his response even more violent and unpredictable.

Sergei Lavrov

The Foreign Minister of Russia since 2004, he is reportedly very close to Putin, and shares his hard-line views. He has been Russia's spokesperson, justifying the war in each forum and also resorting to nuclear and escalatory threats as clear warnings to the Western powers not to get directly involved.

Sergei Shoigu

Very close to Putin, he has been Russia's Defence Minister since 2012, but was reportedly side-lined due to his ineffective direction of the war. One of the senior commanders also suggested that he should "be shot for incompetence."

General Valery Gerasimov

The Chief of General Staff of the Russian Army, he has coordinated the war effort since inception, but was unable to attain complete victory.

General Aleksandr Dvornikov

A veteran of the Syrian and Chechen wars, he was called in as an overall commander to coordinate Russian forces in the Ukraine war. He gave it new direction since March 2022 and shifted the focus away from Kyiv and towards Donbas and the South. His tactics attained slow and steady gains initially, but was stung by reverses following the Ukrainian counter-offensive.

OTHER PLAYERS

President Joe Biden

The 46th President of the United States, he has provided moral and materiel aid to Ukraine to enable it to continue the fight, at the same time making it clear that the USA will not get directly involved. He helped keep NATO and the Western allies united, in the battle against Russia, and staved off Russia's ill-concealed nuclear threats. Has a personal animosity towards Putin, which reflects in his stance.

Jens Stoltenberg

The Secretary-General of NATO since 2014. Under him, the movement to permit Ukraine to join NATO intensified (though Ukraine has not been granted membership as yet). He stood firm in refusing to grant Russia veto over NATO membership during the pre-war negotiations. NATO now has been galvanized and strengthened by the Russian invasion.

Olaf Scholz

The German Chancellor tried to balance Germany's requirement of Russian gas with the need to stave off Russian aggression. Initially reluctant to help Ukraine (the initial offering of aid was only 5,000 helmets) German support grew as the war progressed and Ukrainian gains intensified. He also sharply increased the defence budget thus bolstering Germany's preparedness in case of future aggression.

Xi Jinping

The Chinese Premier called Putin "my closest friend" and promised a "friendship without limits", when they met at the Beijing Olympics just a fortnight before the launch of Russia's invasion. Although China has stood by Russia in the UN and other forums, its support has waned as the war stalled and floundered. Xi has similar visions for his country, and the outcome of Putin's invasion could be a litmus test for his own plans.

Prime Minister Narendra Modi

The nuanced stance that PM Modi took for India during the Ukraine war was based purely on national interests and paid rich dividends. India's position, spearheaded by the dynamic Foreign Minister S Jaishankar, ensured that we could balance ties with the West and still do business with Russia. PM Modi's call to Putin during the SCO summit that "today's era is not an era of war" was indicative of India's desire and willingness to help bring the war to an end.

TIMELINE OF EVENTS

Background

10th Century: Russian and Ukraine are part of the Kievan Rus Empire, centred around modern-day Kyiv.

1783: Russia formally annexes Ukraine and amalgamates it with the Russian Empire.

1917–1921: The Russian Revolution.

1922: The Communist Party takes over. Russia; Ukraine and other states merge to form the USSR.

1941-1945: World War II. Nazi Germany invades the Soviet Union. The greatest battles are fought on Ukrainian and Russian soil. The battles of Kiev and Kharkiv see a loss of over 800,000 Soviet and German soldiers.

1945-1991: The post-war years. Ukraine and Russia are the two main states of the Soviet Union and are in the forefront of the Cold War.

1991: The Soviet Union collapses and its member-states, including Russia and Ukraine become separate states.

24 August 1991: Ukraine becomes an independent nation. The date is henceforth celebrated as Ukraine's Independence Day.

1991-2004: Ukraine and Russia remain close with Ukraine tilting heavily towards Russia.

2004: Pro-Russian candidate Victor Yanukovych is declared President of Ukraine amidst allegations of vote-rigging. Popular protests called the Orange Revolution erupt. He is forced to resign and re-elections take place.

2005: Pro-western candidate Victor Yushchenko elected as President of Ukraine. Ukraine veers towards EU and indicates it wants to join NATO.

2013: Pro-Russian candidate Yanukovych again wins the presidential elections. Suspends talks for joining EU and veers back towards Moscow. Riots and protests erupt in Kyiv against his decision.

February 2014: Yanukovych removed from power by protests. Pro-Russian and anti-Russian rallies and riots erupt across the country.

March-April 2014: Armed men seize the Parliament building in Crimea and declare independence from Ukraine. Using this as a pretext, Russia annexes Crimea.

April 2014: Pro-Russian separatists in the Donbas region of Luhansk and Donetsk provinces declare independence. Fighting erupts between separatists and the Ukrainian army. Russian forces actively aid the separatists but deny it.

April 2014 onwards: Fighting between separatists and Ukrainian forces begins in the Donbas region. Over 18,000 fighters killed on both sides in the fighting which continued for over eight years.

February 2015: The Minsk Agreement is signed between Ukraine, Russia and the separatist groups of the Luhansk People's Republic and the Donetsk People's Republic. A ceasefire comes in place, but both sides accuse each other of violating the agreement and tensions remain.

2019: Volodymyr Zelensky, a former comic actor, is elected President. Promises to join NATO and EU and has it enshrined in the Ukrainian constitution.

January 2021: Move to join NATO intensifies. Russia protests and warns Ukraine against it, citing a threat to its own security. The warnings are ignored.

March 2021: Russian troops are inducted from the Siberian border and concentrated along Eastern Ukraine borders for 'training exercises.'

August-October 2021: Russian troops conduct exercises in Belarus. They remain on Belarus soil. They are now poised to enter Ukraine from the north as well and directly threaten Kyiv.

December 2021: Russia demands that NATO pulls back its troops and offensive weaponry from Eastern Europe and provide written guarantees that Ukraine will never become a part of NATO. NATO refuses to accept Russian demands.

January 2022: Talks between Russia, Ukraine, the USA and European leaders to defuse the situation. Telephonic talks between President Joe Biden and Putin and also the Russian Foreign Minister and US Secretary of State fail.

Early February 2022: Intelligence agencies indicate a likely Russian invasion. The USA and other Western embassy staff are evacuated from Ukraine.

10 February 2022: Putin attends the Olympic Games in Beijing as a special guest. Meets Xi Jinping and the two leaders announce a "friendship that has no limits".

21 February 2022: Russia recognizes the provinces of Luhansk and Donetsk in the Donbas region as 'independent'

24 February 2022: Putin authorizes 'Special Military Operations'. At 5 in the morning, Russian troops begin their invasion of Ukraine.

The War

24 February 2022: Russia launches 'Special Military Operations' in Ukraine and attacks along three main prongs, (with an additional thrust in the Donbas). Kyiv declares Martial Law. Russian airborne operations try to capture Hostomel airport near Kyiv in the first day of the war itself but are pushed back by Ukrainian forces with heavy casualties.

27 February 2022: Russian troops advance from the north towards Kyiv, from the north east towards Kharkiv, from the east in the Donbas, and from the south in Crimea moving towards the major cities.

28 February 2022: A 64-kilometre-long Russian convoy approaches Kyiv from Belarus. Inexplicably, the column halts for a few days when it is just 30 kilometres from the capital.

02 March 2022: Kherson surrenders. The first major city to fall. The cities of Kharkiv, Melitopol, Mariupol, Sumy, Chernihev and others are surrounded and heavily bombarded, but hold on. Russia is unable to capture any other major town, stalling its advance.

First Week March 2022: The Russian convoy moves again. Russian troops approach Kyiv from the north and north east in two prongs and begin isolating it from both sides of the Dnieper River. The suburbs of Bucha, Irpin and Brovary are captured and the city is subjected to heavy artillery and missile strikes.

17 March 2022: Lyiv, a town just 20 kilometres from the Polish border, where Western arms are received, is targeted by air and missile strikes, which destroys vast quantities of newly-received Western equipment. Russia uses Kinzhal hypersonic missiles in a clear warning that it is willing to escalate the conflict.

End March 2022: Russia abruptly announces a withdrawal from the Kyiv sector. Its troops move back from Kyiv with reports of atrocities and mass graves being discovered in the suburbs of Bucha and Irpin. Russia states that it has withdrawn from Kyiv to focus on the Donbas which was "the original aim of the campaign".

First/Second Week April 2022: Russia launches Phase II of the offensive. Operations intensify all along the south and east. In the south, the Russians make headway along the entire coastal belt along the Sea of Azov, and surround the port cities of Melitopol, Mariupol and Mykolaiv. Russian troops reach as far as Zaporizhzhia in the north.

14 April 2022: MOSKVA, the flagship of the Russian Black Sea Fleet, is hit by two Neptune anti-ship missiles and is sunk. This is a major loss to Russian naval capabilities and prestige.

17 April 2022: Mariupol, the gateway to the South, falls after an 82-day siege. The defenders of the 36 Marine Brigade and the Azov Battalion are forced out of the city and take refuge in the Azovstol steel plant till they are forced to surrender on 17 May. This is a major success for the Russians and gives them control over the entire coastal areas up to Kherson.

Mid May 2022: Ukrainian forces counter attack in the north east and retake the town of Kharkiv, pushing the Russians back across the border. This is the first major success of the war and Ukrainian units reach as far as the Russian frontier.

May 2022: Russian attacks intensify all along the Donbas as Russia shifts focus there.

June-July 2022: Russia makes gains in the Luhansk province of the Donbas in slow but steady actions, supported by heavy fire power. The advance is only around two or three kilometres per day, but the major towns and vital villages are captured one by one. Izium, Kupyansk and other communication centres all fall into Russian hands.

Early June 2022: Sievierodonetsk, the key city of the Donbas, falls. Russians gain control over all of Luhansk province. They now shift their focus towards Donetsk province to the south as part of their aim to seize all of Donbas.

Early August 2022: Ukrainian troops launch an offensive in the south towards Kherson. It cannot be recaptured, but Russian troops are pushed eastwards behind the Dnieper River. The counter-offensive recaptures around 500 square kilometres of occupied territory, and also forces Russia to halt actions in the east and transfer troops to the south to stabilize the situation there.

09 August 2022: Attack on Saki air base destroys eight fighter jets, almost half of Russia's naval aviation resources. This strike, almost 100 kilometres deep in the Crimea is not admitted by Ukraine, but underscores its new-found long range strike capabilities.

12 August 2022: The area around Zaporizhzhia sees heavy fighting during Ukraine's counter-attack and the nuclear plant comes under artillery fire raising fears of a nuclear radiation leak. Both sides accuse the other of the firing.

24 August 2022: Ukraine celebrates its Independence Day amidst attacks from Russia. The war completes six months.

End August–early September 2022: Ukraine secretly prepares for its own counter-offensive, beefed up by the arrival of trained reservists and sophisticated equipment from the West. US intelligence provides vital information of the gaps in Russian positions. Russia remains unaware of the impending offensive till it is too late.

05 September 2022: Ukrainian counter-offensive begins in Kharkiv region and makes stunning headway. In less than a fortnight, they recapture around 6,000 square kilometres of occupied territory, and retake the important towns of Izium, Kupyansk and Balakliya. Russian troops are pushed back to the Oskil River. This offensive also puts paid to Russian plans to take over all of Donbas.

21 September 2022: President Putin orders partial military mobilization to call up 300,000 reservists who have served in the army. This is seen as a sign that the war is not going well and leads to thousands of men fleeing Russia to avoid military service.

23-27 September 2022: Russia conducts a referendum in the provinces of Luhansk, Donetsk, Kherson and Zaporizhzhia (approximately 15 per cent of Ukraine's territory) asking "Are you in favour of secession from Ukraine and joining the Russian Federation?" The referendum was termed as 'sham and illegitimate' but as per Russian reports, 93 per cent in Zaporizhzhia, 87 per cent in Kherson, 98 per cent in Luhansk, and 99 per cent in Donetsk voted to join Russia, setting the stage for their formal annexation.

26-29 September 2022: Explosions rupture the gas pipelines Nord Stream I and Nord Stream II, carrying gas to Europe. Both sides accuse the other of sabotage

03 October 2022: Putin signs a decree to formally amalgamate the regions of Luhansk, Donetsk, Kherson and Zaporizhzhia into Russia. This illegal annexation is not recognized by any other nation.

04 October 2022: Ukrainian troops follow up their counter-offensive with the capture of Lyman, denying the Russians a major logistical base. The offensive in the south also makes headway.

08 October 2022: A truck laden with explosives blows up on Kerch bridge, the crucial 19-kilometre-long bridge linking Russia with Crimea.

10-15 October 2022: Russia responds by carrying out a series of missile and drone attacks in Ukraine targeting its power and water infrastructure. Over 30 per cent of Ukraine's power stations are destroyed.

End October–Early November 2022: The Ukrainian counter offensive in the South makes headway. Recaptures areas along the west bank of the Dnipro River and approach Kherson

12 November 2022: Recapture of Kherson. A major victory for Ukraine.

November–December 2022: Both sides consolidate defensive positions with onset of winter.

PREFACE

With the Russian invasion of Ukraine on 24 February 2022, war returned to Europe after 70 years. Since 1945, the continent had not seen any large-scale fighting, as the traditional arena shifted towards Asia and Africa. This war revisited the sites of some of the historical battlegrounds of World War II, following its ebb and flow and matching the same long-drawn timelines.

What exactly did Putin hope to attain with this war? Yes, Russian security concerns at Ukraine joining NATO was the major factor. There is no doubt that if Ukraine joined NATO, the alliance would come to Russia's doorstep, and from its soil, missiles could hit Moscow in three or four minutes. NATO's blatant expansion to the east, in spite of promises not to do so, was the major cause of the war. On hindsight, Russian security concerns should have been taken into account. No less a personality as Henry Kissinger, the doyen of strategists, warned successive US Presidents that a NATO expansion and a disregard for Russian concerns would create a backlash. When the backlash came, none expected such a violent one. In spite of the Russian build-up, most expected that a closed-door solution would be found, in which Russia would be given some concessions and would back down, for the time being at least.

However, the scale of the invasion took the world by surprise. It was expected that Russian action would come in the east and south, directed largely towards Donbas, the scene of fighting since 2014. Instead, it attacked all along the 2,400-kilometre-long frontier, including the northern border with Belarus and even headed for Kyiv. Though much is made of the Russian withdrawal from Kyiv, that operation was actually quite a brilliant and audacious one. Had Russian paratroopers succeeded in capturing Antonov airfield, just 30 kilometres from Kyiv, the course of the war would have been different and they could have entered the capital in the first few days itself. However, the rapid Ukrainian reaction denied them the airfield and the ground offensive towards it ultimately failed. That denied them the swift victory, they were hoping for. The Ukrainians fought back determinedly to hold back the Russian thrusts and the war entered a slow phase of attrition.

The second phase of the Russian attacks in the period from April to August has often been glossed over. That was the time when the Russians focused on the south and the east and, in spite of heavy casualties, captured area almost 200 kilometres deep along a 1,200-kilometre swathe from Kharkiv in the northeast to Melitopol in the south—over a fifth of Ukraine's prime land. Like the Germans, who occupied much of the Soviet Union (including all of Ukraine) in 1941-42, they discovered that holding it was more difficult than occupying it. A 'referendum' was held in the occupied provinces of Kherson, Zaporizhzhia, Luhansk and Donetsk to formally amalgamate them into Russia. That 'referendum' or amalgamation of Ukrainian territory into Russia has not been accepted by the rest of the world, but it could just become a *fait accompli.* The captured areas would become part of Russia in much the same manner that Crimea did after its annexation in 2014.

The Ukrainians have not taken it lying down. They have proved themselves to be brave and determined fighters, fighting for their homeland. Their counter-offensive in September in the south towards Kherson and in the northeast from Kharkiv recaptured lost territories in weeks, which the Russians had taken months to capture. It was a brilliantly executed counter-stroke which pushed the Russians on the back foot, and raised the distinct possibility of a Russian defeat in the war—and it not a defeat, at least the improbability of a Russian victory.

The war seems to be settling into a stalemate. Both sides have dug down in fortified and well defended positions which are difficult to breach. The conflict in the Donbas has raged since 2014, and been in a stalemate for almost eight years with Russian-sponsored separatists and the Ukrainian forces holding positions along a roughly delineated 'Line of Control.' It is likely that a new Line of Control will come up between Ukraine and Russia along which the war will continue in a state of 'frozen conflict.'

However, it is not just the military aspects of the conflict. No other war in recent times, not even the ill-fated US invasion of Afghanistan and Iraq, has impacted the world in so many ways. The economic costs of this war are tremendous. It is not just the damage caused to Ukraine and Russia, which is estimated to be around $ 600 billion; it has virtually touched every nation on the planet. Energy and grain shortages have put half a billion people at risk of food-scarcity and could plunge the world into a recession. Russia's cutting off gas supplies to Europe in return for the sanctions imposed upon it, heralds a cold, bleak winter, which could test Western resolve. Of course, the humanitarian costs of the war are incalculable. Over 6 million refugees have been created, the largest number of displaced people since World War II, and some of Ukraine's most beautiful cities lie in ruins.

At the time of writing, November 2022, there is no clear end in sight. There are different ways in which the war could end—by a victory for Ukraine in which it pushes Russia back to its February 2022 boundaries; by a victory for Russia in which they hold Ukrainian territory successfully and force a negotiated solution on their terms; a stalemate with both sides holding on to their positions where the war goes on interminably in a state of 'Frozen Conflict'; or even a horrendous escalation in which NATO and other countries enter the war leading to another world war. In this case, with both sides bristling with nuclear weapons, the 'Armageddon Scenario' is glaringly plausible.

This book explores all these aspects and looks at the impact on the global power structure and on India. We are grateful to the panel of experts who have shared their views and provided deep insights on different facets of the war. We are also grateful to the Institute for the Study of War and '*The Economist*' and other sources from where the maps used in this book have been taken. We have tried to trace the course of the war, from the beginning to the present state, and the direction it could take. In the fluid ongoing state, it is difficult to discern how it could end. After all, a war which one thought would be over in a fortnight has continued for over eight months, and could carry on for some time to come. Like the World War, it will change Europe irrevocably, leaving its impact across much of the world…, and changing the course of the 21st century.

Ajay Singh

December 2022

New Delhi

1

THE BACKDROP TO WAR

"Russia and Ukraine at War – It is inconceivable."

—Mikhail Gorbachev

The Conjoined History of Russia and Ukraine

When Russia invaded Ukraine at 5 a.m. on 24 February 2022, full-scale conventional war revisited Europe after almost seven decades. At the heart of the war lies the intertwined history and geography of Russia and Ukraine.

Ukraine occupies a unique place in Europe. Second only to Russia in size, it lies in the centre of Europe with the massive land mass of Russia to its east and the states of Poland, Romania and Moldova to the west. Its unique position gives it control over both Eastern and Western Europe and its shoreline and ports allow it to dominate the Sea of Azov and the Black Sea. Its rich fertile soil provides most of the world's wheat and corn. This rich land, with its vibrant culture, provides a buffer between Russia and Western Europe and has been wooed by both, though it has traditionally been a part of Russia and has always been inclined towards it.

The two nations have a conjoined history going back to the 10th century. At that time, Russia, Ukraine and Belarus were all part of the Kievan Rus—the medieval region comprising the lands of the three nations which was centred around the area of modern-day Kyiv. Kyiv is called "the cradle of Russian civilization" and has influenced Russian culture as much as Moscow itself. Over the millennia, the Russian, the Belorussian and the Kievan empires came together and drifted apart, but still remained close socially and culturally. It wasn't till the 18th century, when Russia emerged as the strongest imperial power of Europe and formally annexed Ukraine in 1783 that Ukraine became part of Russia and with the intermingling of population and culture literally became one. Even then, the Russian Empire traditionally considered the Ukrainians (and Belarusians) as ethnically Russian and referred to them as "little Russians"—a condescending view that was opposed by many Ukrainians who wanted to preserve their own distinct identity.

With the eruption of the Russian Revolution in 1917-21, the Communist Party of Ukraine, joined hands with the Communist Party of Russia and willingly merged (with other Caucasian states) to form the USSR in 1922. Ukraine, with its rich granaries and mineral wealth, was the bread basket of the Soviet Union, but it paid a heavy price for it. In the 'Thirties, Stalin set out to privatize farms and convert its vast agricultural lands for industry, in the process unleashing the great famine of 1932-33 which claimed over three million lives in Russia and Ukraine. That holocaust still lingers in the Ukrainian consciousness and even today, Ukraine has a name for it—The Holodomor famine, or killing by starvation.

Ukraine was in the front lines during World War II. When the German armies crossed the frontier into the Soviet Union in May 1941, the first battles of the war were fought around the Ukrainian front. German panzers cut through the flat countryside and encircled Kyiv and Kharkiv (then Kiev and Kharkov) in wide envelopments that decimated over 700,000 Soviet soldiers in the first three months of the war. In fact, though we remember the titanic battles of Moscow and Stalingrad, the major battles of the Eastern front were fought on Ukrainian soil (both during the German advance and their subsequent retreat) and it was the Ukrainian people that suffered most in the carnage. Many of the sites of this war—Kyiv, Kharkiv, Crimea, the Dnieper River and others find an echo in the Great War. In many cases the two combatants (although one nation then) re-fought the battles on the same soil on which they had once fought another adversary.

For over 70 years, Russia and Ukraine shared a conjoined history as part of the USSR, including the tumultuous days of the post-war era and the Cold War. Then, in 1991, the Soviet Union imploded spectacularly. The eleven states that composed it, including Russia and Ukraine, became independent nations. With the dissolution of the Soviet Union, Ukraine inherited a vast stockpile of nuclear weapons, the third largest in the world with over 1,700 warheads and 3,000 tactical nuclear weapons that were left behind on its soil. It surrendered its entire arsenal in 1994, in return for security guarantees from Russia, Europe and the USA and became a non-nuclear state. The two nations followed their own courses—independent but often complementary.

Even though Russia and Ukraine became independent entities, they were still held together by common bonds. Russia was the 'big brother', and in many ways had a say in Ukraine's internal affairs. However, in the new Millennium, a subtle shift came over Ukraine. It was slowly shedding its pro-Moscow stance and veering towards Europe, hoping to join the European Union. For Russia, that shift was disturbing. It installed their own man as the President—Victor Yanukovych, a staunch pro-Russian—even rigging elections and poisoning his opponent to ensure victory. Yanukovych veered Ukraine back towards Russia. It was quite apparent that he was "their man" and his decisions were dictated by Moscow. In 2013, he withdrew from an earlier decision to join the European Union and refused to sign the European Union Association Agreement that would have made Ukraine part of the European Union. Instead, he moved back towards Russia and the Eurasian Economic Union.

The movement to join the European Union had been gathering momentum within Ukraine for many years now, especially amongst the younger generation, and this decision was met with widespread protests. A wave of demonstrations and protests broke out in November 2013 in Maidan Nezalezhnosti—Independence Square in Ukraine—which was also called the Euromaidan protests. They spread across the country as pro- and anti-Russian rallies erupted across the country, reaching as far out as Kharkiv, Odessa and the Crimea. Over 200 demonstrators were killed as government authorities clamped down and that spurred even greater protests. Eventually, the pro-

Europe lobby won and Yanukovych capitulated and fled to Russia in February 2014, leaving it in the hands of an interim government. Flush with the victory of the Euromaidan protests, Ukraine tilted even more strongly towards the European Union and proposed joining NATO, an action that would take it out of Russia's orbit, and make it completely entrenched with the West.

The Actions in Crimea and Donbas—2014-2021

The turn of events in Ukraine was not taken lightly by Russia. The protests had also seen a large number of pro-Russian rallies, especially by the eastern regions of the Donbas and the southern peninsula of Crimea which had a large Russian-speaking population. In February 2014, pro-Russian supporters launched their own violent protests in the Crimea. They seized the parliament building and the airports and virtually held the local government to ransom. As the local authorities tried to suppress them, Russia used this action as a pretext, and on 27 February sent troops to "save Russian-speaking people". Russian paratroopers captured strategic sites across Crimea and installed a pro-Russian government. Things moved rapidly thereafter. In March, a referendum was held in Crimea in which an overwhelming 90 per cent of the population voted for independence from Kyiv to join Russia. Crimea was declared 'independent' and formally incorporated into Russia on 18 March 2014.

Russia has been claiming Crimea as "Historically Russian"—as part of the old Russian Empire—since 1991. Its crucial position abutting into the Black Sea was vital to its own maritime interests. The annexation of Crimea was illegal and orchestrated, and though it drew international condemnation and sanctions, it had little effect on an unrepentant Russia. Russian passports were issued, the Hryvnia replaced by Roubles, and the process of "Russification" began. In a *fait accompli*, Crimea became part of Russia.

Around the same time, they also incited unrest in the largely Russian-speaking eastern provinces of Donetsk and Luhansk, which together made up the Donbas, setting off a civil war between pro-Russian separatists and Ukrainian forces that lasted eight years. This war in the Donbas is the precursor to the war that erupted in 2022.

In April 2014, the activities of the pro-Russian separatist groups in Donbas increased. Their ranks swelled to over 20,000-30,000, which included a large number of Russian 'volunteers.' The unrest swelled to a full-fledged insurgency, actively encouraged and abetted by Russia. Although Russia denies it, there is no doubt that it actively participated in the conflict. Russian soldiers and Spetznaz operatives were captured, and units and formations operating there were identified, including their elite 76th Guards Air Assault Division. Under the pretext of 'humanitarian aid' large convoys of arms and equipment were sent in from Russia to beef up the separatist groups who fought under the banner of "Novorossiya"—New Russia. A Russian surface-to-air missile in their hands hit Malaysian airlines Flight MH–17, which was mistaken for a

Ukrainian transport aircraft and crashed, killing all on board. The civil war in Donbas between the Ukrainian forces and separatists raged for eight years with neither side being able to gain control.

In an attempt to stop the fighting, the Minsk Agreement was signed between representatives of Ukraine, Russia, the Luhansk People's Republic and the Donetsk People's Republic along with the Organization for Security and Cooperation in Europe in September 2014. This initial agreement (also called the Minsk Protocol) failed to stop the fighting and a revised agreement was signed in February 2015—Minsk II. Both sides agreed to a ceasefire, release of prisoners and granted self-government to certain areas of the Donbas, while recognizing Ukraine's sovereignty over it. In the ceasefire that followed, the fighting subsided, but it never stopped altogether. Donbas became a zone of 'frozen conflict' with tensions rising and ebbing, but never being resolved completely. The platform that Russia had established in the Donbas and Crimea would help them in the invasion, and they would use the same model in this war.

In 2019, Volodymyr Zelensky was elected President of Ukraine, ironically on the promise that he would end the fighting. This 44-year-old had no experience of politics and had attained fame as a stand-up comedian and his roles in television comedies. His most remembered role was in the series 'Servant of the People' in which he played the role of a high-school teacher who gets elected as President of Ukraine through a series of flukes, and then fits into the role with the premise "You only have to be good to lead." The unassuming Zelensky would play the same role in real life and prove his mettle in the war—the same war he hoped to avert—where his leadership would give steel to his countrymen to withstand the Russian invasion that came in February 2022.

By 2019, both sides accused the other of violating the Minsk Agreement, and the Donbas began simmering once again. Russia began issuing Russian passports to residents of the Donbas, which was seen as the first step towards the annexation of the region, and a clear disregard of Ukrainian sovereignty. On 14 September 2020, President Zelensky approved Ukraine's new National Security Strategy that included "a distinctive partnership with NATO, with the aim of membership". An amendment was made in the Ukrainian constitution that enshrined its decision to join EU and NATO. Ukraine was now conclusively moving away from Russia and towards NATO.

Ukraine applied for full membership of NATO (though it would be refused at this juncture). If Ukraine joined NATO, it would bring the alliance right to Russia's borders. Putin insisted that the clause be withdrawn and demanded guarantees that Ukraine would never join NATO, something that could not be formally given. As round after round of negotiations faltered, Putin ratcheted the pressure, sending troops towards the border. Europe was moving closer and closer towards war.

Russia and NATO

At the heart of the war lie two issues—the Ukrainian decision to join NATO, and the volatile, mercurial personality of Vladimir Putin. This invasion has been the brainchild of Putin, the former intelligence officer who has ruled Russia with an iron fist since 1999, first as prime minister and then as president for an unprecedented three terms (after changing the constitution to virtually make himself president for life). This ex-KGB officer saw the break-up of the Soviet Union as "The greatest geo-political catastrophe of the 20th century" and hoped to take Russia back to the glory and former position of the USSR.

It was his desire to make Russia take on the mantle of the former USSR that pushed his ultra-nationalistic agenda ruthlessly. He crushed the Chechnya uprising with tanks and heavy artillery, virtually flattening Grozny. Then he took Russia to war with Georgia, which he defeated in 12 short days in August 2008. He also orchestrated the annexation of Crimea in 2014 and the encouragement of separatism in Ukraine's eastern provinces. His engagement in the Syrian civil war in 2015, helped his ally, Assad, to cling on to power, re-asserted Russian influence on the Middle East and eased out US presence in the region. For good measure, he tried to influence the US Presidential elections to ensure that Donald Trump would win, an action that earned him the personal animosity of Joe Biden, Trump's opponent, and the eventual winner.

Under his watch, Russia had grown at an impressive 7 per cent, largely due to gas and oil revenues. It had cosied up to China and had begun exerting itself in Afghanistan, Central Asia and Europe. For Putin, NATO expansion right up to Russia's border was a direct threat. If Ukraine joined the alliance,

NATO troops would be on Russia's flanks, and missiles would take just three or four minutes to hit Moscow. As he himself put it, "Can't they see this? After this we have no place to go. We can't go backwards anymore."

In many ways, he was right. It has been explicitly promised to Mikhail Gorbachev himself that NATO would not expand 'one-inch eastwards' after the dissolution of the Soviet Union. At that time, in 1991, its boundaries stood along the borders of Germany. In the decades after that, Poland, Hungary, the Czech Republic, Bulgaria, Rumania and the Baltic states of Estonia, Latvia and Lithuania were all co-opted in the alliance. When Estonia and Latvia joined in 2004, NATO's borders touched Russia for the first time in its northern areas. Had Ukraine joined, NATO would be at Russia's doorstep.

Putin's demand that Ukraine be refused membership of NATO and that NATO's offensive weaponry in the Baltic states bordering Russia be withdrawn, was thus justified. Perhaps, Putin's initial posturing was just a way of buttressing his demands. After all, he too would not have wanted a full-scale war that would send the just recovering Russian economy back into the doldrums. However, the written guarantees that Ukraine would never join NATO, which was demanded by Putin, could not be given, and Europe headed inexorably towards a war that no one really wanted.

The Build-up to War

The first signs of a Russian military build-up came in February 2021 when around 3,000 paratroopers were deployed around the Ukrainian border for 'exercises.' Around the same time, the activities of the separatist groups of the Donetsk People's Republic also increased. Small arms and mortar fire on Ukrainian positions began once again, to be followed by retaliatory fire. The ceasefire it the Donbas, always fragile, was effectively breaking up.

At the same time, NATO conducted their DEFENDER EUROPE 21 exercises, one of the largest in decades, which involved 28,000 troops from 27 nations. In response, Russia deployed around 40,000 men along the Ukrainian border, and built up its garrison in the Crimea. Russian ships moved into the Black Sea and the first naval confrontation took place in the Sea of Azov on the night of 15 April 2021 when three Ukrainian vessels were blocked from entering the waters of the Kerch Straits which the Russians claimed as theirs following their annexation of Crimea.

By end April, around 60,000 troops of the 41st and the 58th Armies were moved from the Siberian frontier towards the Ukrainian border, once again in the time-honoured garb of 'exercises.' The exercises were conducted perilously close to the border, raising hackles across the world. By May, Russia announced that the troops would be withdrawing and returning to their permanent bases. In effect, only about 3,000 or so troops were moved back. Most of the units were simply moved around laterally, creating the impression of movement, but in effect, remaining in the border areas with their heavy equipment and weaponry.

In October a second and even more significant build-up of troops followed.

Around 30,000 soldiers were sent on 'exercises' to Belarus on the northern border of Ukraine, ostensibly to practice with their Belorussian allies. The Russians took great pains to stress that the soldiers were merely exercising and had no offensive intentions. It was the largest build-up of troops ever seen in Europe since World War II and sent alarm bells ringing across the world.

By early November, the signs were clear. The 8th and 20th Guards Armies and the 4th and 6th Air Defence Armies joined the fray, and the concentration along the borders increased to around 110,000-120,000 troops. Additional troops also moved into the Crimea with heavy offensive weaponry. US intelligence warned of a likely invasion, and estimated that it could take place by January 2022. For a change, the intelligence reports were right, but as it is often the case with unpalatable news, they were not taken too seriously.

Efforts to defuse the crisis continued. On 7 December 2021, US President Joe Biden and President Vladimir Putin spoke via video conference where Putin demanded 'reliable, legal guarantees to preclude NATO from expanding towards Russia or deploying offensive weapons in countries bordering it." Russia also handed over a set of demands that included:

- The USA and NATO would not deploy troops in ex-Soviet states.
- NATO would not expand any further eastwards.
- NATO would not deploy any additional forces in Eastern Europe.
- Refrain from any military activity in Ukraine or other state in Eastern Europe, the Caucasus and Central Asia.

The demands were actually quite flagrant. It is quite likely that the demand for denial of NATO membership to Ukraine had already been agreed to behind closed doors. However, giving written guarantees for it, and agreeing to Putin's other demands (which were actually not quite unreasonable, seeing the scale of NATO expansionism) would be seen as tantamount to surrender. Another frosty call followed between Biden and Putin on 30 December "to de-escalate tensions" in which Biden warned of "serious costs and consequences" including unspecified sanctions. Further talks followed, including a meeting of NATO-Russia, which got delegates from all 30 NATO countries and Russian representatives to the table. That meeting was a disaster. Russia stuck to its stance of 'written security guarantees'. NATO held on to its position that "Russia does not have a veto on whether Ukraine can become a NATO member.

It has to be NATO and Ukraine that decides on membership." The lines were now being clearly drawn.

In January 2022, Russia began a gradual evacuation of its embassy staff from Kyiv—another clear indicator of what was afoot. By mid-January, it was estimated that Russia had built up around 127,000 troops, along with 35,000 Russian-backed separatists in Donbas and around 3,000 soldiers in rebel-held Eastern Ukraine. It also moved 36 Iskandar short range ballistic missiles near the border, many of them within striking distance of Kyiv. By late January, the headquarters of Eastern Military District along with combat units from the 5th, 29th, 35th and 36th Combined Arms Armies along with the 76th Air Assault Division and 98th Airborne Division moved to Belarus—an indicator that the Russians would use the proximity of Belarus to attack Kyiv from the north. As per US estimates, Russia had assembled 83 battalion tactical groups, almost 70 per cent of their combat strength, for the invasion and predicted the attack to come any time after mid-February. Americans were warned to leave Ukraine immediately. The US intelligence had also correctly assessed that Russia would need 175,000–200,000 troops for the invasion but that the present strength would not be sufficient to capture and hold the large tracts of Ukrainian territory the Russians had set their sights on. That assessment would prove to be right.

As the Russian preparations continued, Ukraine too began mobilizing its forces. According to Oleksii Reznikov, the Minister of Defence, Ukraine held 250,000 troops, of which 125,000 had been deployed in the Donbas conflict since 2014, and were battle hardened. In addition, there were 400,000 veterans and 200,000 reservists who were willing and available to be inducted with just a short period of training. As events would show later, the ready availability of highly motivated Ukrainian defenders would make all the difference.

The first shipments of foreign arms and aid also began arriving. In January, the first consignment of FGM—148 Javelin Anti-tank missiles, precision guided munitions, machine guns and small arms and specialised radio and communication equipment reached Lyiv—the trans-shipment hub in western Ukraine where Western arms were stored and then distributed into Ukraine. Stinger surface-to-air missiles, which had played such a vital role in the Afghan Soviet war, also arrived. Other NATO nations also chipped in. Estonia, Latvia and Lithuania provided anti-tank missiles and air defence systems. Germany, reluctant to get involved in the conflict, initially, provided 5,000 helmets, an offering that provoked a derisive snort from Zelensky, "What will they give us next—blankets?" The UK and Canada began a military training program that would train reservists and make them combat ready in a few months; and provided 2,000 new generation light anti-tank missiles to help stave off the anticipated Russian armour onslaughts. As the war progressed, newer and more sophisticated weapons would find their way to Ukraine and prove decisive in the battles ahead.

Even as the clock ticked, NATO began bolstering its eastern flank by sending 2,000 additional troops to Germany. This was followed by an additional 3,000 troops to Poland, and F-15 jets to Rumania. Spain and the UK sent additional warships to the Mediterranean and the Black Sea, and Eurofighters and F-35s jets were deployed in Bulgaria as part of NATO's expanded air surveillance mission. At the same time, the USA made it clear that it would not get directly involved in the war, but would provide complete support and strike Russia with "sanctions as never before."

Within Russia too, the media began increasing their justification of the coming war. Ukraine was accused of violating the ceasefire agreement in Donbas and "spreading Russophobia as the first step to genocide". The Russian propaganda of the Ukrainian government being "run by neo-Nazis" was gathering momentum. 'Demilitarisation and denazification' became the catchwords, though there was little evidence to justify them.

In the midst of all this, Putin still found time to attend the Winter Olympic Games at Beijing in early February 2022, where he met his ally, Xi Jinping, and was wined and feted as a special guest of honour. It is quite likely that he shared his plans with the Chinese premier and perhaps even got a *de facto* expression of support. Both sides of course deny it but the fact that Xi Jinping was the last major world leader whom Putin met just before launching his invasion is a little too much of a coincidence. In any case, Putin conveniently waited for China to complete its prestigious Games before launching his own invasion.

In the Donbas, the fighting escalated. Russia moved in around 2,000 advisors and trainers to coordinate the actions of the militia, and ramp-up their activities. Shelling of Ukrainian positions by the Donetsk and Luhansk militia intensified with almost 60 artillery and mortar attacks daily. Even as these attacks were taking place, Russia announced that Ukraine had been attacking civilians with mortar and machine gun fire, forcing them to leave their homes and flee to safe zones in Russia. It also claimed that Ukrainian artillery had destroyed a border post inside Russia. The Ukrainians denied these activities and it is quite likely they were mere propaganda, or stage-managed by the Russians themselves, as part of 'false flag' operations.

Events moved fast thereafter. On 21 February, Putin signed a decree, recognising the breakaway Donetsk and Luhansk provinces as independent states paving the way for their ultimate amalgamation into Russia. He also sent Russian troops into the Donbas as a "peacekeeping mission to save the lives of Russians from the neo-Nazis of the Ukrainian government".

It was becoming increasingly clear that Russia was poised to attack. As the last round of negotiations failed on 22 February, a vicious denial of services and cyber-attacks hit Ukraine's financial and transport network. Its internet was downed, breaking communication. All along the border, satellites and local civilians reported an intensification of tank and troop movement headed towards the border with an ominous 'Z' marked on their sides. This letter would become the symbol of the Russian offensive.

At 5 a.m. on 24 February, Russian troops debouched from their concentration areas along the border and began moving in to Ukraine from the north, the east and along the south. Putin's 'special military operation' had started. The war that everyone knew would happen, but still hoped would never take place, had begun.

REFERENCES

"Annexation of Crimea," Uaberexplained.com. 29 March 2022.

"Crimeans vote over 90 % for Russia," *Reuters*, 8 March 2015.

"Don't give Putin a Veto over NATO Expansion," https://www.washingtonpost.com 21 Jan. 2022.

"EuroMaidan Rallies in Ukraine," *Kyiv Post*, 21 Nov. 2013.

"Everything you need to know about the 2014 Ukraine Crisis," Vox, https://www.vox.com 03 Sep. 2014.

"Invasion of the Soviet Union, June 1941," https://encyclopedia.ushnm.org

"NATO conducts 'STEADFAST DEFENDER 21' War Games amidst Tensions," https://m.economictimes.com

"NATO's response to Russia's invasion of Ukraine," https://www.nato.int 23 Sep. 2022.

"Putin Announces Donetsk and Luhansk Recognition," *BBC News*, 22 Feb. 2022.

"Putin says Russia has 'Nowhere to Retreat' over Ukraine," *CNBC*, 21 Dec. 2021.

"Putin wants 'de-Nazification, but how much is Ukraine Nazified?," https://www.indiatoday.in 24 March 2022.

"Putin–Soviet Collapse 'a Genuine Tragedy," *NBC News*, 25 April 2005.

"*Russia and the Former Soviet Republics*," Thomas McCray.

"Russia issues List of Demands to Lower Tensions," https://www.theguardian.com 17 Dec. 2021.

"Russia moves units into Ukraine, NATO says," Michael Gordon, *The New York Times*, 5 June 2015.

"Russia's War on Ukraine, Timeline of Cyber-attacks," https://www.europa/.europa.eu 08 June 2022.

"Russian Military Build-up along the Ukrainian Border," https://crsreports.congress.gov, 07 Feb. 2022.

"Timeline of NATO's Expansion since 1949," *ABC News*, 09 May 2022.

"Ukraine and pro-Russian rebels sign Ceasefire Deal," *BBC*, 05 Sep, 2014.

"Ukraine says Donetsk Operations underway," *BBC News*, 15 April 2014.

"Ukraine, Nuclear Weapons and Security Assurances," Arms Control Association, Feb. 2022.

"Ukraine–History, Kyivan Rus," *Encyclopaedia Britannica*, 5 March 2020.

"Ukraine–The Famine of 1932-33 (Holodomor)," https://www.britannica.com

"Xi meets Putin ahead of Beijing Winter Olympic Opening," *South China Morning Post*, 04 Feb. 2022.

2

THE WAR

"I (have) decided to launch a Special Military Operation and pursue the demilitarization and de-Nazification of Ukraine."

—Vladimir Putin, 24 Feb. 2022

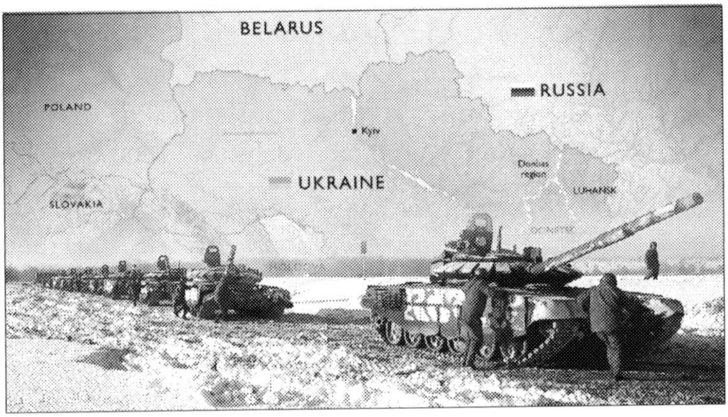

PLANNING AND PREPARATION

"The Best Laid Plans often come undone"

The War Begins

At 5 a.m. on the morning of 24 February, Russian troops debouched from their assembly areas along the Russian-Ukraine border and entered Ukraine along three main axes—from the north and north east; from the east; and from the south and southeast. The Russian invasion of Ukraine had begun.

Preparations for it had begun months earlier. Around 120,000 troops of the 41st Combined Arms Army had been inducted from Siberia and concentrated along the border since November. Another 30,000 troops were engaged in 'exercises' in Belarus, a Russian ally, from where they could enter Ukraine rapidly from the north. Around 40,000 troops had already been garrisoned in the Crimea since 2014, when Russia annexed the peninsula, and were poised to advance northwards. Besides, the Russian-backed separatists in the Donbas region of Eastern Ukraine had been beefed up with additional Russian troops and had stepped up their attacks on Ukrainian positions. As a prelude to war, a vicious information campaign was launched against the Ukrainian leadership and government, ostensibly to justify the coming invasion. Cyber-attacks and denial-of services attacks on government and military sites disrupted finance, transport and communication services and downed the internet hours before the actual attack, cutting off substantial segments of the communication and information networks. The Russian build-up and preparations had been picked up by satellites and Google maps, and was monitored virtually on a real-time basis. Though the invasion was expected, the eventual scale caught many by surprise. Russia attacked virtually all along the Ukrainian frontier in the largest offensive seen in Europe since the Second World War.

On the face of it, it was expected that the Russian Army would sweep through Ukraine and reach Kyiv in a week or so. After all, the Russians have the fifth largest army in the world, with 900,000 men in uniform and over two million reservists. Its defence budget of $ 61.7 billion was ten times that of Ukraine's $ 5.9 billion. It held 12,420 tanks, 7,500 artillery pieces and over 1,500 fighter aircraft, against Ukraine's force of around 209,000 active personnel, 2,500 tanks, 2,040 artillery pieces and just around 150 effective fighter aircraft. Like the campaign in Georgia in 2008, it was expected that the Russians would reach their objectives within a fortnight or so—or a month at the most. Possibly most of the Russian troops expected to be back home for Easter, just as the German soldiers who had invaded USSR in May 1941 were sure that they would be back home for Christmas.

Ukraine was isolated and alone. No European nation, or the USA was willing to get directly involved, and their support was restricted to military aid and equipment, political and moral support and the exertion of pressure on Russia through sanctions and global isolation. Yet, the Ukrainian Army, hardened by eight years of battling separatism in Donbas, put up a stiff resistance that stalled the Russians at every juncture. They revealed courage and tactical acumen, individually and collectively, that perhaps surprised the Russians who were half-expecting a walkover. Their leadership too stood up to be counted, and President Zelensky provided an example of wartime leadership that will go down in the annals of history. Of course, the Ukrainians held the defender's advantage. They were in their own territory, knew each inch of the land and were fighting for their homes and hearths. They could replace their losses by calling up reservists, and virtually every able-bodied male joined the war effort. They improvised beautifully too. Distilleries switched from making beer to making Molotov cocktails, pizza delivery drones and children's quad copters were modified to act as surveillance and early warning drones. They held on with a determination that very few expected. Eventually after months of dogged defence they followed up with their own counter-offensive in September directed at the northeast and the south, which suddenly changed the complexion of the war.

The Russians made a series of baffling tactical and strategic decisions which prevented them from achieving their aim swiftly. A war, expected to last for a week, went on for months, forcing the Russians to push in even more troops and firepower to achieve their aims and sucked them into a brutal war of attrition. The rapier thrust the Russians hoped to strike became a sledgehammer blow. For starters, the Russians made the cardinal error of moving along too many thrust lines—along the north, the east, the south—in an area separated by over 1,600 kilometres. Perhaps they hoped to emulate the German offensive of 1941 which entered the Soviet Union along three widely spread axes which addressed each part of the country with one thrust in the north towards Leningrad, one in the centre towards the prized objective, Moscow, and one in the south towards the Caucasus. However, unlike the Germans, their thrust lines lacked cohesion. Each thrust line seemed to have its own commander, and it was only in April that General Aleksandr Dvornikov was appointed the overall commander to give central direction to the war. There also seems to have been a measure of overconfidence. The troops were not told their objectives—perhaps for reasons of security, and half-expected to be welcomed as 'liberators.' Perhaps their intelligence got the 'pro-Russian' sentiment wrong, and many of the soldiers were taken by surprise in the initial days when civilians began firing on them. From some accounts, ceremonial uniforms were also recovered in captured tanks and vehicles. Perhaps they were preparing for a victory parade in Kyiv after a short, victorious war. In any case the assessment of the Russian planners, both in terms of their own capabilities and the Ukrainian will to resist, was grossly wide off the mark.

Plus, the Russians did not even attempt to control the skies even though they easily out-matched the Ukrainian air force in quality and quantity. It was expected that a 'shock and awe' campaign of air power would be unleashed to suppress Ukrainian air defence and to keep their aircraft on the ground. Surprisingly, only around 75 aircraft were committed—largely Sukhoi-25 ground attack aircraft. There was no determined attempt to destroy the Ukrainian air force and air defence sites, nor were concentrated air strikes made on value targets. Russia never gained control of the skies, nor were its aircraft seen actively in support of ground troops. The neglect of the air war was one of the baffling aspects of their campaign.

Even the timing of the offensive was awry. In February–March, the spring thaw sets in and the snow begins to melt, turning the ground to slush. Surely Putin and his generals would have been aware of that. After all, Russian history is full of stories of how 'Marshal Mud' and 'General Winter' defeated Napoleon's and Hitler's armies, who were traversing along the same route (albeit from opposite directions). Or perhaps the decision was taken by Putin himself, who wanted to postpone the offensive till after China's Olympic Games were over and none of his generals could contradict him. One has to only look back to India's great victory in the 1971 Bangladesh liberation war to realise the impact of timing. Mrs. Indira Gandhi, the then Prime Minister, had asked the Army Chief to launch an offensive into East Pakistan in April. He refused, on the grounds that the monsoons would be setting in, and the ground of East Pakistan would be flooded impairing movement. Plus, the passes in the north would be open at this time, which would enable the Chinese to intervene. He requested for time till 15 November to launch the offensive in East Pakistan, and the results, as they say, became history. Had one of Putin's generals revealed the same professional integrity, the offensive would not have got bogged down in the way that it did in the initial days. The slushy ground forced the Russian columns to stick to the roads where they could easily be ambushed and halted. The videos of Russian tanks and trucks being hit by missiles and artillery while strung out in long lines along the road showed the effect of the awry timing. In fact, it was only in the later months, when the ground conditions improved, that the Russians could make sizeable headway in the south and the east.

Logistics also played a major role. From some accounts, the Russians had faulted in their logistic planning and had not catered for the fuel and ammunition that the campaign would require. The Russian concept of logistics relies heavily on using railroads and pipelines to push forward supplies and their units and formations are notoriously short of trucks. Also, since they were road bound, they had to clear the towns and cities that stood at the road junctions. They were unable to capture most of the major towns in the initial thrust, which stalled the forward movement of their logistics columns. Capturing towns and cities thus became increasingly important, and much of the offensive force was sucked in to the battle of the cities, making the Russian progress was slow, expensive and, more-often than not, inconclusive.

Once again, one cannot but help compare this offensive to the 1971 Indian campaign in East Pakistan. There too, Pakistan had occupied all the major towns and cities as strong points. The Indians took a simple decision. Instead of attacking these virtual fortresses, it simply bypassed them leaving a small force to contain them, and moved deeper towards Dacca, creating a psychological paralysis in the minds of the defenders. Perhaps the Russians could have taken a leaf out of this book and not got themselves sucked into the battle of the cities. That was what eventually spent the offensive. It is however quite significant that when the Ukrainians launched their own counter-offensive in September, they followed more innovative tactics, in which their mobile forces simply raced ahead to depth objectives, causing psychological dislocation and cutting off their opponents from the routes of withdrawal, while the infantry cleared the by-passed objective. That was one of the reasons for the stunning speed of the Ukrainian counter-offensive and the manner in which it recaptured territory in days, which the Russians had taken weeks and months to occupy.

The Overall Offensive Plan

Ukraine is the second largest country in Europe; next only to Russia in size, with whom it shares a 2,600-kilometre long land border. To its north lies Belarus, a Russian ally, and to the south lie the Sea of Azov and the Black Sea. The Dnieper River, which is the lifeline of the country, runs from north to south, flowing through its capital city, Kyiv, and cuts southwards down to the Black Sea. The areas east of the river adjoining Russia comprise some of its richest agricultural and industrial lands—areas that Russia seemed to have its eyes on. By all accounts, Russia hoped to push on towards the line of the Dnieper River and then simply carve the rich territories into their own land.

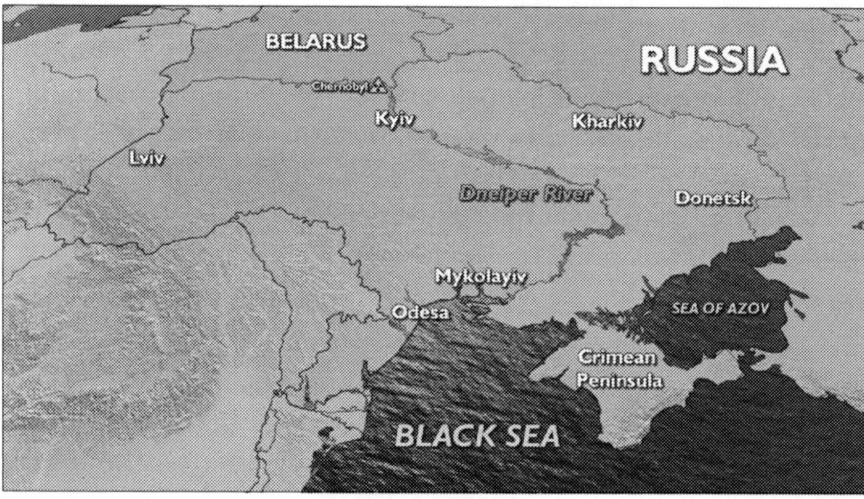

The Area of Operations

The long border with Russia has its challenges. Kyiv lies a good 380 kilometres from the eastern Russian frontier, which forced it to attack the capital from Belarus in the north. In its northeast, Kharkiv, Ukraine's second largest town, just 80 kilometres from the Russian border along with the towns of Sumy and Chuhiv, form the gateway into the heart of Ukraine. To the east, lies the Donbas with its provinces of Luhansk and Donetsk, an area which held a large Russian-speaking population and where a Russian-sponsored insurgency has been raging since 2014. Much of the Russian attention was focused on the Donbas after their attempt to capture Kyiv failed, which they called "the original aim of the campaign". To the South, its 1,600-kilometre-long coastline with its port towns of Mariupol, Mykoliav Kherson and Odesa, were its most critical areas, essential for maritime trade with the rest of the world. The coastline was broken by the Crimea, a diamond-shaped peninsula that projected into the Black Sea and was vitally important to both the Russians and the Ukrainians. The entire frontier between Russia and Ukraine was over 1,800 kilometres long, but the Russians, in their initial enthusiasm, decided to address all of it virtually simultaneously.

The jury is still out as to what exactly Putin hoped to achieve by this offensive. In many ways, it was a completely needless war. After having recognised the provinces of Luhansk and Donetsk as independent states, he had set the ground for them to be amalgamated into Russia. Crimea in any case had been annexed in 2014. The main demand of Ukraine not going in for NATO membership had already been agreed to informally. All this would have led to a change in regime. one of Putin's major aims. in which Zelensky would be replaced with an amenable pro-Russian president. Even if he did want military action to demonstrate Russian might, he could have gone in for limited action focusing only on the Donbas and southern sector, where his troops would be concentrated, the logistic lines would be shorter and the population would not be so hostile. Those aims could have been attained relatively easily.

Instead, he decided to go in for the all-or-nothing option in which the Russian army attacked virtually along a 1,400-kilometre-long frontage, striking Ukraine from the north towards Kyiv, from the east towards Kharkiv, from the southeast in Donbas and all along the coast line in the south. This ambitious offensive was perhaps designed to reach the line of the Dnieper River and cut off the rich Eastern region from the rest of the country. Simultaneously the capture of the coastal areas would have cut Ukraine from the Black Sea and the Sea of Azov, crippling its economy. The focus of the offensive, at least in the initial days, seemed to be Kyiv, whose capture would seize the nerve centre of the government and be the symbol of their complete victory. In conjunction, the three thrust lines would be able to take over the capital, seize the coast and the rich lands east of the Dnieper River and virtually carve Ukraine into three.

The thrust lines were:

- **The Northern Front.** This offensive was launched from Belarus and directed towards Kyiv, approximately 400 km from the frontier. It actually had two prongs. One, the Northern Thrust, comprised of troops of the Eastern Military District from the 29th, 35th and 36th Combined Arms moved along highway M01, the main highway from Belarus to Kyiv keeping east of the Dnieper River (which cut Kyiv in two). Another thrust line, the north-eastern thrust by the 41st Combined Arms Army and the 2nd Guards Combined Arms Army approached from the northeast, keeping east of the river. Both thrust lines were to converge on the town and isolate it.

- **The Eastern Front.** This was a thrust towards Kharkiv (the second largest town in Ukraine) launched by the Central Military District with the 1st Guards Tank Army and the 20th Combined Arms Army. Its aim was perhaps to capture Kharkiv and then head towards the Dnieper River where it would link up with the northern thrust. This thrust actually had two components. The major one came in from the northeast towards Kharkiv; the other from the southeast from the

Donbas region with the 8th Combined Arms Army and the 1st and 2nd Army Corps of the Russian Separatist forces operating in the Donbas.

- **The Southern Front.** This was launched from Crimea (which was already occupied by around 30,000 Russian troops) by the Southern Military District with the 58th and 49th Combined Arms Armies. It moved northwards from Crimea and fanned out along the coast to capture the coastal areas and the port towns of Odessa, Mariupol, Melitopol and Kherson. It would move in almost 200 kilometres deep and seize the vital town of Zaporizhzhia which had the largest nuclear plant in Europe.

Just one glance at the map reveals that the thrust lines were widely separated and not even complementary. In a way, it was akin to the German plan for the invasion of the USSR in 1941, where they attacked on three thrust lines along the entire frontage of the Soviet Union, with the northern thrust heading for Leningrad, the central moving towards Moscow, and the southern towards the Crimea and Caucasus. Like that plan, it did divide Ukrainian reaction by forcing them to commit troops virtually along the entire frontier with Russia and its ally, Belarus. It split the Russian resources along a front almost 2,000 kilometres wide and prevented them from making a decisive thrust along any of the thrust lines. The greatest weakness of this plan was that it was a little too ambitious, and while all three thrust lines made initial headway, eventually none of them could completely achieve their objectives. We will follow the progress of each of these thrust lines as we go along.

REFERENCES

"2022 Russian Invasion of Ukraine," Wikipedia, https://en.wikipedia.org

"Captured Documents Imply Ukrainian Invasion Planned," https://www.forbes.com, 03 March 2022.

"Road to War: US struggled to convince Allies and Zelensky," https://www.washingtonpost.com, 16 Aug. 2022.

"Russia's Possible Invasion of Ukraine," https://www.csis.org, 13 Jan. 2022.

"Ukraine Reveals Russian Military Plans for 'full-scale' Invasion," https://www.atlanticcouncil.org, 20 April 2022.

"Why has Russia Invaded Ukraine and what does Putin Want?," *BBC News*, https://www.bbc.com, 09 May 2022.

THE RUSSIAN OFFENSIVE IN THE NORTH: AT THE GATES OF KYIV

"I don't need a ride. I need ammunition"

—President Zelensky when offered a helicopter to leave Kyiv

The three thrusts moved out from the Russian and Belorussian frontiers almost simultaneously. From the very onset it seemed that Kyiv was the major target. Being the capital city and the fact that it housed President Zelensky and his government of 'neo-Nazis', it had an allure that Putin could not resist. A swift capture of Kyiv would have broken Ukrainian morale and brought the war to the swift and complete conclusion that Putin hoped for. But their major thrust emanated from Belarus, a different country altogether, which made problems of communication, coordination, and logistics even more difficult. Plus, it was separated by over 600 kilometres from their Eastern thrust line and thus not complementary to the rest of the offensive.

The Russians were well poised to encircle Kyiv from the north and the north east if only they moved fast. However, Kyiv would not be an easy target. This ancient town, with its spires and cobbled streets, was the largest in Ukraine and covered an area of over 800 square kilometres. Its warren of streets and alleys could suck in any attacker, and its underground sewage and subway tunnels enabled defenders to move undetected from one part of the city to another. Most importantly, the Dnieper River ran through the city from north to south, dividing it in neatly in two—the eastern and western parts. Capturing the city would thus require great coordination and use up major resources.

The Russians planned their advance on two prongs on either side of the river. From the north the 29th, 35th and 36th Combined Arms advanced along the M01 highway from the Belarus frontier, keeping west of the river. The 41st Combined Arms Army and the 2nd Guards Combined Arms moved in from Russia to approach the town from the north east keeping east of the river. Their move would be more difficult. They had to clear the towns of Sula and Chernihiv en route, and also go through the Pripyat marshes which were notoriously difficult to cross. The two prongs were to advance simultaneously and encircle the city from both directions, isolate and invest it before its capture. However, as time would reveal, the north-eastern thrust would be unduly delayed and that would eventually delay the isolation of Kyiv and put paid to plans for a swift capture.

The Russians had an even more ambitious plan to take over the city on the first day of the operations. An airborne assault was planned to capture Hostomel, a suburb 30 kilometres to the northwest of Kyiv, which had the crucial Antonov airfield. Its capture would give them an airhead to build up troops by air and enable them to seize the town in a swift, shock operation. Had that attack succeeded, the war would have taken an entirely different course.

At 8 a.m. on 24 February, around 30-35 MI-8 troop-carrying helicopters, escorted by K-52 'Alligator' attack helicopters flew low across the border and approached Hostomel, carrying soldiers of the elite NVD and Spetznaz special forces. Flying low, they reached Antonov airfield on the outskirts of Hostomel, virtually undetected, and swooped down. Ukrainian air defence guns and MANPADS downed three helicopters, but the Russian paratroopers landed, fanned out, rapidly overcame members of the National Guard there, and secured the airfield and its runway for the main force to follow.

The main force comprising paratroopers of the elite 11 Guards Air Assault Brigade or 31 Guards Air Assault Brigade (the unit has not been identified) were waiting and ready in their 18 Ilyushin IL-76 aircraft in airfields in Belarus to swoop down and take over the airfield, once it had been secured by the initial pathfinder force. The Ukrainians responded swiftly. Their 4th Rapid Reaction Brigade based around Kyiv, launched a rapid counter-attack with tanks and infantry combat vehicles that eliminated the pathfinder force and prevented the follow-up transport aircraft from landing. The Russian heli-borne force, comprising some of their best troops, was cut off and suffered heavy casualties as the Ukrainians closed the area and finally eliminated or captured them.

Though the airborne operation had failed, Russian mechanized units were racing towards the town. The initial plan was perhaps that the mechanized column would link up with the paratroopers at the airfield, secure it for the follow-on main force, and then launch a concerted attack on the town while it was still relatively unprepared. From the Belarus border, Kyiv was just 180 kilometres away and the route was virtually undefended. Elements of the 37th Guards Motor Rifle Brigade and 6th Guards Tank Regiment reached Antonov airfield by the evening of 24 February. In the furious fighting that took place, which many describe as the most intense of the war, Antonov airfield changed hands thrice in two days. In the fighting, the world's largest aircraft, the Antonov AN-225 'Mariya', was destroyed in its hanger. This Soviet-era aircraft was the only one of its kind in the world; a piece of aviation history and source of Ukrainian pride. Hostomel finally fell into in Russian hands, but the Ukrainians destroyed the runway and made it inoperable, ending any possibility of a Russian airborne attack.

With the airborne assault failing, the onus of capturing Kyiv lay with the large land columns that were closing in towards the town from both the north and the northeast. The northern column moved along the M01 highway, the shortest and easiest route to Kyiv. The column from the northeast hit the abandoned town of Chernobyl, the site of the world's largest nuclear disaster. Chernobyl has been abandoned since 1986, its leaking reactor encased in steel and cement, but the movement of tanks and soldiers in the area released increased quantities of radioactivity in the air.

As the Russians were closing in on the capital city, air and missile strikes rained down on Kyiv, perhaps to soften it before the main assault. The TV tower collapsed when hit, power plants damaged and other key targets hit.

Russian saboteurs infiltrated the city and three paratroopers were killed near the Parliament building, leading to speculation that the Russians intended to assassinate Zelensky. Within the city, Mayor Vitali Klitschko called up reservists and all able-bodied males and distributed 18,000 rifles for 'a fight to the finish'. Molotov cocktails were prepared and distributed, and anti-tank defences and steel 'hedgehogs' came up on the crossroads and main arteries leading into the city. It now seemed a matter of time before Kyiv would fall, and the USA even offered President Zelensky a helicopter to take him to safety. His reply, "I don't need a ride, I need ammunition" will go down as a classic of wartime leadership. Had Zelensky fled, as did Afghan President Ghani when the Taliban approached Kabul, the story of the war would have been much different.

By 28 February, the situation was dire. A 64-kilometre-long column of tanks and trucks carrying around 30,000 troops was approaching the city along the main road from the north. Another force was closing in from the northeast. It seemed but a matter of time that the two forces would close in and tighten the noose.

And then, inexplicably, the 64-kilometer-long column stopped.

The column had been barrelling down the road from Belarus to Kyiv, undeterred by sporadic air and artillery attacks, when it halted around the evening of 28 February. Even today, it is unclear why it halted the way it did. The halt has been attributed to faulty logistics. Ostensibly, they ran out of fuel. Russian units and formations are known to be light in load-carrying trucks and can cater for an advance of just around 90 kilometres, before being replenished by follow-on supply units and pipelines. That seems unlikely. After all, the column would have catered for enough fuel for the advance to contact, and had not fought any major action that would have depleted its fuel or ammunition. In all probability, the column halted while it awaited the thrust line from the northeast to move forward for a coordinated attack on the town.

The north eastern thrust line found the going more difficult on the way to Kyiv. It had to clear Sumy and Chernihiv, two border towns en route to Kyiv. The Russians entered both towns, but were unable to completely occupy them. Very often the defenders would simply melt away, ambush the vehicles in the narrow roads, and, once the Russians withdrew, simply occupy the positions once again. Though Sumy was almost completely reduced to rubble, Chernihiv held, earning the title of 'Hero City' for its stanch defence. The battles were an indicator of the heavy fighting that awaited the Russians if they entered Kyiv. Yet, in spite of delays, the Russian prong advanced and on 04 March reached Brovary, a suburb around 30 kilometres northeast of Kyiv. Brovary and other suburbs were occupied on 06 March and the Russians started fanning out to isolate the town as a prelude to its capture.

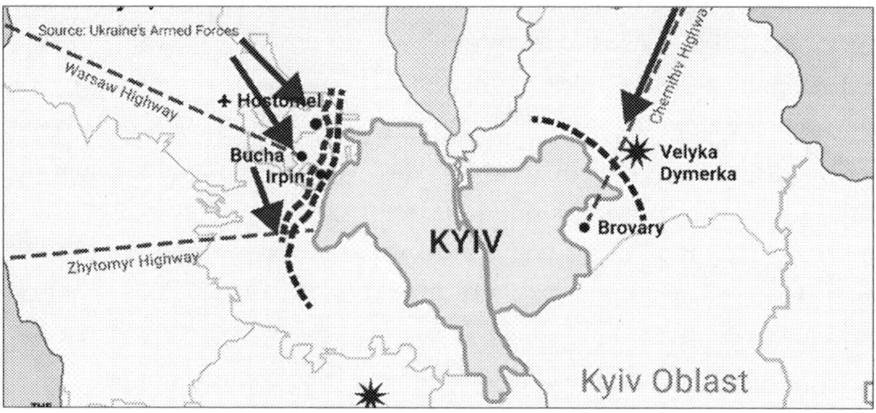

The Russian Advance Towards Kyiv

The main column approaching from the north, which had halted 30 kilometres away from Kyiv for eight crucial days, finally began moving on 7 March and moved to contact Kyiv. The halt and needless delay had given the defenders precious time to prepare obstacles and defensive lines, move up reserves and additional troops into the town. It also allowed the Western countries to fly in much-needed arms and equipment, especially anti-tank missiles and surface-to-air missiles, to strengthen the defences. As the column resumed its move, it approached Kyiv and then fanned out to begin the process of encircling the town and isolating it. The suburbs of Irpin, Bucha and Hostomel were captured as Russians came within 20 kilometres of Kyiv. In the east, the suburb of Brovary fell into Russian hands as did other critical townships. Kyiv was being slowly isolated from the northeast and the southwest and the crucial highways leading to it—the Warsaw, Zhytomyr and Chernihiv highways were blocked one by one. Artillery and rocket batteries occupied gun areas, and for the first time artillery fire struck the outskirts of the town, unleashing their deadly destructive power. With the Russian concept of massed artillery fire, it was felt that they would use their artillery to simply reduce the town to smithereens before their infantry moved in, in much the same manner that they had done with Grozny in 1991 and with some of the rebel towns in the Syrian war. A psychological campaign was launched on social media and television calling upon the defenders to surrender and emphasising that the Russian battle was with the "neo-Nazis of the Government" and not the people. Chechen and Syrian fighters, known for their brutality, were inducted around the town, in a throwback to earlier, more barbaric times, when a besieged town would be threatened with large-scale destruction if it did not surrender in time.

The capture of the suburbs would have given the Russians an idea of the bitter fighting in built-up areas and all the problems it entailed. Sniping and ambushes took a heavy toll and apparently their logistics too failed to reach the forward troops in time. (To get an idea of the scale of the problems, it required 80 trucks travelling 200 kilometres to carry ammunition for just one artillery salvo). The town itself had a perimeter of around 800 square kilometres and it is unlikely that the Russians would have had the resources to isolate a town of that size effectively. Its capture, of course, would have required twice as many troops and the scale of casualties and destruction would have been horrendous. The Russians could never completely isolate Kyiv, and to prove a point, Zelensky invited UK Prime Minister Boris Johnson and UN Secretary-General Antonio Guterres to visit the town, which only highlighted the Ukrainian resistance.

Though humanitarian corridors were established to permit movement of civilians, there was great damage to civilian lives and infrastructure. Throughout the first two weeks of March, the Russians continued firing and launching missile strikes into the city (as per Russian accounts, the scale of attacks in the city was deliberately reduced to prevent civilian casualties and only 'military target' inside the city were attacked) but the much-anticipated attack did not come. Perhaps the Russians had already overstretched themselves by then. The Ukrainians took advantage of the lull to launch their own counter-offensive on 22 March and began retaking the lost suburbs one by one. The Russians were gradually pushed back from the outskirts of the town, but surprisingly, the Ukrainians did not meet with the kind of resistance that was expected. In most cases the Russians simply withdrew, leaving behind scenes of carnage and destruction. In Irpin and Bucha, bodies of shot civilians and mass graves were found, prompting calls for investigations into war crimes. Slowly, each of the outlying areas was retaken by the Ukrainians as the Russians continued withdrawing from the town.

Then on 29 March, Russia abruptly announced that it was withdrawing its forces from the Kyiv area to 'focus on the original aim of the campaign—the Donbas in the East'. That explained the reason for the lack of resistance as the Ukrainians entered the lost areas around the town. The Russians moved back in relatively good order and by 6 April were back across the border. The Ukrainians retook the occupied areas, in spite of the mines and demolitions left behind by the Russians, and the threat to Kyiv receded. Russia claimed that its withdrawal was planned and that there was never any intention to take Kyiv; those actions were merely to draw Ukrainian forces from the area of decision, the Eastern front. However, that was just a cover-up. After all, the Russians would not have committed almost 30-35,000 of their best troops had it not been a definite objective. The Russians did have plans for taking over the town, but they had miscalculated badly in terms of manpower, supplies and resources. Once the air-borne assault on Hostomel failed, any hope of a rapid land assault to take Kyiv had little chance of success.

Kyiv was never a viable objective and even had the land offensive not halted the way it did, it is unlikely that the Russians would have been able to capture a town of that size. They would have been sucked into the 'Battle of Zelenskygrad' in much the same way that the Germans had been sucked into a needless battle for Stalingrad in the winter of 1942. Also, had they entered Kyiv; their troops would have suffered very heavy casualties and would have been in danger of being cut off by a Ukrainian counter-offensive that could have disrupted their supply lines. (Once again, akin to the manner in which the Soviets cut off the entire German Sixth Army in Stalingrad and then decimated it in detail.) Their decision to withdraw from Kyiv, though belated, was a correct military decision.

The jury is still out as to what Russia hoped to attain by its actions towards Kyiv. For one, by opening the Northern front from Belarus towards Kyiv, the frontage of the offensive increased by over 600 kilometres and became virtually unmanageable. Coordinating the offensive from the soil of a third nation further complicated the logistics and control. The force level that the Russians employed would not suffice for a large town like Kyiv. Perhaps they hoped to capture it in the first few hours through its airborne force, and had they succeeded, it would have been a different story. After their airborne operation failed, the ground forces had a far more difficult task ahead; one that was well beyond their capabilities, and which they recognised, albeit at a belated stage.

Slowly, the action eased around Kyiv. Missile attacks did strike the town from time to time, which continued virtually throughout the war, more as an intimidatory signal than anything else. The town went back to its routine. The trains and trams came back and ran largely on schedule. Traffic and revellers thronged the streets, even though the air raid sirens did go off from time to time. Zelensky and his government continued to oversee the war effort; and from there he maintained his nightly address to his countrymen, at 9 pm on the dot. Visits of world leaders to the town continued, largely as a symbol of support and solidarity, and gradually the threat to Kyiv receded.

Further to the west, the border town of Lyiv, just 19 kilometres from the Polish border, also received considerable Russian attention. Lyiv was the transit point where Western arms were received, stocked and then sent eastwards for distribution amongst Ukrainian forces. Its warehouses were hit repeatedly by Russian rockets and missiles, including long-range hypersonic Kinzhal missiles, which destroyed large consignments of newly-received aid and equipment. The strikes on Lyiv were a clear signal that Russia could escalate the war should the Western powers intervene directly, but though it did cause significant damage initially, gradually the attacks reduced as Russia focused its attention on other sectors.

The action now shifted towards the North-eastern front, in the area of Kharkiv; in the eastern sector of the Donbas; and towards the south along the coastal belt and port cities on the Sea of Azov and the Black Sea, where the Russians did make significant gains. We will see how the action unfolded in these sectors, one by one.

REFERENCES

"At the Edge of Kyiv, Ukrainians on the Counter-offensive," *The New York Times*, 26 March 2022.

"Battle of Kyiv–2022," https://en.wikipedia.org

"Kyiv Region 'Liberated' from Russian Invaders," *Ukrinform*, 2 April 2022.

"Moscow says it will curb Assault on Kyiv: Russian Troops withdrawing," *Times of Israel*, 02 April 2022.

"Russia failed to take Kyiv; was Key Objective," *The Independent*, 30 March 2022.

"Russia forced into Retreat from Ukraine Airport," *The Telegraph*, 31 March 2022.

"Russian Convoy north of Kyiv stretches for 40 Miles-MAXAR," *Reuters*, 01 March 2022.

"Russian Military Convoy advances on Kyiv," *CBC News*, 01 March 2022.

"Ukraine says it Repels Russian Attack on Kyiv Base," *Reuters*, 26 February 2022.

"Why has Russia's 64-kilometer-long Convoy Stopped Moving," *BBC News*, 03 March 2022.

THE NORTH EASTERN FRONT (FEB–MAY 2022): KHARKIV

"Kharkiv—It is the gateway to both Russia and Ukraine"

—A Russian General

German troops entering Kharkiv, August 1941

To the northeast of Ukraine, lies Kharkiv, an old town, steeped in over a millennium of history and culture. Ukraine's second-largest town, it is just 30 kilometres from the Russian border and in a way guards the approach into Ukraine from the northeast. Kharkiv is no stranger to war. During World War II, some of the major battles took place in and around it, when German and Soviet armies clashed for control of this vital town. (Kharkov, as it was known then). It was captured by the Germans in autumn 1941. Around half a million Soviet soldiers were decimated by the Germans in a classical encirclement around the town. It fell back into Soviet hands in the closing days of 1942, only to be recaptured by a stunning counter-offensive by General Manstien, and then was lost again in the summer of 1943 when the Soviet armies began pushing the Germans slowly but inexorably, from their soil. As the World War wrought havoc on this town, it was destroyed only to be rebuilt to its former glory.

This old and beautiful town was again under attack, but this time from the opposite direction, and from a former sibling, Russia. As in World War II, the town became the site of advances, retreats and counter-offensives that would help decide the outcome of the overall war. On the very first day, 24 February, the town was reached by Russian forces that had concentrated in the area of Belgorod, and advanced into Ukraine, in conjunction with the other thrust lines. Kharkiv, Ukraine's second-largest city, just 30 kilometres from the Russian border was the gateway to the east, and had to be cleared to enable the Russians to move up to the Dnieper River and the rich lands of Eastern Ukraine.

By 25 February, the Russians reached the northern suburbs and began taking over the villages in the perimeter. The town was subject to a series of artillery and missile attacks and Kharkiv, along with Mariupol, suffered most extensively at Russian hands. The softening-up process killed an estimated 2,000 residents, including Yevgeny Malyshew, a bi-athlete, who was a member of the Ukrainian national team. The intensive shelling also killed a 21-year-old Indian student, Naveen, S.G., a student of Kharkiv National Medical University, as he stood in line to buy groceries. Almost half the 8,000 Indian students in Ukraine were located in Kharkiv and Sumy, and it is to the credit of the Indian government, that all of them were evacuated safely, except for this one unfortunate casualty.

The Russians made their first major effort to seize the town in the early morning of 27 February as armour and infantry closed in after an intensive artillery barrage. A large column of tanks and military vehicles penetrated the lines and entered the city, almost reaching the town square. This attack was beaten back in a much-publicised ambush which halted the column and attacked them with drones and artillery fire. The remnants were counterattacked by Ukraine's 92 Mechanized Brigade and forced to withdraw, leaving behind seven tanks and APCs.

Even as Kharkiv was being addressed, further to the northeast, the smaller town of Sumy was similarly reached by the Russians in the early hours of 24 February. In the surprise of the initial attacks, the Russians captured half the city by 26 February, only to be evicted by a Ukrainian counter-attack by the end of the day. Sumy, like Kharkiv, held on, and their stubborn defence largely reduced the Russian threat in the northeast.

Kharkiv remained cut off and settled down to a long hard grind. Raids and attacks on the town continued, practically on a daily basis. Russian paratroopers launched a major raid on 2 March, but they were rapidly counter-attacked and not allowed to establish a foothold. The fighting in Kharkiv turned into confused street fighting, with individual battles raging at every street and crossroad. The Ukrainians held on and succeeded in pushing back each ingress. Even the Russians who entered the city got a rude welcome, not the warm reception they had been told to expect. Videos emerged of a civilian coolly walking up to a Russian tank, as its crew looked confusedly around, lifting his rocket launcher, firing and destroying the tank and calmly walking away. Two soldiers of the 3rd Motor Rifle Division were killed and 28 others hospitalised when "a kind, elderly lady" handed out cakes to them, which later turned out to be laced with cyanide. The reception at Kharkiv was a foretaste of what was to come in other cities as well.

As attack after attack stalled, Major General Vitaly Gerasimov, the Deputy Commander of the 41st Combined Arms Army, moved ahead to urge his troops forward, and was killed in a sniping attack. A major factor of this campaign was the inordinately high killing of senior Russian officers, whose locations were detected when they used unsecured communication networks. US intelligence also helped identify and target senior commanders and provided advance information of Russian movement and plans.

For much of March and early April, the city remained besieged. Then in mid-April, the Russians withdrew from the Kyiv sector and renewed their focus in the east. The actions to capture Kharkiv intensified as many of the troops who were released from Kyiv were sent to this sector. Villages around the town changed hands with bewildering frequency, with villages being captured and retaken in the course of a single day. The dreaded Russian artillery and rocket batteries subjected the town to terrible shelling which took a horrible toll of civilian lives. Over 60,000 civilians were evacuated in humanitarian corridors, but those who remained faced the firing virtually daily for over three months.

The tide changed around the first week of May. On 06 May, the Ukrainians launched a counter-offensive along a broad front, north and south of Kharkiv. The offensive, spearheaded by the 92nd and 93rd Mechanized Brigades, successfully recaptured around 40 villages around the town, and forced the artillery batteries to move away. The Ukrainian offensive advanced east of the town, a manoeuvre that could have cut off the Russians from their supply lines in Belgorod within Russia. By the second week of May, the Russians began withdrawing from Kharkiv in much the same manner they had withdrawn from Kyiv. By most accounts, the Russians did not fight a delaying battle, but concentrated on preserving their supply lines. The Ukrainians pushed eastwards and reached the line of the Siverskyi Donets River where, in a major action, they destroyed a Russian pontoon bridge and cut off their routes of retreat. In the chaotic withdrawal that followed, the Ukrainians claimed to have decimated two complete battalion tactical groups and captured much of their heavy equipment. The Ukrainians advanced virtually up to the border and reconnaissance units of the 227 Battalion posted selfies of themselves standing by the border pillars, which were flashed across the world as proof of Ukrainian victory at Kharkiv.

The Russian pull-back from the Kharkiv region was announced in much the same way as their pull-back from Kyiv. The Russian spokesman of the Defence Ministry simply announced that the Russians were pulling back to "better positions." It did not hide the fact that along two major fronts—Kyiv in the north and Kharkiv in the northeast—the Russians had been unable to attain any of their objectives and were forced to withdraw. The success of the Ukrainian counter attack had revealed the vulnerability of the over-extended Russians. In a way, their withdrawal from these areas shortened the front considerably and they could focus on the prime objectives of Donbas in the east, and coastal areas of the south.

With the Ukrainians retaking the areas around Kharkiv and north-eastern Ukraine, the overall threat reduced considerably. This would have a long-term impact. Later, in September, the Ukrainians would use the same area around Kharkiv to launch another counter-offensive and this time the results would be even more decisive. The second Kharkiv counter-offensive of 22 September, would perhaps change the course of the entire war.

REFERENCES

"2 Russians killed, 28 hospitalized, after being poisoned"; Scully Rachel, *The Hill*, 04 April 2022.

"A large column of Russian vehicles pushing in to Sumy", *The Kyiv Independent*, 27 February 2022.

"Ex-Biathlete of Ukrainian National team dies in War"; *Odessa Journal*, 01 March 2022.

"Heaviest fighting in Ukraine, in and around Kharkiv"; *CNN*, 26 February 2022.

"Indian Student killed in Shelling in Kharkiv"; *The New Indian Express*, 02 March 2022.

"More than 60,000 evacuated from Kharkiv, says Governor" *Nova Chas*, 8 March 2022.

"No Indian left in Kyiv," NDTV.com, 02 March 2022.

"On the front lines of the Battle of Kharkiv", *BBC*, 10 May 2022.

"Russian Armored Vehicles meet tough Resistance in Kharkiv," *Wall Street Journal*. 27 February 22

"Russian pullback from Kharkiv," *The New York Times*, 09 May 2022.

"*The Battles of Kharkov–1941-43*", Casemate Publishers.

"Ukraine claims it killed Russian General during fighting in Kharkiv", *The Independent*. 08 March 2022.

"Ukraine has won Battle of Kharkiv," *The Guardian*, 14 May 2022.

"Ukrainian soldiers clash in fierce fight near Sumy", *The Kyiv Independent*. 24 February 2022.

THE RUSSIAN OFFENSIVE IN THE SOUTH

"It is not just a battle for the coast; it is a battle for Ukraine's future"

—Oleksiy Reznikov, Ukrainian Minister of Defence

The war in the south actually began when Russia annexed the Crimean Peninsula in March 2014 following the Maidan protests (See 'The Backdrop to War'). As the protests intensified, pro-Russian supporters (actively aided by Russia) seized the Parliament building. Russia used this act to remove the government council and install a pro-Russian government; conduct a referendum (in which over 90 per cent overwhelmingly voted to join Russia) and formally annexed Crimea into Russia. The annexation was resoundingly criticised by the West, which unleashed a raft of sanctions that had little effect. It did not change the *fait accompli.* Crimea, came back under Russian sway and they soon garrisoned 20,000 troops there and built up their naval and air elements in the strategic peninsula.

In the winter of 2021 as tensions rose, Russia concentrated its forces for an invasion of Ukraine, and placed an additional 20,000 troops in the Crimea. They would be used for an invasion from the south to seize the critical coastal areas and ports along the Sea of Azov and the Black Sea. Additional troops also built up in the Donetsk region, from where they could advance from the East and trap the Ukrainians in a pincer. The Russian aim seemed to be the seizure of the entire coastline, right from Mariupol in the east to Odesa in the west a swathe of over 400 kilometres. It was an ambitious plan; if it had succeeded it would have cut off Ukraine from the sea, made it land-locked and completely dependent on Russia.

On 24 February, troops of the 58th Army, the 8th Guards Combined Army, and the 22 Army Corps moved from their bases in Crimea and advanced northwards towards the Ukrainian mainland. They had to cross the narrow Isthmus of Perekop to enter the mainland and in one of the first actions of the war, the Ukrainians destroyed a vital bridge on the Isthmus to slow the Russian advance. Vitali Shakun, a combat engineer responsible for the demolition, detonated the explosives while on the bridge, killing himself but denying that vital bridge to the Russians. He was awarded a posthumous 'Hero of Ukraine'—Ukraine's highest gallantry award—for his act.

Though delayed, the Russians continued their advance northwards, from the Crimean Peninsula into the mainland. They soon secured the North Crimean Canal, a canal emanating from the Dnieper that supplied 85 per cent of Crimea's drinking water, which had been blocked by Ukraine after Russia took over the Crimea in 2014. The resumption of drinking water in Crimea was heralded as a major victory by Moscow, and a sign that their initial offensive was going well.

The Russian southern offensive moved upwards in three prongs. One moved eastwards towards Mariupol, the vital port town just 30 kilometres away from the Donbas. The thrust towards Mariupol was reinforced by a detachment of Russian troops and fighters from the Donetsk People's Republic, who moved out of Donetsk to approach Mariupol from the east. Another thrust line moved northward towards Melitopol and then further on towards Zaporizhzhia, the site of Ukraine's largest nuclear power plant. Perhaps that thrust line was designed to link up with the eastern thrust line, a manoeuvre that would carve out the entire eastern areas of Ukraine and bring it under Russian control. The third thrust moved westwards towards the port towns of Kherson and Mykolaiv. Taken together, the three prongs of the southern offensive would have carved a swathe of land over 200 kilometres deep all along the coast and seized the entire coastline along the Sea of Azov and the Black Sea along with its vital ports.

Further to the west, an ambitious amphibious assault was planned on

Odesa, Ukraine's major port on the Black Sea. Half of Ukraine's exports and imports moved through this port and it was the last major city on the coastline. Beyond Odesa, the route was open to Transnistria and Moldova. Russia also had its eyes on the large Russian-speaking population of Transnistria, and perhaps one of the eventual goals of the offensive was to reach Transnistria and amalgamate it into Russia like the other Ukrainian regions it had annexed. The loss of Odesa would have been comparable to the loss of Kyiv or Kharkiv and its defences were hurriedly built up as residents sandbagged the perimeter, mined the vulnerable areas along the shore, and prepared hedgehog defences along the crossroads. A barrage of 60 missiles hit Odesa which severely damaged its infrastructure in the initial days. Satellite images detected a complete amphibious brigade along with a large naval component which seemed to have assembled for the assault. By some accounts, the assault on Odesa was to have been launched at the very onset of the operation but the much-anticipated amphibious assault was called off at virtually the last moment.

The Southern Sector

The Russians set out to dominate the coast by launching missile strikes from their warships in the Black Sea. Islands along the coastline were also seized. Snake Island, a major base, just south of Odesa, was approached by MOSKVA, the flagship of the Black Sea fleet, with an ultimatum to surrender. Its defenders replied with the classic, "Russian warship, Go f—k yourself", a slogan that emblazoned itself in social media, T-shirts and coffee mugs, even in a postage stamp. Roman Hybov, the soldier of the Ukrainian border guards who reportedly made the defiant statement was later awarded the 'Hero of Ukraine' award. Yet, contrary to initial reports, the 13 soldiers who were defending the rocky outcrop of Snake Island, did not die fighting to the last man and last round. They surrendered instead and were taken into captivity, to be later released in a prisoner swap.

In the first few days of the war, the Russian advance was rapid. The 22 Army Corps moved almost 80 kilometres northwards and on 26 February, laid siege to the town of Enerhodar and occupied the Zaporizhzhia nuclear plant, the largest power plant in Europe. That was a huge blow for Ukraine and put its largest nuclear power plant in Russian hands. During the cross-firing, a fire broke out in one of the training facilities of the complex, but fortunately was controlled in time. None of the stowage buildings or the main reactors were affected and there was no radiation leak, but throughout the occupation of the plant, fears of inadvertent shelling or damage to the crucial nuclear plant remained.

The Russian thrust line, moving westwards, rapidly captured Kherson on 02 March, which became the first major city to be captured. The international airport came into Russian hands, its mayor was arrested, and the municipal administration replaced with a pro-Russian council. Like the other towns invested by the Russians, Kherson suffered tremendous damage from the strikes that preceded its capture. Concurrently, the Russians also approached the towns of Melitopol and Berdiansk. Russian forces captured Berdiansk on 28 February 2022, and seized six Ukrainian patrol boats in the harbour; one of the major successes of the southern campaign. Melitopol, a vital ship-building centre, was attacked on 25 February and captured after heavy fighting on 11 March. One by one, the port towns began falling into Russian hands and slowly the control of the entire coast was seized.

The Russians discovered that occupying a town was a far cry from holding it. Their troops were subject to sniper attacks and ambushes. Resentful civilians attacked them with Molotov cocktails and other expedients. One video circulating on social media showed an old woman offering a packet of sunflower seeds to a bewildered Russian soldier telling him to put it in his pocket, so it would sprout sunflowers when he was killed and buried in their soil. Another video showed a Russian tank approaching a town square, with its commander telling the local population to stop resisting. A civilian calmly walked up to the tank with a rocket launcher and fired on the tank setting it ablaze. It seemed that the Russian soldiers were actually taken by surprise by the level of anger and resentment amongst the local population. They were perhaps half-expecting to be greeted as 'liberators.'

The Southern Thrust

The third prong of the southern offensive moved eastwards in the direction of Mariupol, just 30 kilometres from the Donbas. This was launched in conjunction with attacks from the pro-Russian separatists of the Donetsk provinces, who approached it from the east. The Russian offensive was actually remarkably successful. It captured areas along the coastline almost 200 kilometres deep, and took control of most of the major cities, including Kherson, Mykolaiv, Melitopol, Zaporizhzhia, and Berdiansk. Virtually all of Kherson and Zaporizhzhia Oblasts were in their hands. From here they could go westwards towards Odesa, move northwards to link up with their eastern thrust line, and also be able to form a land bridge to connect the Donbas with the Crimea. It was quite a major achievement, but one prize still eluded the Russians. Mariupol, the crucial port town in the east which still held on. The story of its defence and ultimate fall is one of the most stirring stories of the war.

The Battle for Mariupol

Mariupol is the largest city of the Donetsk Oblast, the southern province of the Donbas, which is largely controlled by Russian-backed separatists of the Donetsk People's Republic (DPR). It is one of the largest Russian-speaking cities of Ukraine but after the siege of the city which destroyed over 95 per cent of its infrastructure and killed an estimated 1,400 civilians, most of the Russian-speaking population, switched to Ukrainian, rather than speak the language of 'the invader'.

The city is also a major industrial hub and home to Ukraine's largest steel plant, the Azovstal Iron and Steel Works. Located just 30 kilometres from Donetsk, its capture was essential to provide the Russians with a land bridge to Crimea.

The city was in the forefront of the war since May 2014, when the uprising in Crimea and Donbas began. Militants of the Russian-backed DPR took control of the city and forced Ukrainian troops to abandon it. That very month, Ukrainian troops recaptured the vital city, which then faced repeated attacks by the DPR fighters who vowed to capture it. Fighting continued for months till the ceasefire came into place with the signing of the Minsk Accord and the conflict was finally frozen.

One of the major groups involved in the recapture and defence of Mariupol was the Azov Battalion, a Ukrainian volunteer militia, with openly neo-Nazi and ultra-nationalist views. They even sport the SS insignia on their badges and give the Nazi salute. Members of the Azov Battalion, along with the 36th Marine Brigade and members of Territorial defence forces held the city even now. As one of Putin's goals of "de-Nazification of Ukraine", Mariupol and its defenders became an important ideological and symbolic target, besides its strategic importance as the gateway to the Crimea.

On 24 February, Russian artillery pounded the city in a foretaste of what was to come. The same day, Russian forces, along with their supporters of the DPR, advanced from the Donetsk in the east, hoping to capture the border town with a swift land attack. This force was halted near the village of Pavlopil, and in a major encounter, was forced to withdraw with the loss of 22 tanks and armoured personnel carriers. At the same time, the Russians launched an amphibious assault about 70 kilometres to the west of Mariupol on the night of 25 February, deploying around 2,000 marines who established a beachhead and then began moving towards Mariupol.

By 01 March, Russian and DPR forces advancing from the east linked up with the Marines moving in from the west and by 02 March, Mariupol was completely surrounded. A naval blockade from the sea completed the encirclement, and slowly the noose around the town tightened. The Russians called on the defenders to surrender, an offer that was rudely rebuffed. The city was rapidly running out of food, fuel, and supplies. The last cellular tower was hit and all mobile and internet communications were completely cut. As the city was being bombarded into submission, an estimated 60-70 artillery and missile strikes took place daily in the worst days of March. The mayor appealed for a humanitarian corridor to enable citizens to leave the war zone. Over 200,000 civilians were evacuated, but most still remained and the war continued around them for months to come.

Throughout March, Mariupol remained under siege, subject to attacks virtually every day. On 20 March, DPR forces broke through the inner line of defences and captured the international airport, cutting off the last tenuous link with the rest of the world. The few supplies that were flown in by air also stopped now. Russian fighters reached the city centre, and captured the railway station, the radio and television buildings, and other important communication centres. Russian units entering the town were soon engaged in house-to-house battles, sniping and bitter street fighting, akin to what must have gone on during the bitter siege of Stalingrad in the winter of 1942. Amongst the over 2,000 Russian casualties in the town was Major General Oleg Mityaev, the Commander of the 150th Motorized Rifle Division who was killed trying to lead yet another unsuccessful attack into the town.

By end March, even though Mariupol remained notionally under Ukrainian control, its forces had run out of food and ammunition, medical supplies and even clean drinking water. The situation was dire and on 04 April 267 Marines of the Ukrainian naval forces surrendered *en masse.* (The Russians claim that 2,000 had surrendered). This act caused tremendous acrimony amongst the fanatical Azov Battalion, whose members accused the Marines of cowardice. With this surrender, which was done without informing the defenders still holding out, a vast gap came up in the positions. There was no coordinated line of defence now and the remnants of the Marines and the Azov Battalion fought in isolated pockets of resistance, with virtually each man for himself.

Mariupol was a shattered city, but the beleaguered defenders still held on desperately. The 36 Marine Brigade tried to break out of the ring around them, but were cut down by fire and many were killed or captured. The remnants, mainly from the fanatical Azov Battalion, finally holed up in the Azovstal Steel Plant, "The Fortress within the City". On 20 April, Putin announced the 'liberation of Mariupol' but refused to order to storm the plant, choosing to exhaust the defenders into submission instead. Even as the Azovstal steel plant held out, the Russians began clearing the rubble and on 09 May, Russia's Victory Day, held a victory parade in the streets of Mariupol.

The 82-day long battle of Mariupol finally ended on 17 May when the last bastion, the remnants in the Azovstal Steel Plant, finally surrendered and were led into captivity in buses emblazoned with the infamous 'Z'. Its stubborn defence was very much like the role the German 6th Army played in Stalingrad in the winter of 1942. Though cut off and virtually decimated, the 6th Army held on for three months tying down Soviet troops that could have been used elsewhere. Similarly, Mariupol tied down 10-12 battalion operating groups for months and divided the Russian forces east and west of the city.

Mariupol was the city that suffered the most during the war. Over 95 per cent of the town was destroyed and over 20,000 civilians reportedly killed during the fighting for the city. The capture of Mariupol, though at great cost, was one of the notable Russian successes of the war. With this, the land route all along the coast to Crimea was open. It now gave the Russians full control of the Sea of Azov and provided an unbroken stretch of eastern and southern Ukraine around the size of Greece. The area extended 800 kilometres from Luhansk in the east to Kherson on the Black Sea. The Russians set about fortifying the positions, erecting barriers, and digging trenches to stave off the Ukrainian counter-attacks. They installed pro-Russian mayors and placed their own governing bodies in the captured territories to 'Russify' them.

The Russians also suffered a huge loss of prestige and naval capability when the flagship of the Black Sea Fleet, the MOSKVA, was sunk in a missile attack on 14 April. It was patrolling off the Black Sea coast when it was hit by two Neptune anti-ship missiles fired from the coast. The ship caught fire and the crew was evacuated, but it sank while being towed away. The Russians denied that it had been hit by missiles, attributing the loss to an internal fire, but satellite imaging confirmed that the ship had indeed been hit by missiles. Ironically, the MOSKVA was built in the same ports of Melitopol and Mykolaiv in 1983 when Ukraine was part of the Soviet Union, which it now bombed and from where the missiles that sank it were fired from. With the loss of the MOSVKA, Russian ships were now forced to keep a considerable distance from the coast, reducing their ability to influence operations on land, or even launch amphibious operations.

With Mariupol under their belt, the Russians now had a base from where they could advance northwards to link up with the Eastern thrust, or even develop operations further west along the coast towards the prize of Odesa. Though the south with virtually the entire areas of the Kherson and Zaporizhzhia Oblasts had come under Russian control, it at a high cost. They would face the brunt of the Ukrainian offensives when they came in September, but for now, they turned their attention to the next major objective of the campaign—Donbas in the east.

REFERENCES

"Fighting reaches Center of Mariupol", *Radio Free Europe*, 23 March 2022.

"First Ukraine city falls as Russia Strikes more Civilian Targets"; Michael Schwartz, *The New York Times*, 03 March 2022.

"Fourth Russian General killed in Ukraine", MSN, 18 March 2022.

"Melitopol city taken by Russian Army", Marca, Spain, 26 February 2022.

"Putin calls off plan to Storm Mariupol Plant, opts for Blockade instead", Reuters, 21 April 2022.

"Putin reclaims Crimea for Russia and denounces West"; *The New York Times*, 18 March 2014.

"Putin signs Russia-Crimea Treaty," *BBC News*, 18 March 2014.

"Russia says Ukrainian Marines surrendered in Mariupol", *Eurasian Times*, 06 April 2022.

"Russia's amphibious Operations Dilemma, www.navalnews.com, 20 March 2022.

"Russian forces unblock water flow of Canal to Crimea, Moscow says"; Reuters, 01 March 2022.

"Russian Offensive Campaign Assessment," Institute for the Study of War, 28 February 2022.

"Russian troops in Final Stages of Readiness, add to Worries for Ukraine", *The New York Times*, 25 February 2022.

"Russian Troops take Zaporizhzhia Nuclear Plant"; *ABC News*, 04 March 2022.

"Russian-speakers in Ukraine are struggling to learn a new tongue", *The Economist*, 27 August 2022.
"Sinking of the MOSKVA: What we Know", https://www.theguardian.com 15 April 2022.
"Strategic port of Mariupol now Surrounded by Russian forces", *BBC News*, 04 March 2022.
"Surrender of last of Azovstal ends Ukraine most Brutal siege", https://atalayar.com, 21 May 2022.
"The Azov Battalion", *CBS News*, 22 March 2022.
"Timeline–Russia's siege of Mariupol", Max Hundar, Reuters, 30 March 2022.
"Ukraine gives medal to Soldier who told Russian warship to 'go f—" https://www.the guardian.com 29 March 2022.
"Ukraine Marine blows himself to delay Russian Advance, " https://www.ndtv.com, 26 Feb. 2022.
"Ukrainian Forces retake Port City from Rebels'" Reuters, 14 June 2014.

THE CAULDRON IN THE DONBAS

"The Donbas has been frothing and fermenting since 2014. But this is unlike anything I have seen before"

—Unknown Ukrainian Soldier

In the winter of 1942, the German Sixth Army was trapped inside the ruins of Stalingrad, surrounded by Soviet forces. The ring of steel around them closed within which German units and formations were gradually encircled and destroyed. The Germans called it the cauldron. A witch's cauldron that frothed and foamed and swirled; and then trapped and consumed all within it till the final denouement.

The Donbas has also earned the moniker 'The Cauldron'. The Russian offensive in the Donbas has seen heavy, confused fighting, with immense losses to both sides. The tactics followed by the Russians closely resemble those followed by the Soviet-era armies. Slow advances and encirclements, a massive pounding of the trapped forces by artillery, and then an overwhelming assault to finish off the remnants of the defenders. Like Stalingrad and Kursk, the battles involved a series of skirmishes all along the front, and like those two famous battles, the outcome of the Battle of Donbas had a major impact on the war.

The cauldron in the Donbas has been simmering since 2014. In March 2014, as the Maidan protests rocked the country and a strong pro- and anti-

Russian sentiment spread across the nation, the provinces of Luhansk and Donetsk which make up the Donbas too came under the fervour. The population of the Donbas is largely ethnic Russian and a series of pro-Russian riots broke out in the Donetsk and Luhansk Oblasts of Eastern Ukraine. These protests coincided with the Russian annexation of Crimea and were undoubtedly orchestrated by Russia. Russian-backed separatists of the Donetsk People's Republic and the Luhansk People's Republic seized government buildings, held officials hostage, and launched a widespread campaign of armed conflict against the Ukrainian forces under the banner of 'Russiyana'.

Ukraine responded by launching what it termed as "Anti-Terror Operations" against the separatists' groups in April 2014. Security forces were pushed in, and a series of military operations regained control of the Donbas and pushed the separatists back to the Russian-Ukraine border. With their proxy groups on the back foot, Russia intervened directly. It sent in convoys of 'humanitarian aid' to help the "oppressed, Russian-speaking population". It also pumped in Special Forces personnel and advisors to help the separatists, along with vast quantities of military aid that were smuggled in through humanitarian convoys. Although Russia staunchly denies it, the presence of 'Little Green Men' operating within Ukrainian soil has been an open secret since 2014.

The Minsk Agreement signed between Ukraine, Russia and the separatist groups finally brought a ceasefire in the Donbas, but it was violated blatantly by both sides. No less than 29 separate ceasefires were signed, but it did stop the fighting. Separatists intensified their activities on Ukrainian forces and both sides fortified their positions by developing a vast network of trenches, bunkers, and tunnels, in the areas they controlled, creating a *de facto* 'Line of Contact' running between the two sides. The static trench warfare along the Line of Contact, became 'a frozen conflict' which continued at low levels interminably, and claimed a soldier every day or so.

Donbas continued to simmer. Then in 2021, when Russia built up troops along Ukraine's borders, the Donbas erupted again. Separatist groups increased their activities against Ukrainian security forces, undoubtedly coordinated by Russian forces. As the security forces reacted, and violence increased, Russia used this as a pretext to formally recognise the Donetsk People's Republic and

Luhansk People's Republic as 'Independent states,' on 22February. The very next day, it sent in troops to "protect the Russian-speaking population". The pot was reaching boiling point and erupted on 24 February when Russia launched its invasion of Ukraine.

The Offensive

When Russia launched its offensive across Ukraine in 22 February, a thrust line also headed eastwards from the Donbas, comprising the 8th Combined Arms Army with the 1st and 2nd Army Corps along with fighters of the separatist groups operating in Donbas. Surprisingly, this sector did not see any large-scale fighting till around mid-April, with the two sides largely confined along the Line of Contact. It was only after Russia withdrew from Kyiv and announced its intention to focus on the Donbas, "The original aim of the campaign", that the Donbas erupted again. Troops from Kyiv, Sumy and the north-eastern sectors were transferred there as Russia built up a force of around 60,000 men—three armies comprising over 75 battalion tactical groups, along with around 14,500 fighters of the DPR and LPR. Approximately 18-20,000 mercenaries from Syria, Libya, Ethiopia, and the infamous Wagner Group also joined the fray, as Russia prepared for a decisive battle to take over the Luhansk and Donetsk provinces.

Around a third of the Ukrainian army, most of them battle-hardened veterans with years of combat experience in the Donbas, were deployed in the Donbas. Around six brigades, along with reservists, foreign volunteers and partisans, were build up there—a force estimated to be 40-50,000 men. Russia held a strong numerical superiority and had the attackers' advantage of being able to concentrate its forces at the point of decision. Most importantly, it had the firepower. It had a 10:1 superiority in guns, and almost 40:1 in ammunition, and their dreaded artillery and rocket batteries could rain massive volumes of fire on the defenders. The Ukrainian inferiority in artillery—both in ammunition, guns, and ranges—was a crippling disadvantage which would even out only in the later stages of the war, when sophisticated Western artillery like the HIMARS, with greater ranges and lethality would be made available to them.

On 18 April, Russia began an intensive bombardment of positions in

Luhansk, Donetsk, and Kharkiv Oblasts. The impact of the concentrated fire could be felt as far as Mariupol and Kharkiv, as the front lines were churned by a continuous barrage of artillery fire. The Battle of Donbas had begun.

The Russians advanced in a slow creeping movement along the entire front in the Luhansk and Donetsk regions. They did not go in for deep grandiose manoeuvres, as they had in the initial days. Instead, they advanced slowly and steadily, in the wake of intense bombardments that churned entire villages and defensive positions that could be mopped up by the following infantry. It was a slow, expensive battle, but using these tactics they crept forward at 3-5 kilometres a day

The Russians took over the major towns of Popikka, Popasna, Kremina, and Rubizhne and by mid-May had reached the line of the Donets River, the line roughly separating the Donbas region from the rest of Ukraine. As the Russians attempted to force a crossing across the river they were violently counter-attacked by the Ukrainians, who destroyed the pontoon bridge they had established and virtually eliminated two complete battalion tactical groups trying to get across. Around 500 Russian soldiers were killed and were eventually forced to withdraw with heavy casualties.

The Russians repaid the favour just a few days later. They had captured most of the existing bridges on the Donets River, and the Ukrainians established a pontoon bridge a few kilometres to the north to supply their forces and also enable them to withdraw. This bridge was detected and destroyed by Russian artillery fire, which cut off most of the Ukrainian forces east of the river.

Ukrainian forces still held on in towns and villages, fighting grim, isolated battles all along the front. Like the battle of Kursk in March 1943, it turned into a brutal war of attrition which could only be won by the side with greater staying power. The Russians resorted to a series of small encirclements which cut of Ukrainian units and sub-units and then pounded the trapped forces with intense fire power. The grinding tactics paid dividends as the Russians slowly but steadily extended their sway, concentrating first on Luhansk in the north and then towards Donetsk to its south.

The two major objectives that would enable the Russians to gain control over the Luhansk were the twin towns of Sievierodonetsk and Lysychansk which were astride both sides of the Donets River, with Sievierodonetsk to the

Area of Major Fighting in Donbas

east of the river, and Lysychansk to its west. The two towns formed the major administrative and communication centres of the Luhansk. Sieverodonetsk came under major attack in mid-April from the 4th Guards Tank Division in early May, when it was encircled and its outlying villages captured one by one. The first direct assault came in on 27 May. The Russians established a foothold; were thrown back, again entered the town, and then continued fighting—street by street, crossing by crossing, block by block—for over a month before they could eventually take over the bombed-out town. The Ukrainians launched a violent counter-offensive to retake this vital town, which failed. By mid-July, Ukrainian troops were ordered to withdraw from Sieverodonetsk and move west across the Donets River to the twin town of Lysychansk. It was a controversial order, but the withdrawal helped save the beleaguered troops and also enabled them to occupy more defensible positions on the other side of the Donetsk River.

With the capture of Sieverodonetsk, Russia rapidly took over the communication hubs of Lysychansk and Lyman, and gained control of all of Luhansk Province. They had attained one of their major objectives of the war, and now could focus on the Donetsk. The units had a much-needed operational pause in the first two weeks of July and then renewed their offensive in the Donetsk Province. Almost 70 per cent of Donetsk was already in their hands, and as per plan, the entire region was to be occupied by end-August to enable them to hold a referendum in the Donbas, and then annex the areas in the same way they had annexed Crimea in 2014.

Securing the Donetsk proved more difficult than the Luhansk. Over a period of six weeks from mid-July to August, the Russian war machine crept on inexorably, taking village after village and overrunning position after position. More discerning observers would have noticed that Ukrainian resistance was reducing. Artillery firing, even in counter-bombardments, was a trickle, and no new reinforcements were being sent into the area. Not known to the Russians, the Ukrainians were building up their own strength for an offensive that would come around September and preserving men and ammunition for it.

In August, the first Ukrainian offensive burst out of Kherson region in the south (See The Kherson Offensive) The offensive was heavily publicised, and did make some headway (but not as much as it was purported to have made); but it alarmed the Russians sufficiently to pause their own offensive and send some of their best troops to the south to help stabilise the situation.

Even now, for the Russian, things seemed to be going as per plan, as they were so fond of reporting. A little slow, but according to plan, all right. They had secured the Kherson and Zaporizhzhia regions of the South, all of Luhansk and most of Donetsk in the east—almost 20 per cent of Ukraine's area. Their success glossed over the fact that their men had been fighting for over seven months without a pause. Their units were depleted—most had lost over 25-30 per cent of men and equipment. They held a ragged and tired front across 1,200 kilometres. It was a situation that could explode any moment..

And explode it did. The Russians had taken their eyes of the ball and focused in the south where the Ukrainians had launched the offensive in the Kherson sector. They had even depleted the east and north-eastern sectors to send reinforcements there. Then in the first week of September, the Ukrainians launched their counter-offensive in the northeast that burst through from the area of Kharkiv, taking the Russians completely by surprise. The offensive raced through Russian positions and retook the areas in a matter of weeks what the Russians had taken months to capture. (The Ukrainian offensives are covered in detail in subsequent chapters).

The war had just changed course again—this time in Ukraine's favour.

Areas under Russian Control at the End of Phase II

REFERENCES

"Bloody River Battle was third in Three Days", *BBC News*, 13 May 2022.

"Inside the Frozen Trenches of Eastern Europe", *TIME*, 26 April 2022.

"Massive Bombardment signals Russia's Renewed Offensive", *Forbes*, 21 April 2022.

"New Ceasefire enters force in Donbas"; TASS, 29 December 19???

"Putin announces Donetsk and Luhansk Recognition", *BBC News*, 22 February 2022.

"Putin claims Russia was forced to Defend Russian speaking Population", *The Interpreter*, 12 October 2016.

"Russia deploys 20000 mercenaries in Battle for Ukraine's Donbas", *The Guardian*, 19 April 2022.

"Russia pours in more troops in the East", Adam Schrek, Associated Press, 21 April 2022.

"Russia's Cauldron Tactics Tipping Donbas Battle in its Favor", *The Guardian*, 27 May 2022.

"Russian Battalion wiped out trying to cross River of Death", Parker Charlie, *The Times*, 14 May 2022.

"The Stalingrad Cauldron", The University Press, https://kansaspress.ku.edu

"The War Report: Armed Conflict in 2014;" Bellal Annyssa; The Oxford University Press.

"Ukraine says Donetsk Anti-Terror Operation underway", *BBC News*, 15 April 2014.

"Ukraine Struggles to Combat Russia's Artillery Superiority", *The Kyiv Independent*, 01 August 2022.

THE UKRAINIAN COUNTER-OFFENSIVE IN THE SOUTH: THE MATADOR'S CAPE

"There is no place for them on Ukrainian soil. If they want to survive, it is time for the Russian military to surrender or flee."

—President Vladimir Zelensky, 29 August 2022

The Planned Ukrainian Offensive

The Russian advance in the Donbas had taken over Luhansk Province after three months of slow battle and then turned its attention towards the adjoining province of Donetsk. The war turned into a long battle of attrition, in which the Russians, with their greater resources, would eventually prevail. The Ukrainians had been received more muscle with over $ 40 billion of Western aid and an influx of weaponry, including the long-range HIMARS artillery system from the USA. They had also inducted over 200,000 reservists, who had been trained and amalgamated in the front lines. They were keen on breaking the stalemate and there was growing talk of a counter-offensive to recapture their lost territories.

During the southern offensive of February-May, the Russians had taken over most of the Kherson, Zaporizhzhia, and Mykolaiv oblasts and captured the important cities on the coast, including Kherson, Melitopol, Mariupol, and Mykolaiv. They reached as far as Zaporizhzhia in the north (site of Ukraine's largest nuclear reactor) and taken over the area from Kherson to Donetsk province. This was a loss of some of Ukraine's most vital territories that threatened to cut it off from the sea.

A Ukrainian counter was definitely on the cards. They had last achieved a major success in June when they managed to recapture Kharkiv and pushed Russian troops back across the border in that sector. Since then, they were on the back foot. Pushing the Russians back from the Donbas region was not feasible. The Russians were well deployed there and entrenched in fortified positions. A counter-offensive was thus planned in the south with the aim of reaching the Mykolaiv-Zaporizhzhia-Kherson line and recapturing the town of Kherson. That would provide a huge boost to morale and unbalance Russian actions in the east. Most importantly, it would keep the Russians away from Odesa, the only port still in Ukrainian hands, and divert them from their offensive in the Donbas.

Russia had captured the entire area along the coastline of the Sea of Azov during the initial days of the war and Kherson, in fact, was the first major Ukrainian city to fall. Russia controlled 95 per cent of the Kherson Oblast and over 70 per cent of the Zaporizhzhia Oblast and had occupied the entire coastline. In the areas they held, the process of 'Russification' had already begun. Municipal councils were replaced with pro-Russian members; Russian passports were issued (with newly-born children being granted automatic Russian citizenship). Pay and pensions was issued in roubles instead of the Ukrainian hryvnia, and statues of Lenin had come up in the town squares. Militarily, there was a pause in the actions in the south as the Russians focused on the Donbas.

In the South, both sides had established defensive lines roughly along the line of the Inhulets and the Dnieper rivers. Raids, sniping, local actions, and artillery duels continued. Partisan action in the occupied territory had also intensified which had reportedly claimed over 100 Russian soldiers. In Kherson, a bomb placed in a café frequented by Russian officers killed seven high-ranking officers. These were mere pinpricks. The Ukrainians had been planning a major offensive around July to divert attention from the East and also "retake all the occupied areas of the south, including Crimea".

In early July, messages were passed to the residents of Kherson and Zaporizhzhia to evacuate their homes or stay in protective shelters for an impending offensive. Western media too, was agog about this great offensive which would change the war. The defence minister, Oleksii Reznikov, announced that Ukraine was amassing a million-strong force for the counter-offensive (a little exaggeration since the entire Ukrainian security forces did not have so many men) and that the entire Kherson region would be free by September. The Ukrainian offensive was to move along a 100-kilometre long swathe from Mykolaiv in the north to Kherson in the south and simply clear the area from Russian occupation. These ambitious claims were touted, and widely publicised, but the underlying aim was even more subtle; it aimed at drawing Russian attention towards the south and deplete their forces elsewhere.

The Counter-offensive

The Ukrainian counter-offensive began on 24 July when Ukrainian artillery began targeting Russian positions using their newly-acquired HIMARS systems. The long ranges and precision munitions of these systems allowed them to strike deep on the rear of Russian positions, an advantage they did not have earlier. In the opening salvoes, artillery attacks targeted ammunition dumps and command posts, destroying three of them in a week. Artillery fire also damaged the Antonivka Bridge and other critical bridges on the Dnieper River, cutting off supply lines to the Russian forces west of the river and forcing them to withdraw.

The withdrawal of the Russian forces was hailed as a great success and Ukraine claimed to have retaken 44 villages in the first month of the offensive, including the vital villages of Lozove and Andrivka, which overlooked the Dnieper river crossings. They followed the same tactics used by the Russians, making small creeping movements supported by artillery fire, and taking small objectives. Though the outlying villages were retaken, none of the major towns, especially Kherson, which was the aim of the offensive, were severely threatened. The recapture of Kherson would have been a major morale booster, especially since Kherson was the first town to fall into Russian hands in the early days of March. The advance forced the Russians to send in 12 battalion tactical groups from the north-eastern sector to add to the 13 battalion tactical groups that they had in the area. (As events would show, the side-stepping of Russian troops to this sector was one of the major aims of the Ukrainian operation). With over 25 battalion tactical groups in the area, the Ukrainians offensive slowed down and they were unable to penetrate the Russian defence lines which were prepared along geographical features, well dug-in, and heavily fortified. Slowly, the Ukrainian offensive began petering out and actions were more at the local level rather than coordinated activities along the entire front. Again, all this was part of an overall plan.

Area of Ukrainian Counter-Attacks in the South

The Ukrainians achieved a major success when an explosion ripped through Saky airbase in the city of Nevofedorivka, around 100 kilometres deep inside Crimea on 09 August. That blast destroyed around eight Sukhoi ground attack fighters and some helicopters, almost half of Russia's Black Sea naval aviation resources. Ukraine did not take responsibility for the blast, but could not resist warning the Russians of the dangers of smoking on the base. Russia claimed the blast was the result of an accident, but the Black Sea Fleet Commander was sacked a week later—the highest ranking General to be removed. Another blast hit the headquarters of the Black Sea fleet killing an unspecified number of senior officers. These attacks would have definitely hurt, and the Ukrainian ability to strike target deep in the rear, coupled with an intensification of partisan activity, further divided Russian reaction.

Another crisis also arose when Russian and Ukrainian troops exchanged fire near the Zaporizhzhia nuclear plant, the largest in Europe. The plant is strategically located on the Kakhovha Reservoir on the south bank of the Dnieper River and thus controls the Dnieper River crossings. Heavy artillery and small arms fire set a training facility ablaze, damaged the radiation sensors and shells landed dangerously close to the nuclear storage facilities. Predictably, both sides blamed each other. The fires were put out before they could cause much damage but raised fears of a radioactive leak which could easily engulf all of Europe in a Chernobyl kind of nuclear disaster.

On 20 August, the Russians launched their own Southern offensive which recaptured some of the lost areas in the Mykolaiv oblast. That offensive was largely to strengthen their defensive positions and did not advance deeper into Ukrainian lines towards the west. Russia also began posturing from Belarus in the north and resumed strikes on Kyiv, thus reinforcing the threat to the capital. By end-August, the Ukrainian counter-offensive seemed to have run its course without achieving any of the aims it had set for itself. Then, on 29 August, President Zelensky announced that the counter-offensive in the south was being reactivated and Ukrainian activities intensified in the sector. The much-touted Ukrainian aim to recapture Kherson was again announced in the Ukrainian Parliament and on the official website of Operational Command South, the military headquarters responsible for actions in this sector.

All this was part of a grand deception plan. After all, if one is to launch an offensive, it is not advertised as broadly as the Ukrainians did, and the Russians should have smelt a rat. However, they did not and allowed themselves to be diverted towards the south, and sent their best units there. The initial actions in the south were those of a Matador's Cape—designed to distract while the main action took place elsewhere. As the widely-publicised actions continued in the south, another grand offensive was launched just a week later on 06 September. This offensive was not directed in the south. It fell 600 kilometres away in the northeast, in the area of Kharkiv. The deception tactics followed by the Ukrainians enabled them to meet rapid success, which would virtually change the course of the war.

The actions of the Kharkiv offensive will be covered in detail in the subsequent chapter. What stood out was how well it was coordinated with the southern offensive which enabled both offensives to make impressive gains. The Kharkiv offensive burst out in September and retook over 6,000 square kilometres in just a month or so. The Ukrainians used the dislocation it caused to renew their own offensive in the south, which had been halted for a while, but now gathered momentum.

In mid-September, the Ukrainians renewed their push to the south. Some Russian units had been sent back to the North-eastern sector to stem the rot there, and the Russians were divided in both sectors. At the same time, around end September, Russia held a 'referendum' in its occupied territories and formally annexed Kherson, along with Zaporizhzhia, Luhansk and Donetsk regions. Two days later, on 02 October, the Ukrainians pushed ahead with their own offensive. They advanced in a wide sweep from north to south on the west bank of the Dnipro River that rapidly recaptured vital villages north and northwest of Kherson. The Ukrainians secured the western bank and the crucial bridges on the Dnipro River, in effect cutting off 15-20,000 Russian troops west of the river. The Ukrainian advance forced the Russians to blow up a dam on the Inhulets River to slow down their advance. Long-range artillery strikes also hit logistics depots, ammunition dumps, convoys, and bridges, cutting off supply and reinforcement routes. Russian commanders requested permission to withdraw to more defensible positions which was refused by President Putin, who was still smarting from the reverses in the northeast, and could not afford any further setbacks in this sector. Yet, within a month, the Ukrainians reclaimed over 2,400 square kilometres in the south.

By early November, the Ukraine offensive had captured most of the outlying positions around Kherson and were in a position to launch an attack on the town. Russia began evacuating citizens and grudgingly announced that "a grave situation has arisen". On 09 November, Russia aanounced that it would be withdrawing its troops from the city and move to better positions on the East bank of the Dnipro River. Kherson was a vital symbolic and strategic target, and the only provincial capital to be captured by Russia. The loss was a major setback, and would affect its hold not only on the coastal areas, but Crimea as well.

The Ukrainian offensive had made impressive gains in the South and in the East. Both sides occupied defensive positions roughly along the line of the Dnipro River in the South and the Oskil River in the East. The war was in a critical phase. Winter was approaching, and both sides had a window till around November or so to attain their objectives. After that, Marshal Winter would arrive, and the entire front would become a long war of attrition.

REFERENCES

"Fighting rages near Russian held Nuclear Plant in Zaporizhzhia", Reuters, 08 September 2022.

"Half of Russia's Black Sea Fleet Combat Jets out of Operation", Reuters, 19 August 2022.

"How HIMARS help Ukraine", *Al Jazeera*, 26 July 2022.

"How Russia is Imposing its Rule in Occupied Ukraine", *BBC News*, 11 May 2022.

"Kherson: Russia to withdraw troops from key Ukrainian City", BBC News, 9 November 2022

"Putin ups the ante, to Mobilize 3 Lakh troops", *Times of India*, 22 September 2022

"Russia annex 4 Ukrainian Territories", *Times of India*, 30 September 2022

"Russian Offensive Campaign Assessment," Institute for the Study of War, 4 October 2022.

"The Russian Occupation of Ukraine's Southern Region", Hedenshog Jakob, SCEEUS, 2 June 2022.

"Ukraine announces Offensive Operations across the South", *The New York Times*, 29 August 2022.

"Ukraine claims precise hit on Russian Military Unit in Occupied Kherson", *CNN*, 11 July 2022.

"Ukraine has One Million ready to Re-capture South", *The Times*, 10 July 2022.

"Ukraine says 2400 square kilometers liberated in the South", *CNN*, 7 October 2022.

"Ukraine strikes Antonivka Bridge, essential for Russia's Supply Lines in Occupied South," *CBS News*, 27 July 2022.

"Ukraine tells Residents to leave Occupied South due to Counter-attack Plans", *The Times*, 10 July 2022.

"Ukraine's growing 'Reserve Army' Getting Ready", https://news.sky.com 23 May 2022.

"Ukraine's long-awaited Southern Counter-offensive Begins with a Bang in Crimea", *POLITICO*, 10 August 2022.

"Ukraine's Southern Offensive was Designed to trick Russians", *The Guardian*, 11 September 2022.

"Zelensky tells Russian forces to flee as Ukraine starts Counter Offensive in Kherson", Reuters, 29 August 2022.

THE UKRAINIAN COUNTER-OFFENSIVE IN THE NORTHEAST: REACHING THE FRONTIER

"We were given our objective and told to just move. We didn't stop, we didn't sleep, we didn't eat. But we moved 90 kilometres and captured our objective in just three days."

—Ukrainian tankman from 92 Mechanized Brigade

The Kharkiv sector, northeast of Ukraine, had seen some bitter fighting in the early days of the war. This area is no stranger to war. It had seen some of the bitterest battles of World War II and had been captured and recaptured thrice by both the Germans and the Soviets. Its key position, just 80 kilometres from the Russian frontier, provided the gateway to both Ukraine and Russia and was significant to both.

Kharkiv, the second-largest town of Ukraine, had been hit by the Russian offensive in the very first day of the war. It held on for over three months, till a Ukrainian counter-offensive in May reclaimed the area and pushed back the Russian forces back to the border. That victory was one of the major Ukrainian victories of the campaign and helped stabilise the entire North-eastern sector. (See 'The North-eastern Front: Feb- May 2022).

For two months the sector was static, as the Russians focused on the Donbas and made slow, excruciating progress in the Luhansk and Donetsk provinces. They also made headway in the south with the capture of Mariupol and coastal areas up to Kherson. All this came at a cost. Its troops were tired and depleted, and their equipment suffered from constant usage and lack of maintenance. According to some Western sources, Russian casualties were in the region of 65-90,000 soldiers. Russia maintained that it had lost just around 6,000 soldiers killed, as per their Defence Minister Sergei Shoigu. By some accounts, most units had lost almost 20-25 per cent of their strength and no new reinforcements were forthcoming. Kharkiv was a relatively dormant sector and had settled into a stalemate of artillery duels and occasional raids by both sides. This would change abruptly, as the Ukrainians launched their decisive counter-offensive here in conjunction with their offensive in the south.

The planning for the Ukrainian counter-offensive had been going on for months. The ideal time frame was identified as around August-September which would give a window up to November or so before winter set in. The Ukrainians had suffered heavy casualties as well, (reportedly around 14-16,000 till October) especially in the Donbas battles where they were losing almost 100-150 soldiers every day. Ukrainian morale, too, had suffered from the reverses in the south and the east and they needed a victory to galvanize their army and ensure that the Western allies remained committed to the war and continued to supply them with arms and aid. An estimated 60-80,000 reservists had been trained and amalgamated into front-line units. They had gained proficiency in the newly-acquired Western weapons, like HIMARS long-range artillery which had a distinct qualitative edge over the earlier Soviet-era weaponry. Their air defence too was raised with HARM anti-radiation missiles which downed one aircraft and two helicopters on the first day of the offensive, in effect negating the Russian use of their superior air power.

Most of all, they had access to US intelligence which provided them with the exact location and dispositions of the Russians and identified the weak spots in their deployment. Based on inputs provided by US intelligence, two broad options emerged; to strike in the south towards Kherson and the coastal areas, or to strike in the northeast towards Kharkiv. After much deliberation, it was decided to launch an offensive on both locations, first in the south, then in the northeast. The timings were deliberately staggered to disrupt Russian response and cause even further dislocation.

In early August, the Ukrainians launched their offensive in the Kherson sector, moving in a swathe from Zaporizhzhia to Kherson (See The Kherson

Offensive). Over a period of a month, the offensive pushed the Russians back across the Dnipro River, along a rough line Zaporizhzhia-Melitopol-Kherson. Though that offensive regained sizeable territory, it could not recapture Kherson or any of the major towns but the Kherson offensive was widely publicised as part of an overall deception plan. It forced the Russians to pull out around a dozen battalion tactical groups from the northeast and eastern sectors, including crack units like the 1st Guards Tank Army, and send them to reinforce the south, leaving large gaps in their defences. While Russian eyes were being diverted to the south, the offensive force was preparing for a launch in the Kharkiv sector.

The Ukrainians concealed their offensive forces well. They had shifted some of their forces to the south, (to add to the impression that their focus was there) while retaining the bulk of their mechanized forces. Artillery firing and other actions in the Kharkiv sector had also reduced while they built up their offensive force in great secrecy. Even their preliminary attacks were conducted with relatively little armour and heavy equipment to conceal their true strength. They did succeed in lulling the Russians into complacency in this sector.

The offensive began on 06 September with long-range artillery strikes hitting Russian ammunition dumps, command and control centres and headquarters deep in the rear. In the wake of intense artillery barrages, the main thrust was launched in the direction of Balakliya, a vital road and rail junction which had been identified as the weak spot in the Russian front lines. Through the hole punched in the forward lines, two prongs pushed forward, one towards Kupyansk on the north and another towards Izium in the south, headed for the Oskil River. This would recapture the two vital communication centres and cut off the Russians east of the river.

On the morning of 06 September, Ukrainian Special Forces along with tanks and combat vehicles of the 92 Mechanized Brigade moved out of their hideouts around the small village of Pryshyb and raced eastwards, rapidly reaching the small town of Verbibky. Mechanized columns raced through the town and special forces occupied key locations forcing the Russians to abandon their equipment and flee. Leaving a small force to mop up and hold the town, the mechanized forces continued eastwards towards their initial objective,

Balakliya—a small town with a population of around 26,000 that sat astride a key river crossing and was a key rail and road junction of the critical T2110 and P78 highways.

In an overnight battle, the Ukrainians took control of Balakliya. The speed of the advance took the defenders by surprise (later identified as 18 Guards Motor Rifle Brigade) and the town was rapidly captured. Mechanized forces entered and isolated that town, while special forces seized critical buildings and junctions. Balakliya fell on the 7th itself, with many of the Russians changing into civilian clothes and trying to flee on bicycles. Even as the mopping up was in progress, the Ukrainians raced further eastwards with their mechanized forces, seizing the key villages of Volokhiv Yar and Semenivka along the route. In most cases, the Russian defenders were taken by surprise and did not put up much of a fight. According to some Ukrainian sources, there was so much disorientation amongst the Russians that a column of Russian trucks actually came up to Ukrainian tanks asking for directions without realising who they were, and were rapidly disarmed and captured. The advancing 92 Mech Brigade linked up with troops of the 113 Ukrainian Territorial Defence Brigade, advancing on a parallel axis and the combined forces now advanced towards the main objective—Kupyansk.

The Ukrainian Offensive

Kupyansk, a small town on both sides of the Oskil River, was the *de facto* headquarters of the Russian regional command. It was also a vital rail and road hub, through which supplies for the entire eastern front were routed. The town had been captured by the Russians in the very first few days of their offensive—on 27 February—but its 195 days of occupation would soon come to an end.

The capture of Kupyansk was surprisingly swift. In most cases, the defenders were taken by surprise by the rapidity of the Ukrainian advance and as per radio intercepts, many local commanders sent frantic messages up the chain of command asking for directions rather than act on their own initiative revealing a rigidity which has been a characteristic of Russian armies. The 1st Mechanized Battalion captured the city centre on the afternoon of 09 September and by the end of the day, the Ukrainians had seized control of the entire western riverbank of the Oskil River and the bridges astride it. Russian soldiers trying to escape across the river were targeted with machine gun and mortar fire, causing many to leave behind their heavy equipment and try to swim across. By 10 September, Kupyansk was completely cleared and back in Ukrainian hands.

Even as Kupyansk was being addressed and captured, another prong of the Ukrainian offensive headed southwards towards Izium, another vital rail and road junction, which could provide the gateway to the Donbas. In a repeat of the actions at Kupyansk, Izium was attacked by mechanized forces, which bypassed the initial defences and raced deep into the rear. As per an Ukrainian tank trooper "We did not sleep or eat for three days. We were told to just keep moving for Izium and reach there in any way possible." The tactics paid off. Izium was reached on 9 September and captured by the 11th. It was an action reminiscent of another battle fought in Izium, way back in 1942—the Second Battle of Kharkiv—in which the Germans defeated the Soviet armies and caused over 200,000 deaths in a single battle.

With the fall of Izium, the Ukrainian defence ministry put up photographs of its soldiers in the town square with an emoji of grapes ('Izium' means 'raisins' in Ukrainian). Just a week after the offensive had commenced, Zelensky raised the Ukrainian flag in the town square, with the promise that "it will soon come up in every town and village of the Russian occupied areas."

The Ukrainian advance was actually quite stunning. In just under a fortnight, they had retaken over 6,000 square kilometres, area that had taken the Russians months to secure. The Russians acknowledged the scale of their defeat, stating simply that their units had "redeployed to better defensive positions." The Russian forces were forced to retreat east of the Oskil River to avoid being cut off, leaving behind 338 pieces of military hardware, much of which came intact into Ukrainian hands. By Ukrainian accounts they captured over a brigade's load of equipment and the hated 'Z' sign of the Russians was painted over with the white cross of the Ukrainians and their equipment pressed into service against their former owners. As per Ukraine's Operational Command East, which oversaw the offensive in this sector, "Russia is now the largest supplier of equipment to Ukraine."

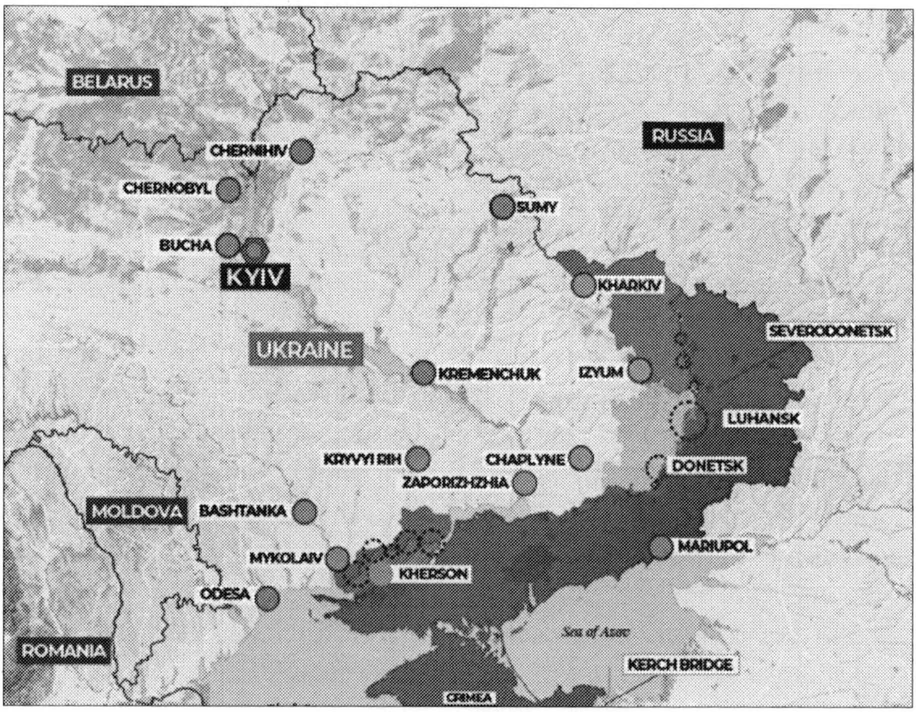

The Situation in Mid-November

The Ukrainians followed up their success at Izium and Kupyansk by moving forward rapidly to the line of the Sieverski Donets River and soon established bridgeheads across it. This cut off the Russians west of the river, forcing them to withdraw, leaving behind their heavy equipment. From here, they were in a position to carry the offensive ahead to retake the province of Luhansk which the Russians had captured with much difficulty over the past three months. The Ukrainians pushed ahead and by 02 October captured Lyman, a transport and logistics hub which was essential for the resupply of Russian troops. The loss of Lyman was a major setback, more so since it came just a day after Putin had declared the Donbas region, where it is located, as part of Russia. With the fall of Lyman, Russian positions in both Luhansk and Donetsk were seriously threatened.

The Russians consolidated themselves along the line of the Oskil and Donetsk rivers, and the Ukrainian offensive lost momentum after a month or so of heavy fighting. They had made impressive gains. The north-eastern and southern offensives managed to retake over 6,500 square kilometres in just around a month, area which had taken the Russians four months to occupy. The offensive weakened the Russian hold on the rest of Donbas. More than that, it also proved that Putin's declaration of Kherson, Zaporizhzhia, Luhansk and Donetsk as Russian territory, following a 'referendum' there, was premature, and the offensive captured vast swathes of territory that were now "officially Russian". The success of the offensive, for the first time, brought about the belief that a Russian defeat was a distinct possibility, and that in many ways, raised the stakes.

The Russians still held on to 600,000 kilometres of Ukrainian territory (now Russian territory, after the referendum) which they would not give up in a hurry. The depth positions were held with better units and were well fortified and defended. Moreover, their strength would be raised by over 200,000 conscripts that were hastily drafted for military service following Putin's announcement of 'partial military mobilization'. Russia launched local counter-attacks to stabilise the situation and halt further Ukrainian advances, as both sides dug in. Russia sharply escalated the strikes into Ukraine, even as it ramped up its nuclear rhetoric, as part of its 'escalate to de-escalate' strategy. The military reverses suffered in the Ukrainian counter-offensives only made the Russian response more violent and unpredictable. (See next chapter, 'The Russian Response').

Just like the Germans had invaded Russia in May 1941 hoping for a swift victory, but got trapped in a quagmire for four years, the Russians too have miscalculated. With winter setting in after November, no large-scale campaigning will be possible and both sides seek to consolidate their positions in the east and south (which is now the major arenas of the war). Winter could bring about a stalemate where both sides hold positions along rough geographical boundaries, which would be a 'Line of Contact'. Unless a negotiated truce comes up, action along this Line of Contact would continue in a long war, but which will weaken both Russia and Ukraine.

REFERENCES

"After reclaiming key Logistics Hub, Ukraine presses on," *Times of India*, 03 October 2022.

"Crimea Saki Air Base, Seven Russian Warplanes Destroyed", https://www.cnn.com, 11 August 2022.

"More than 14000 Casualties to date, but Number likely Higher", *United Nations News*, 9 September 2022.

"Over 90K 'Irrecoverable losses' in Ukraine," *The Moscow Times*, 12 October 2022.

"Putin ups the ante, to mobilize 3 Lakh troops", *Times of India*, 22 September 2022

"Russian Offensive Campaign Assessment, 11 September. understandingwar.org

"The 90-kilometer-long journey that changed the war in Ukraine", Henry Foy, *Financial Times*, 28 September 2022.

"Ukraine punches through Russian lines as surprise offensive retakes land in the East"; *CNBC*. 11 September 2022.

"Ukraine's new Offensive is fuelled by Captured Russian Weapons," Yaroslav Trofimov, *The Wall Street Journal*, 5 October 2022.

"Ukrainian Balakliya-Kupyansk Offensive;" Mylola Bielieskov, *Eurasiona Daily Monitor*, Volume 19, Issue 133.

"Ukrainian forces capture Key Town", *The Kyiv Post*, https://www.newsweek.com 10 September 2022.

"US to supply more Missiles after Kyiv success with Anti-Radiation Weapons", *The Eurasian Times*, 17 October 2022.

"We retook 6000 square kilometres in September, Says Zelensky" *BBC*, 12 September 2022.

THE RUSSIAN RESPONSE: SOUND, FIRE AND FURY

"I would demote them to Privates, strip them of their awards, and send them barefoot to the front, with gun in hand, to wash the disgrace with their blood."

—Ramzan Kadyrov,
Chechen Warlord, on Russia's Generals

The Ukrainian counter-offensive definitely put Russia on the back foot. Perhaps it caught them by surprise, since there was no coordinated military response to it, though there were local counter-attacks launched to recapture lost ground. After the initial Ukrainian advances, the Russians did hold on to both the south and the east, as the Ukrainians paused and did not over-extend themselves. There was however a violent intensification of missile and rocket strikes in their cities that were designed to intimidate, rather than have any real military value. A suicide drone also struck President Zelensky's home town of Krivyi Rih, and missiles hit as far as Odesa. These were largely symbolic strikes, nothing more.

Even though Russia still held on to over 600,000 square kilometres of their territory, the speed of the Ukrainian advance changed perceptions about the war. Even within Russia, the scale of the defeat was being acknowledged on social media and television with murmuring that "the war is not going our way". Influential sources blamed the military for incompetence, with the defence minister, Sergei Shoigu, coming in for the heaviest criticism. The

Chechen commander, Ramzam Kadyrov, ridiculed the military saying "senior officers should be stripped of their rank and sent to the front barefoot, to atone for their sins." Though Putin was still insulated, fingers were slowly pointing in his direction as well. The precariousness of his political position raised the stakes and the unpredictability of his response.

On 20 September, Putin accelerated the war effort by announcing a 'partial military mobilization' to call up 300,000 reservists who had earlier served in the army. It was the first such call-up in Russia since World War II, and was not even used in Afghanistan. It meant that men and women between 18-60 who had previously done military duty would be called-up, given a brief period of training for 3-6 months and then sent to augment the front lines.

The Russians had indeed miscalculated their requirement of troops. The 200,000-odd they had sent for the invasion were not enough for a campaign of this nature whose front line now extended over a frontage of 1,300 kilometres. Nor had they anticipated such stiff resistance. The tired and depleted units desperately needed reinforcements and the only way to make it up was through mobilization. The conscripts who would be sent to reinforce them would be hurriedly trained and not very motivated. Russian morale seemed to be the greatest problem. Their soldiers often seemed disillusioned and war-weary, in contrast to the highly motivated Ukrainians fighting for their homeland.

The move for 'partial mobilization' was widely unpopular, reflecting the lack of support for the war, even within Russia. As soon as it was announced, young men started leaving the country in droves, driving to adjoining countries like Georgia and Kazakhstan. A prominent 27-year-old rapper, Ivan Petunin, jumped to death from his high-rise apartment to avoid conscription and mobilization officials were shot at and threatened.

There was one more card to play. Between 23 and 27 September, Russia conducted a 'referendum' in the occupied provinces of Luhansk, Donetsk, Kherson and Zaporizhzhia—area that comprised about 15 per cent of Ukraine territory—asking one simple question on ballot paper, "Are you in favour of secession from Ukraine and joining the Russian Federation?" The referendum was considered 'sham and illegitimate' and not recognised by any other country. By many accounts, it was conducted at gunpoint. However, as per Russian reports, an astounding 93 per cent in Zaporizhzhia, 87 per cent in Kherson, 98 per cent in Luhansk and 99 per cent in Donetsk voted overwhelmingly to join Russia, paving the way for its formal amalgamation. Even when the Russians had annexed Crimea in 2014, they had set the stage with a similar referendum.

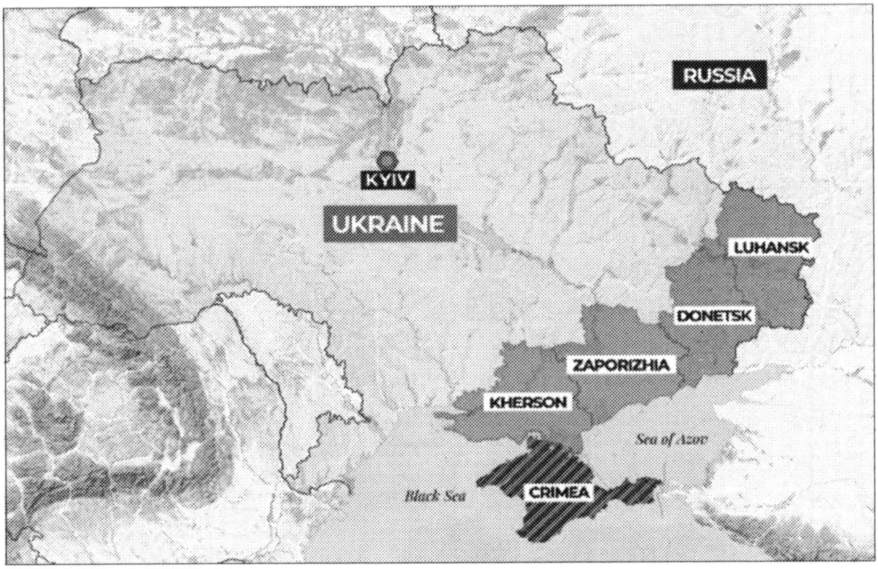

Provinces where Referendum was Held

With the massive 'Ayes' of the referendum in place, a glittering ceremony was held at the Great Kremlin Palace on 03 October where Putin signed treaties with the Russian appointed representatives of the provinces that declared them "as part of Russia, and its people, forever". With this, Putin formalized what was termed as "Europe's largest land grab since World War II". It was followed by a massive rock concert in Moscow's Red Square with billboards proclaiming, "Donetsk, Luhansk, Zaporizhzhia, Kherson—RUSSIA."

The formal amalgamation of the occupied territories raised the stakes considerably. It implied that these areas were part of Russia, and any attack to retake them by Ukraine or any of its allies, would be deemed an attack on Russian soil. The area would also come under Russia's nuclear umbrella and an attack on it could invite the use of nuclear weapons. Putin followed it up with a blatant threat to use nuclear weapons, implying that even strategic nuclear weaponry could be used, in what was a blatant case of nuclear blackmail.

Needless to say, Ukraine did not accept the referendum or annexation and vowed to press ahead with its attacks till the last inch of Ukrainian territory, including Crimea, was cleared. In fact, Ukrainian attacks were already underway in both Kharkiv and Kherson, now officially Russian territory. In the wake of the battlefield success, Zelensky signed a decree stating that any talks with Vladimir Putin were "impossible", but they were open to dialogue with another president of Russia. The war was fast becoming a personal conflict for Putin.

The success of the Ukrainian offensive and the manner in which Russia has reacted to its own admitted lack of success on the battlefield put the war in a whole new phase. Besides making a Ukrainian victory a tantalizing reality, it isolated Russia even further, which came under increasing pressure from even China and India to end the war. Prime Minister Modi gently reminded Putin at the Shanghai Cooperation Organization meet at Dushanbe that "this is not the era for war", and "there can be no military solution, and that India was ready to contribute to peace efforts". Though world pressure was building up for an end to the fighting and a negotiated settlement, both sides stuck to their guns, with Russia insisting that it would negotiate, but not on the occupied territories, and Zelensky insisting that negotiations could commence only after 'the last inch of Ukrainian territory, including Crimea, is vacated". The war seemed poised to enter another difficult phase.

The War Escalates

The 19-kilometre-long road-and-rail bridge across the Kerch Strait linking the Black Sea to the Sea of Azov was one of Putin's pet projects. Constructed at a cost of $ 3.6 billion, it provided the lank link from Russia to Crimea and had been inaugurated with much fanfare, with Putin himself driving the first truck across it in June 2018.

This symbol of Russia's annexation of Crimea would become the next target of the war. At 6 in the morning of 08 October, a truck loaded with explosives crossed over from the Crimean side and was detonated on the bridge. The blast of the explosion tore apart two sections of the bridge and sent them crumbling into the icy waters of the Sea of Azov. The blast also hit a goods train moving on the adjoining rail section, and set ablaze seven oil tankers carrying much-needed carrying fuel supplies to Crimea and disrupting raid and road connectivity to the south.

Though the damage to the bridge was rectified and traffic resumed in a few days, albeit far more slowly, it was a devastating symbolic blow, coming as it did in the wake of the Russian military reverses in the northeast and the south. Ukraine did not claim responsibility for the blast, but posted jubilant messages on social media, including one showing the burning bridge accompanied by a video of Marilyn Monroe singing, "Happy Birthday to You." The significance was not lost on anyone. Just a day earlier, Putin had celebrated his 70th birthday (in a formal but slightly subdued manner) and this was Ukraine's gift to him.

The loss of the bridge has been called comparable to the loss of the MOSKVA, whose sinking severely impacted Russian naval capabilities. The bridge forms the only land link from Russia to Crimea, and the entire supply chain right from Mariupol in the east to Melitopol in the west could be further affected, hampering operations along the entire south. More than that, the loss of prestige, coming in the wake of widespread military reverses, heightened the pressure on Russia to call off the war.

Russia responded with widespread sacking, removing three senior military officers in just a week. Another officer, Air Force General Sergei Surovikin, took over as the overall commander of the Russian forces in Ukraine, but these changes were unlikely to do much to change the unfolding situation on the ground. Predictably, Putin lashed out in retaliation for what it claimed was a Ukrainian terrorist attack by unleashing a barrage of 64 Cruise missiles, targeting 70 vital infrastructure sites in Kyiv and 10 other cities. The attacks specifically targeted Ukraine's water and power infrastructure and destroyed 30 per cent of Ukraine's electricity grid. The situation was grave enough for Zelensky to cut down power supply from 7 to 11 in the morning to save electricity for the long winter months ahead.

In fact, winter was a major factor in Putin's calculations. As both sides hunkered down for the winter months, Putin also raised the stakes in Europe by cutting off gas supply to it, and depriving European nations of almost 40 per cent of their energy requirements. In a tit-for-tat move, Russia blatantly refused to provide gas through the Nord Stream I pipeline, on the grounds that Western sanctions had severely affected its maintenance and upkeep. The pipelines would remain closed as long as Western sanctions were in place. To compound the situation, explosions also ripped holes in the Nord Stream I and Nord Stream II gas pipelines, rendering them inoperable. The shutting off of Russian gas heralded a bleak cold winter for Europe with rising prices, darkened streets, homes devoid of heating and factories closing down due to lack of energy. It could plunge all of Europe into a recession, and severely test their resolve to stand by Ukraine.

Putin's response seems part of his 'escalate-to-de-escalate' strategy. He has raised the stakes further by his nuclear threats, stating that he would use nuclear weapons, and not just tactical devices, even strategic ones, if NATO entered the war. Any attack on Russian territory and the occupied areas now considered Russian territory would meet the same response.

By November, there seems no clear-cut end in sight. As winter sets in, there would be a pause in large-scale offensive actions, as both sides settle down and consolidate their gains. Most analysts predict a long-drawn haul, and the war could go on to the next year, or even beyond. There are no definite timelines in which the war could end, nor any clear-cut end state. However, there are four likely scenarios in which the war could end:

- Russia attains its military aims.
- Ukraine's counter-offensive pushes the Russians out of Ukrainian soil and emerges victorious.
- The war enters a stalemate with each side holding on to their territories, and becomes a long drawn out 'frozen conflict.'
- NATO enters the war and sparks off a European confrontation.

There is another 'worst-case scenario', one in which the Third World War is sparked off and China too enters it by using the moment to further its claim on Taiwan. This scenario would be akin to the actions of Germany and Japan in World War II, and though unlikely, cannot be completely ruled out. The following chapters will explore these scenarios one by one.

REFERENCES

"98000 Russians enter Kazakhstan after call-up" *Indian Express*, 28 September 2022.

"Bridge linking Russia to Crimea targeted. Disrupts key supplies", *The Indian Express*, 9 October 2022.

"Crimea bridge blast kills 3, cuts off Key Supply Artery", *Hindustan Times*, 09 October 2022.

"Crimea Bridge: Excitement and Fear in Ukraine after blast," *BBC News*, 8 October 2022.

"Moscow pledges full Protection to area Annexed by Russia", *Times of India*, 26 September 2022

"PM tells Zelensky: No military solution, India ready to help" *Indian Express*, 04 October 2022.

"Putin allies slam Russian Defense Minister, Military Brass for 'incompetence," *Times Global, The Times of India*, 07 October 2022.

"Putin ups the Ante, to Mobilize 3 Lakh Troops", *Times of India*, 22 September 2022

"Russia annex 4 Ukrainian Territories", *Times of India*, 30 September 2022, "Ukraine War: Putin announces annexation of four Regions", *Outlook*, India; 17 October 2022.

"Russia begins breakaway polls in Occupied Regions", *Hindustan Times*, 24 September 2022.

"Russia gets new General as Blast damages Bridge to Crimea", *Times of India*, 9 October 2022.

"Russia targets Kyiv, 10 other cities in biggest Missile Attack", *The Indian Express*, 11 October 2022.

"Russian Suicide Drones hit Zelensky hometown as Kyiv eyes further gains"; *The Indian Express*, 03 October 2022.

Russian Rapper kills Self to avoid Fighting", *Times of India*, 03 October 2022

"Ukraine's NATO entry could lead to WW III: Russia", *Times Global, The Times of India*, 14 October 2022.

"Will not bluff on Nukes: Putin escalates the war", *The Indian Express*, 22 September 2022

"Zelensky signs decree, rules out negotiation with Putin", *Indian Express*, 05 October 2022.

3

SCENARIOS OF THE ENDGAME

"*There will be no negotiations till Russia withdraws from Ukrainian territory*".

—**Zelensky**

"*The territory is ours. It is non-negotiable*".

—**Putin**

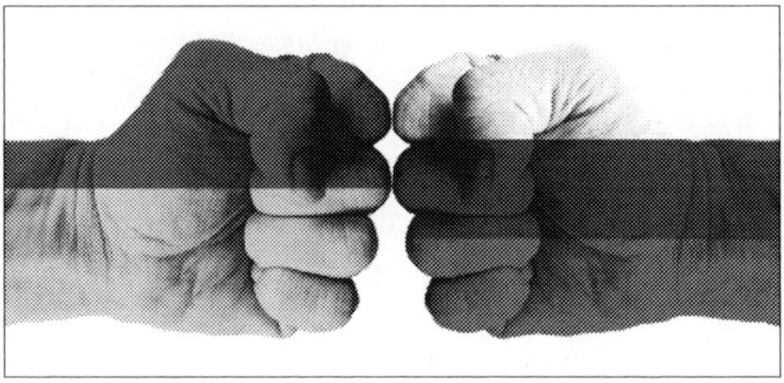

Almost a year of war with no clear signs of how it could end. A war which no one really believed would take place and when it did break out, expected to be done and dusted in a week, still rages on inconclusively. From the initial heady days of the invasion on 24 February, to the determined resistance by the Ukrainians which halted each of the Russian thrust lines, to the slow occupation of the Donbas, and then the Ukrainian counter-offensive in the northeast and the south, which has recovered vast swathes of occupied territory, the war has seen many twists and turns. The offensive pushed Russia on the back foot, more so since it has claimed the provinces of Kherson, Zaporizhzhia, Donetsk, and Luhansk as 'Russian territory' after the 'referendum' held there. The war entered another phase. Where could it go from here?

After months of war, both armies are exhausted and depleted. The continual attrition has taken a taken a toll of men and equipment, even though Ukraine has received aid and trained reservists to make up its losses and Russia's partial military mobilization would make another 200,000 or so conscripts available to fill their tired and ragged lines. With winter setting in and then the melting snow and slushy ground of spring, the dreaded *Rasputitsa,* there would be a pause around November or so till around March. Both sides will make maximum gains and perhaps even bring the war to a conclusion before that but it seems difficult. It will be a long war, akin to the titanic struggle between Germany and the Soviet Union from 1941 to 1945 that moved from one extreme to the other. It is difficult to predict the timelines or even the manner in which the war could end. Let us explore some of the likely scenarios.

SCENARIO 1: The Russians launch a fresh offensive and attain their military objectives

After months of sustained action, the Russians have taken over most of the Donbas and the southern regions, including most of Luhansk and Donetsk and virtually the entire coastline along the Sea of Azov. The Ukrainian counter-attacks have pushed them back from some of the occupied territories, but they still hold 15 per cent of Ukrainian soil, which they consider their own. The Russian war machine is weakened but still a formidable force. The Russians could consolidate and launch a fresh offensive, perhaps even into the next year. Should the Russians re-start their offensive with fresh troops or even with the infusion of around 200,000 recently-mobilized conscripts, they could try to regain the entire area of the Donbas, perhaps go back again towards Kharkiv in the northeast. They could even push ahead in the south towards Odesa, the one vital port on the Black Sea which the Ukrainians still hold. The capture of this port would block all Ukrainian access to the sea and give the Russians the launch pad to develop operations further west towards Moldova. Here they could take over the Russian-speaking areas of Transnistria in much the same way they took over the Donbas. Should they achieve this, they would attain their original aim of gaining control of a swathe of land over 200 kilometres deep from Kharkiv to Odessa, block Ukraine completely from the sea, and make it land-locked and dependent on Russia for all future trade.

The Russians could also launch a fresh thrust towards Kyiv from Belarus, along the same axis that they had used in the initial days of the war and strike the nerve centre of Ukrainian resistance and political leadership. After all, Belarus is still a staunch Russian ally, and troops are still positioned on its soil but that battle could well go the same way as the German campaign for Moscow or Stalingrad and would be long and expensive. However, if Russia regains some of its lost territories in the south or the east, it would give Putin his military victory, consolidate his hold on the occupied areas, and push the Ukrainians back on the defensive.

Likelihood. This is the end state Putin would have desired when he set out on the war. The gains the Russians made in the east and in the south have come over months and at a huge cost. While Russia has had reverses in both the northeast and the south, it can hold on. The generals are under pressure to show some results, and perhaps with the infusion of additional troops, maybe additional divisions on the Siberian border (which were used by the Soviet Union in December 1941 to drive the Germans back from Moscow) they do have the capability to launch a fresh offensive. Perhaps even Kyiv could be a likely target, and the pounding of the city shows a renewed focus there. The likelihood of a renewed Russian offensive is high, though one cannot predict the gains it could make, or in what time frame.

SCENARIO 2: A successful Ukrainian counter-offensive pushes the Russians back into their own territory

The Ukrainian offensive has made sizeable gains both in the east and in the south. Buoyed by their success, and replenished with Western arms and freshly-trained reservists, the Ukrainians could continue their offensive to recapture the lost cities of Kherson, Melitopol, Zaporizhzhia, and the crown jewel, Mariupol, in the south. This would push the Russians back into the Crimea, but evicting them from there would be virtually impossible. Concurrently, they could continue operations to retake the lost areas of the Donbas by launching a pincer movement from the south from Mariupol and in the north from Kharkiv. Like the Russian advance to capture these areas, their movement of the Ukrainian forces to recapture these territories could be slow and tortuous, since the Russian positions there are held by frontline troops who are well supplied and equipped. However, they will be able to inflict continuous attrition on Russian positions and logistics with long-range strikes, which they seem to have mastered.

Should the Ukrainians attain decisive gains in the south and east, they could even reach the Russian frontier. That would put them within reach to strike Russian bases at Smolensk and Belgorod, hampering resupply to all Russian troops inside Ukrainian territory. The Ukrainian aim of getting the Russians back to the pre-2014 boundaries (less Crimea) would thus be attained. It would, of course, provoke a massive retaliation from Russia in the form of air and missile attacks across Ukraine, but in spite of increased nuclear threats, hopefully more balanced minds within the Kremlin will ensure that it stops short of using nuclear weapons. This military defeat could increase the unrest within the population especially as news from the front percolates through increased casualties. As more and more fingers point towards Putin and his handling of the war, he could be removed in a palace coup (though he could be still propped up as a face to show a united front, but with his powers severely curtailed). This could lead to a negotiated solution in which Russia moves all its troops back across the border, but is permitted to hold on to Crimea. Ukraine renounces its aim to join NATO, and defers its intention to join the European Union, thus providing a face-saving exit to Russia and a negotiated end to the war.

The flip side to that, of course, is that Russia will resort to nuclear weapons in case of severe military reverses. That would change the entire complexion of the war.

Likelihood. Although this is the most desirable end state, the ability of the Ukrainian forces to retake all the lost areas is a little 'iffy'. In spite of the flow of weaponry which the West helpfully provides to keep the war going, they too have been severely weakened after months of war. The Russians have developed strong defensive lines and fortifications along the depth areas which they have occupied which will be very difficult to overcome. Also, there is a fear that the Ukrainian counter-offensive could get over-extended and thus vulnerable to a counter-stroke. A complete Ukrainian victory, in the near term, at least, could be difficult.

SCENARIO 3: The war becomes an interminable frozen conflict, with neither side being able to change the *status quo*. Both sides dig in along the positions they hold which becomes the Line of Contact

In spite of being pushed back by successful counter-offensives, the Russians have been able to hold on along the line of the Seversky Donets River in the east and the Dnipro and Dnieper rives in the south. They have good defensible positions which are well fortified, and can hold on indefinitely. On the Western bank of the rivers, the Ukrainians too have done the same to prevent further Russian advances in the east or in the south. There could be a stalemate along the line held by Russian and Ukrainian troops along which low intensity fighting could continue interminably.

The same situation exists in the Donbas since 2014. Russian separatists and Ukrainian forces have occupied defensive positions opposite each other along a line which is called the Line of Contact. Low-level fighting, artillery duels and raids have continued for over eight years, but the line remained largely static. A similar Line of Contact could come up along the line of the territories that Russia has annexed, and now calls its own. Since Ukraine will never accept it, the fighting would continue but with neither side really able to change the *status quo*. This LOC would become the dividing line not only between Russia and Ukraine, but between Russia and the rest of Europe as well.

Likelihood. This seems to be the most likely scenario. Both sides already seem to be preparing for it by occupying defences along geographical lines in both the south and east. Although Putin will not fully attain his war aims, the occupation of Donbas and the south will give him a measure of military victory. Ukraine will never accept it, but would be unable to change the overall picture. It would be akin to the LOC in Kashmir between India and Pakistan which came up in 1948, and after a while, gradually became the *status quo*.

SCENARIO 4: A NATO-Russia War

NATO is actually the *caucus belli* of this war. It was Ukraine's desire to join it, and the fact that this would have brought the alliance right at Russia's doorstep, that led to the war. Even as the war continues it seems unlikely that Ukraine would be able to join the alliance, in the near future. If Ukraine gets membership, NATO would be sucked directly into the conflict under Article 5 of the NATO charter that states that any attack on any member-state is considered an attack on all. NATO will continue to prop up Ukraine with infusions of arms and aid, which keeps the conflict going. After all, this state suits them where they can continue to weaken Russia 'to the last Ukrainian' without being directly involved. Neither does Russia want a direct confrontation with NATO, one in which they would lose. However, while neither side wants it, they could still slip, advertently or inadvertently into a NATO-Russia conflict that sets off a European, or even a global war.

The crossing of a 'Red Line' could draw NATO into the conflict. It could be the use of a chemical, biological or a nuclear weapon, or maybe even a particularly devastating attack on a civilian target. Should NATO enter the war, Putin has warned that he would use his nuclear weapons. NATO too has warned that any use of nuclear weapons would not go unchallenged even if it brings the world to 'Armageddon.' The use of any nuclear weapon, even a tactical low-yield one, would draw NATO into the war, and send it spiralling towards WW III.

Even an inadvertent strike by Russia into a NATO member's territory could provide the trigger. Should a Russian missile strike on Lyiv, where Western aid is stockpiled and is just 20 kilometres from the Poland border, fall on Poland territory, it would constitute an attack on a NATO-member and draw in all the members. With Sweden and Finland having joined NATO, an inadvertent air or naval confrontation around the Baltic Sea could again provide the trigger. In the turbo-charged environment of the day, a minor incident could rapidly go out of control.

How would NATO respond? The crossing of a 'Red Line' could lead to a limited NATO involvement initially—perhaps the imposition of a 'no-fly-zone' or moving of additional forces close to Russian frontiers. NATO's entry would escalate the situation dangerously, perhaps to the point of no return. It would push Russia, and Putin personally, against the wall, and he could lash out indiscriminately, maybe even using the nuclear option, "against an existentialist threat to Russia". Putin is aware of the power of his threat and this knowledge stays a direct NATO involvement, so far, at least.

Likelihood. It seems unlikely that NATO will get directly involved and thus escalate the situation. Should a situation spiral out of control and lead to NATO involvement, it would mean certain defeat of Russia against their combined might. That could also suck in Russian allies like Belarus and Syria, and even China, which can set the stage for World War III. A NATO involvement would trigger the "Armageddon Response"—a nuclear exchange in a scenario so horrific that it will encompass the rest of the world. This worst-case scenario will be examined in detail in the following chapter.

4

The 'Armageddon Scenario': World War III

"We are closer to Armageddon, than at any time since the 1962 Cuban Crisis."

—US President Joe Biden

History often provides glimpses of the future and a peek into the past can give an inkling of the shape of things to come. There is an eerie commonality of the war in Ukraine and the events of the World War II—and not just in the arena of the battle. The chain of events that led to the war finds an echo here, as do the roles of the major players involved. There is also a likelihood that this war could expand in scope in much the same manner that the Second World War did.

When a proud, nationalistic Germany was humiliated by the Treaty of Versailles following its defeat in the First World War, it laid the seeds for the Second. The mood of the nation set the ground for the rise of Adolf Hitler, who re-armed and revitalized Germany and set it on the road to regain past glory. It began with the annexation of Sudetenland, Poland, Czechoslovakia, and France in 1938-39; and culminated in the disastrous, uncalled for invasion of the Soviet Union in May 1941, which ultimately destroyed the Third Reich. At that time, the Western nations cheered from the sidelines as Soviet and German armies clashed in titanic battles across Ukraine, Russia (both of whom were part of the same Soviet Union at that time) and ultimately within Germany itself. It is significant that while the Western powers continued supplying the Soviet Union with arms, aid and many promises, they actually entered the war in Europe only in June 1944, a good three years after Russia had battled Nazi Germany virtually single handed and weakened it sufficiently to ensure its eventual defeat.

At the same time, when Germany was pushing its nationalistic goals in Europe, Japan was rising in the East as a militaristic power with visions of creating a Greater East Asia Co-prosperity Sphere (something on the lines of China's Belt and Road Initiative) which would project itself as the economic and strategic hub of Asia. As Japan too pushed its agenda in the region, the Western nations led by USA blocked its access to oil, rubber, iron, and natural resources that were essential for its island economy. Japan responded to Western sanctions and pressures by launching a pre-emptive attack on Pearl Harbour in December 1941, hoping to destroy the US fleet, especially its carriers, while they were still docked. The audacious strike had mixed results. It destroyed most of the warships, but could not hit the US carriers that were out at sea. The world plunged into war in both Europe and in the Pacific which ended with the Red Army in Berlin, and culminated in August 1945 with the nuclear strikes on Hiroshima and Nagasaki. Two widely disparate powers, Germany and Japan, bound by a strong sense of ultra-nationalism and common interests, had got together against most of the Western world, and came dangerously close to succeeding.

Fast forward to the 21st century, where war has revisited Europe after 70 years with the Russian invasion of Ukraine. Only this time the roles are reversed. Now it is Russia playing the role of Germany—a fiercely nationalistic Russia with a sense of insecurity that seeks to re-assert itself in Europe. Russia has been the aggressor in this war, with its largely uncalled for invasion of Ukraine, a country, which like Germany and the Soviet Union of the 1940s, shared warm relations and common ties. Ironically, it is Ukraine that is playing the role of the Soviet Union. Battered by the aggressor, it holds out against huge odds, in spite of enormous casualties. Like the Soviet Union of 1941, it has been urged with aid and moral support by the Western powers, but little actual action. And like the actions of the Western powers in 1941-44, they too have let the war prolong to weaken Russia, as it suits their long-term strategic interests.

In the East, China has adopted the mantle of Japan. Like Japan of that time, China is a military and economic power with nationalistic dreams, though it is far stronger than Japan was, both militarily and economically. Its actions have been far more aggressive and militaristic than Japan, and it has pursued it agenda with greater ruthlessness. Like Russia, China seeks to redress so-called 'historical wrongs' as it tries to re-unify areas, which they consider 'historically Chinese', back into its fold. Its perception of these areas extends across the China Sea, Ladakh and, most importantly, Taiwan.

In the worst-case scenario, we see a similar situation, where Russia and China come together to pursue their nationalistic goals against what they perceive as the common enemy—the USA and the West. China has a greater interest in maintaining stronger economic ties with the West, but it is sympathetic to the Russian cause and their two leaders share a lot in common. China has tried to distance itself from the war, especially after Russia's battlefield reverses, but the war in Ukraine finds an echo in China; and could well encourage it to pursue its own agenda in Taiwan.

Let us look at the worst-case scenario, one in which a chain of events sparks off a World War that even draws China and the USA into it, and sucks in all of Europe, Asia and much of the world. It may not take place in the immediate future; hopefully, it will not even occur. But yes, the seeds are in place and a chain of events could just trigger it.

How Could a Global War Unfold?

In a worst-case scenario, the war in Ukraine continues, perhaps into 2023 and beyond, in an endless stalemate. Like the German-Soviet conflict of 1941-45, the battle rages across a vast front and erupts periodically with offensives and counter-offensives from either side. Then, after a long pause in which the

Ukrainians are buoyed by vast quantities of Western aid, and its depleting ranks increased by newly-trained recruits and foreign mercenaries, the Ukrainians launch a major counter-offensive. The counter-offensive strikes the weakest part of the Russian lines (whose location is helpfully provided by US intelligence) and drives the Russians back across the frontier. The Ukrainians come within striking distance of Smolensk and Belgorod, the vital administrative hubs, which provide the logistics for Russian troops in Ukraine. Photographs of Ukrainian soldiers on Russian soil flood the print, television and social media channels and the news of 'the Debacle on the Donetsk' penetrates into Russian media and news channels. The Russian population, hitherto insulated from news of the war, become aware of the setbacks on the battlefield. The conscripts who had been hastily mobilized after Putin's 'partial military mobilization' send back tales of horror from the front lines. The body count rises, and a growing number of body bags make their way back into Russia. Rumblings arise against Putin and the war. Even in the inner coterie, influential party members and powerful oligarchs question Putin's handling of the situation, and he feels an increasing threat to his own position. Like all autocrats, he sees signs of a palace coup all around him and decides to take a gamble to salvage the situation.

He orders his commanders to use tactical nuclear weapons to halt the Ukrainian advance and retrieve the situation. A bright orange flash rips through the darkness of the early morning, as a .3-kiloton nuclear warhead explodes in a low air burst above the Ukrainian bridgehead on the Donetsk River, the vital bridgehead from where the Ukrainians can launch their offensive into Russia. For good measure, he also orders a strike on the town of Lyiv, a small town just 20 kilometres from the Polish border where Western aid is received. Two Kinzhal missiles race at hypersonic speed across the Russian frontier, penetrate the air defence, and hit Lyiv. A missile with a .2 kiloton nuclear warhead in its cone, smashes into the line of warehouses where Western equipment is stored. Another hits a railway siding, damaging it beyond redemption. The effects are disastrous. The twin blasts destroy a massive consignment of Western aid, including six batteries of newly received HIMARS launchers and thousands of rounds of precious ammunition. The detonating ammunition compounds the effect and the town is virtually flattened by the blast.

In the shocked aftermath of the strikes, Russia brazenly denies using nuclear weapons. It claims that the explosions were the result of high-powered conventional munitions, and even hints that the Ukrainians could have been planning to use their own nuclear weapons which detonated prematurely. Residual radioactivity lingering over the area reveals the evidence, but Russia denies it as fabricated charges by the West. They warn the West that should they use 'concocted evidence' to strike Russia, it will be forced to use its strategic nuclear arsenal to retaliate in self-defence. The message is clear.

The attack unnerves the Ukrainian military and political leadership. Russian counter-attacks in the wake of the blast overrun the Ukrainian positions and recapture lost territory. Putin gambles that the Western powers will still be reluctant to get involved, and his 'escalate to de-escalate' strategy will pay off.

He almost gets away with it. The NATO and US leadership consider the responses, and ponder over direct action in Ukraine. After all, Russia has crossed 'the Red Line', but NATO intervention could provoke Putin to unleash a barrage of nuclear missiles, especially if he feels his own survival is at stake. This action cannot be allowed to go unanswered. NATO imposes a 'No-Fly-Zone' over western Ukraine and places all NATO forces in Europe on high alert. US warships and submarines come into the Baltic Sea, dangerously close to the Russian enclave at Kaliningrad. Turkey, another NATO member, blocks access to Russian shipping into the Black Sea, and US and NATO submarines enter the crucial waters.

As the stand-off continues, the inevitable happens. A Russian SU-25 on a photo-reconnaissance mission from Belarus strays into the 'No-Fly-Zone' imposed by NATO. In spite of warnings, the pilot refuses to back off and is shot down by a US F-18 Hornet. In retaliation, Russia fires half a dozen Kinzhal hypersonic missiles into the airbase in Estonia where NATO fighters are based. Estonia is a NATO ally and as per Article 5 of the NATO charter, an attack on any member is considered an attack on all. The die is cast for NATO to enter the fray, and its forces begin mobilizing. Russia calls for general mobilization, in the face of 'unprovoked Western aggression.' Its divisions on the Siberian frontier in the east are hastily pulled back to the European front, and its nuclear forces are placed on the highest state of readiness.

Even at this juncture, NATO does not put 'boots-on-ground' in Ukraine, but merely maintains a defensive posture. Russia has its back to the wall. It knows it cannot win against the combined force of NATO and stands alone, except for its unwilling ally, Belarus, which too is sucked into the war. Putin reinforces his threat of using strategic nuclear weapons, knowing that his 'Armageddon Option' would be a good deterrent.

As this tense stand-off continues, the war still rages, but fortunately does not escalate beyond its soil—not yet. China, watching from the sidelines makes the mandatory calls for peace, but seizes the moment. Xi Jinping, who is more powerful than any Chinese leader before him, after securing another term in power, is all set to consolidate his agenda of 'Greater China.' The once-in-a-lifetime moment to re-unify all areas that are 'historically Chinese' has arrived. Seeing the pre-occupation of the USA and the Western countries in Europe, he gambles that they would not want to get involved in another war in the East. Its naval, land and air forces which had been practising amphibious operations for months now, are given the go-ahead and well-rehearsed drills for an assault on Taiwan are put in place. A spate of cyber-attacks hit Taiwan, bringing down their internet services, communication networks, and even financial and banking networks. Its Air Defence and Early Warning radars which had already given away their frequencies by being activated each time Chinese fighters violated their air space were jammed and rendered inoperable. Chinese fighters attacked Taiwanese airfields, ports, and shore fortifications. While the navy established a blockade over the Taiwan Strait, a flotilla of over 100 landing ships crossed the 180-kilometre-wide straits for an amphibious assault on Taiwan's northern and southern coasts. Its carrier force led by the LIONING, formed a defensive line on the perimeter of the First Island Chain to prevent access of any external naval force into the area. At the same time, the deadly 'carrier killer' YJ-21 hypersonic missiles, potent enough to sink a carrier at 3,000 kilometres, are activated to engage any US naval force moving into the Indo-Pacific region.

As China launches its three-pronged invasion, Taiwanese air and naval forces inflict heavy damage on the invading force and hold it back—temporarily. They could hold on for a while, maybe a month or so, but unless the USA comes to their rescue, their defences would soon be swamped. Almost simultaneously Russia launches another offensive in Northern Ukraine towards Kyiv (obviously pre-planned with China's actions). It warns that any Western interference would be considered an 'existentialist threat' and leaves it free to use its entire arsenal of nuclear weapons. The US President, who has watched Europe and Asia erupt, is in a quandary. The USA has a treaty to defend Taiwan, but the US public and most Congressmen are strongly against a war so far from its own shores. His admirals warn him that in a possible intervention, there would be very heavy losses and the US navy could even lose. Should they focus on the Russian threat in Europe? Do they get diverted towards the Indo-Pacific? Or do they do neither and refuse to get involved in another continent's war? Worse of all, how do they react to the nuclear threat, without further escalation?

The grim scenario could be the hypothetical start to World War III, and already has a lot of commonalities with the events leading to World War II. Could it come about? At this stage, it seems unlikely, but unfortunately, the groundwork is in place, and a series of events could just trigger it off. Putin has repeatedly warned that any NATO entry in the war would lead to World War III and a likely nuclear holocaust, but the longer the war continues, the greater are the dangers of it happening. Whether China exploits the situation for its own actions in the East, remains to be seen. Taiwan is a core interest, as is Ladakh in India, but will they take the gamble to decide the issue by force? Also, how far would Russia go, and how much would China be willing to support it? A lot would depend on how the Ukraine war pans out. Should Russia attain success, it could embolden China to embark on its own adventurism. Should Ukraine hold strong, it may be a deterrent to China as well. The Ukraine war provides fertile ground to draw other nations into it; but that could well have a cascading effect that engulfs the entire world within it.

REFERENCES

"China could attack Taiwan by end of Year, US warns", https://www.telegraph.co.uk 20 October 2022.

"Estonia in NATO", https://nato.mfa.ee

"How did World War II end?" History Channel, 11 August 2020.

"How would we Know when China is preparing to Invade Ukraine", https://www.carnegieendowment.org

"Japan and the Greater East Asia Co-Prosperity Sphere", https://www.taylorfrancis.com

"NATO's response to Russia's Invasion of Ukraine", https://www.nato.int, 18 October 2022.

"Taiwan's top Diplomat: China's Invasion Plan-DW," https://www.dw.com 01 September 2022.

"Treaty of Versailles: Definition, Terms, Dates and WW I," https://www.history.com

"World War II; Dates and Timelines", https://www.historyextra.com

5

Mechanized and Anti-Tank Operations

"The end of the tank? Not by a long chalk. Tanks will not die out; they will evolve instead."

—The Economist

A New Norm of Mechanized Operations

The Ukraine war has debunked quite a few theories about modern warfare. Pundits had been proclaiming that conventional wars would be short, limited in scope, restricted in area and would not involve extensive use of fire power. It was also felt that armoured and mechanized forces would not be employed on a large scale, and, if used, would be largely in open areas and not in urban warfare. However, the widespread use of mechanized forces by both sides and the contrasting manner in which they were utilized by the Russians and the Ukrainians brings out vital lessons on the use of mechanized warfare, in this war and others that would follow.

Russia and Ukraine hold an impressive arsenal of armoured fighting vehicles and both sides fielded them extensively in the war. Russia, holds the world's largest tank fleet of over 12,400 vehicles and their doctrines hinge around deep manoeuvring and wide thrusts along a broad front. Mechanized spearheads have been at the heart of their operations since World War II, during the Cold War and even after the breakup of the Soviet Union. In the Ukraine war, their tank forces, especially the 1st Guards Tank Army, spearheaded the offensive, along all four thrust lines. Around 1,200 tanks or so were reportedly deployed by Russia, mostly the T-72 which formed the workhorse of the fleet (akin to the Panzer IVs fielded by Germany in the World War), T-80s, and T-90s. A regiment or so of their latest T-14 Armata tanks were also reportedly used in secrecy in select areas, largely to assess its battle performance. A vast array of BMPs (largely IIs and IIIs), and other AFVs were also fielded, working together in composite forces based on Battalion Tactical Groups.

The Russian concept of Battalion Tactical Groups is akin to the Indian concept of combat groups. It is a grouping of all arms composed of infantry, tanks, artillery, air defence, combat support and logistics elements. The organization was flexible, and tailored as per tactical requirements, but a typical BTG held around three companies of motorized infantry with each company having 10 BMP II/IIIs carrying seven men each. It could have one or two tank companies, along with self-propelled artillery, Pantsir S-1 mobile air defence systems, engineers and resupply elements. Each BTG had around 7-800 men but since the composition was flexible the figure could go up to 900. It was designed to be a self-sustaining unit and move around 150 kilometres, function independently for six days and be in combat for three days without requiring additional support. Each brigade had two or three BTGs under it. Interestingly, the Russians seemed to have moved away from large divisions and corps, preferring brigade-size formations instead

Ukraine too fielded a formidable array of around 1600 operational tanks, largely T-64s, T-72s and T-90s along with the versatile BMPs. Though both sides possessed similar Soviet-era equipment, the Ukrainians had the disadvantage of both quality and quantity.. However, as time would show, they used their equipment optimally and applied the concepts of manoeuvre warfare far more effectively.

The Russian armoured thrusts in the early days of the war of February-March were expected to simply *blitzkrieg* across Ukraine, much like the German offensive across the Soviet Union in 1941. Their deep armoured thrusts did not materialize. Most of the thrust lines simply ground to a standstill. Sucked into cities, led into ambushes, and cut off from their logistics, the Russians were forced into a long, expensive battle of attrition, which blunted their offensive. Armour did form the spearhead, and accounted for the deep penetrations of over 200 kilometres made by the Russian forces. The less-than-optimal utilization of mechanized forces, at least in the early days, led to a long-drawn-out conflict, and not the swift victory that was hoped for.

The Ukrainians largely used their mechanized forces in defensive roles during the initial days of the war, fighting skilful defensive battles with anti-tank weapons, drones and artillery. However, when they launched their own offensive in September 2022 in Kharkiv in the northeast and Kherson in the south, their use of mechanized forces was far more imaginative. They used them to manoeuvre deep into enemy-held territory and made rapid advances recapturing areas in days, which the Russians had taken months to occupy, with their slow attrition tactics. The use of mechanized forces by both sides brings out valuable, though contrasting, lessons.

The Concentration and Build-up

The bulk of Russian mechanized forces for the offensive concentrated along the eastern Ukraine border for months before the war, supposedly 'exercising.' In the north, around 30 battalion tactical groups similarly conducted joint exercises in Belarus. The two arms of the offensive were ideally positioned for a pincer move that could rapidly encircle Kyiv from the north and the northeast. However, the Russians lost the element of surprise. Their early concentration gave them away and they were detected and monitored at every stage of the build-up.

The concealment of a large mechanized forces has been a problem since the days of 1917. Detection from ground, air and satellite is easy in today's transparent battlefield. Formations, units and even individual vehicles were identified and tracked virtually on a real-time basis. When the Russians resorted to the standard deception tactics of side-stepping units and formations to create a confused jumble for the enemy, their identities were discerned not by sophisticated satellites, but by the humble cell-phone. An army of social media warriors operating along the border posted photos of tanks and equipment, getting details down to the tank numbers and formation signs. More than military satellites, the bulk of the information was received from private operators with cell phones, and entities like Maxar Technologies and Google Maps which could pick up large columns of vehicles and then post the information in the public domain. The Russian concentration and their likely thrust lines were discerned weeks before the onset of the war, which robbed them of the crucial element of surprise, and enabled the Ukrainians to position their own forces to counter the thrusts.

However, when the Ukrainians launched their own offensive in Kharkiv in September, they concealed their mechanized forces far more skilfully. They also deceived the Russians by moving some of their mechanized elements to the south, creating the impression that they meant to launch the main offensive there. In today's environment, deception may be easier to attain than concealment.

The Russian Advance

The Russian offensive was expected to race into the heart of Ukraine and simply overwhelm them in 'shock and awe'. The Ukrainians claim that ceremonial uniforms were discovered in captured tanks and AFVs indicative of a planned victory parade after an easy win. The Russian offensive did advance rapidly in the initial days but was then halted at the cities which had to be reduced to open the axes of maintenance. The Russians should have simply followed the German tactics of World War II when their panzers approached Kiev and Kharkov (as they were then named) in 1941. Rather than enter the cities directly, the German panzer armies launched a pincer that encircled Kiev, trapping its forces inside. As the Soviets pushed in even more men and equipment to break the pincer, a larger encircling move was launched 200 kilometres eastwards in the area of Kharkiv. The twin pincers trapped over 700,000 Soviet soldiers in a ring of steel and decimated them. With the destruction of the Soviet armies in the field, the Germans simply walked into the cities without much resistance.

Had the Russians resorted to similar battles of manoeuvre, perhaps the result would have been different. Instead, they followed the German model of Stalingrad, the site of the greatest defeat of German armies. They pounded against the cities, hammered them into rubble and got sucked into long and expensive battles for suburbs, streets and crossroads. All with the presence of civilians who became the ubiquitous 'collateral damage'.

The Russians traditionally advance on a broad front which allows their tanks to spread out and manoeuvre in different directions. Moving cross-country also enables a tank or a ICV to make optimal use of its mobility and firepower. Their armoured columns were largely confined to roads, often moving in line along designated avenues. The reluctance of the Russians to move cross-country, especially in the early stages of the offensive, is baffling. Perhaps it had to do with the flawed timing of the attack. At the time of the year—March-April—the spring thaw sets in and 'Marshal Mud' arrives. Heavily loaded vehicles sank axle deep into the ground which had turned slushy by melting snow, forcing the crew to abandon them. Similarly, Pakistani tank crews had simply abandoned their tanks when they were bogged down in the flooded fields around Asal Uttar in September 1965.

Tanks versus Anti-tank Weapons: The Gap Widens

Over 4,000 Javelins and 3,500 Next Generation Light Anti-Tank Weapons (NLAWs) were supplied by the USA, UK, Germany and other countries to Ukraine to build up their anti-tank potential. These were augmented by German Panzerfaust 3s, Soviet era RPG–7s and even local expedients such as Molotov Cocktails. As time would show, these anti-weapons more than proved their worth, causing extensive damage at long ranges, and halting the columns of advancing armour.

Footage of some of the tanks reveal extensive damage. In many cases the turrets have been literally blasted from their bodies, indicating that the HEAT warheads of the anti-tank munitions penetrated the armour protection and detonated the ammunition inside. Most of the Russian tanks were fitted with Explosive Reactive Armour panels which were designed to blow off on impact thus defeating the impact. Many AFVs were also fitted with slats—improvised cages of wire mesh and steel strips around the turret to detonate an incoming missile and keep its blast away from its body. However, from most accounts, these did not prove very effective. We do not know as yet how effective the Russian active armour protection system, the Drozd, was. By some accounts, the Ukrainians resorted to bombarding the fighting vehicles with dozens of projectiles to confuse the computer of the active armour protection systems. In most cases, the armour of AFVs—even those with ERA and other protective suites—could be defeated by modern day anti-tank weapons.

Much of it had to do with the warheads and mode of attack. Most of the missiles had tandem warheads, in which the first warhead exploded on hitting the protective suite, but the second warhead could still punch its way through the armour. Javelins and NLAWs with ranges of almost 4,000 metres, using the fire-and-forget mode were especially effective, more so since they used top-attack modes, in which the missiles would first rise about the tank and then dive down, striking it at the top of the hull or the turret where the armour was weakest.

A similar top-attack mode was followed by drones using MAM-Ls anti-tank missiles. The use of drones by the Ukrainians really stands out. Using a combination of cheap, locally made Specter and Punisher drones, they could bring down attacks with pin-point precision. The Specter drone—the observer—loitered over the battlefield, observing and relaying images and coordinates of targets to its handlers. When a target was identified, the Punisher drone, armed with bombs or missiles was launched. It fired missiles from long ranges at target coordinates received from the observer, and more often than not, scored direct hits. Ukraine had received 20 Turkish-made Bayraktar drones, whose four anti-tank missiles were used with telling effect. The later stages of the war also saw the induction of Switchblade—kamikaze drones—loaded with explosives that would home in to a target and slam into it, destroying a $ 4 million tank in a matter of minutes.

Drones often operated at night using thermal imaging systems to home in to tank engines (which very often had their engines on in the cold) and then striking them with guided bombs and missiles. Night attacks were the preferred mode which helped the drone to avoid detection and gain surprise. Aerorozvidka, Ukraine's tactical drone unit, had adopted the Latin motto *'Non dormies'*—You shall not sleep.

It was not for the first time that drones had been used in this manner. Even in the Armenian-Azerbaijan conflict at the Nagorno-Karabakh enclave in April 2020, the Azeris used a fleet of Turkish TB2S and Israeli Harops to overwhelm Armenian armour, artillery guns and air defence systems. Syria lost the bulk of its tank fleet in Idlib when Turkish drones blitzed their armour concentrations in a two-day carnage, using a similar seeker-destroyer combination. This innovative use of drones is a game changer in today's battlefield and will require major changes in armoured tactics to help counter them.

The Russians did learn their lessons as the war progressed and equipped their mechanized columns with all-arms teams using specialized equipment such as the BMPT 'Terminator' which was equipped with machine guns, 30-mm cannons, smoke grenades, and missiles to detect and eliminate any anti-tank teams in the vicinity. They too used drones, often flying over their own columns that would relay information of the terrain and the threat ahead, giving vital early warning and over-the-horizon visibility to the crew. Once the Russians began grouping their armoured forces with adequate surveillance, prophylactic protection, and securing their flanks with their own anti-tank teams, their effectiveness increased manifold.

Russian Tactics and Logistics

Many of the Russian tactics and the initial conduct of operations have been baffling. During their advance towards Kyiv in the first week of the war, a 64-kilometre-long column of tanks and supply vehicles merely halted 30 kilometres away from Kyiv, when the tanks should have moved off the road and begun encircling Kyiv.

As per speculations, the column simply ran out of fuel, but that is not correct. They had definitely catered for enough fuel for the advance to establish contact at least. They halted to enable the complementary thrust, moving in from the northeast, to close it. That delay in isolating and investing Kyiv did cost the Russians dearly. The Russians also faced problems due to paucity of trucks and resupply vehicles. Their logistic doctrines depend on the rapid laying of pipelines and using road and rail networks to ferry supplies to the forward lines. To use the rail and road junctions, they needed to capture the cities that lay astride them. Their inability to capture the cities thus meant their logistics could not be pumped forward and their offensive stalled as a result.

Perhaps they could have taken a leaf out of the book on the Indian advance for the liberation of Bangladesh in 1971. Here, the Indians simply bypassed the towns and moved inwards towards Dacca, causing a psychological collapse. However, there was a difference. The follow-up logistic columns could bypass Pakistani-held towns and move along side roads and tracks. We were guided and aided by the Mukti Bahini, and there was no fear of partisans attacking the supply columns. This luxury was denied to the Russians who faced attacks and ambushes by vengeful parties all along the way.

Even at the tactical and operational levels, there was much to be desired. Although, the Russians have the concept of combined arms and BTGs, their mechanized forces often operated without infantry. The footage of tank ambushes show that the flanks were often not secured. Maybe there was a paucity of training and motivation of the crew (as it emerged later, many were conscripts who seemed unclear of what was expected of them during the offensive). Nor was there adequate coordination with the air force. Their ground attack aircraft; the very potent SU-25s and attack helicopters did not operate in tandem with the mechanized forces in the way they should have. As the war progressed and newer anti-aircraft missiles became available to the Ukrainians, the effectiveness of Russian strike aircraft and attack helicopters reduced considerably. The inability of the Russians to gain control of the skies, cost the ground forces dearly.

During the second phase of the war (after 22 April) when the Russians moved away from Kyiv and focused on the south and the east, mechanized forces were better utilized as the ground hardened with the onset of summer. They did succeed in penetrating deep into Ukrainian territory—in many cases up to 200 kilometres deep. Even in the later stages of the war, as the Russians were sucked into the cities and built-up areas of the Donbas, the use of armoured columns in composite all-arms teams proved very effective. ICVs were the weapon of choice in the clearing of built-up areas, where their infantry could advance under protection and then secure the ground, while the heavier tanks provided fire support. Fighting in built-up areas will be a norm for which mechanized forces must be prepared.

Ukraine's Use of Mechanized Forces

Ukraine did have a qualitative and quantitative disadvantage over the Russians, though both sides fielded virtually the same family of equipment. In the initial days of the war, Ukraine's armour and mechanized forces played a largely defensive role helping funnel Russian armour into ambushes and killing zones where they could be decimated with the combined fire of artillery and anti-tank weapons. They were used extensively in counter-attacks—especially the famous counter-attack by 4th Rapid Reaction Brigade on Russian airborne troops at Hostomel airfield on the first day of the war, which saved the day for Ukraine. The Ukrainian command wisely resisted the temptation to spread their armour in penny packets across the 1,200-kilometre-wide frontage. Instead, they preserved them and concentrated them for their own offensive in Kherson and Kharkiv in September. In the Kharkiv counter-offensive, their mechanized forces raced 90 kilometres in just three days, recapturing area that had taken the Russians months to occupy, demonstrating how effective mechanized forces could be when correctly used.

The Russians are the original proponents of the 'Deep Battle Concept' in which armoured forces strike deep into enemy territory, simultaneously attacking different echelons of defence to create a psychological dislocation of the enemy. The concept was developed by Marshal Tuchachevski, one of the pioneers of manoeuvre warfare in the 1930s, and forms the bedrock of armoured tactics. The Ukrainians took a leaf out of his book for their own offensive.

In September, six armoured and infantry brigades were concealed in the thick forests in the north-east of Kharkiv region, a heavily wooded area crisscrossed with rivers and streams, where the Russians did not expect any offensive action. At the same time, extensive activity was depicted in the south in the area of Kherson which led the Russians to believe that the offensive could come there and divert troops to the region. These actions were akin to the German offensive in 1940 when their armoured formations burst out through the thickly-wooded Ardennes forests, while leading the French to believe that the main offensive would come much further to the north and diverting their forces there.

The Ukrainian offensive spearheaded by the 92nd and 25th Mechanized

Brigades penetrated through the lightly-held Russian front lines with information provided by drones and local intelligence. Light vehicles slipped through the gaps, guided the main forces, and then formed a screen deep in the rear to cut off the retreating enemy. It was a classic case of 'Reconnaissance Pull' where the recce elements simply guided the mechanized forces following in their wake.

Area of the Ukrainian Offensive

When the initial objectives of Balakliya and other forward towns were reached, tanks and combat vehicles isolated the town in a rapid encirclement. The mechanized forces clearing built-up areas with tanks and BMPs raced to the town centre to seize important buildings and road junctions, and provided firepower and protection to their infantry as they cleared the positions. The concept of 'Thunder Runs' which the USA followed in Iraq was quite effectively replicated here as well.

While the initial objectives were being cleared, armour and mechanized infantry did not wait, but raced deeper towards the intermediate and depth objectives like the towns of Kupyansk and Izium. There, once again, similar tactics were followed. The positions were cleared by infantry, while the bulk of the armour moved even deeper. They reached the line of the Oskil River, seized bridges and cut off the Russian route of withdrawal. They moved 90 kilometres in just three days, reaching deep behind Russian lines, and often causing the defences to collapse through sheer psychological dislocation and surprise.

Another skilful use of mechanized forces was demonstrated during their southern offensive in the Kherson region. An equivalent of a mechanized brigade was lined up abreast in the western bank of the Dnipro River and then roared from north to south all along the bank of the river. The following infantry cleared the positions and seized vital bridges, cutting off the Russians on the far bank and forcing them to withdraw.

There is still no official account of the war by either the Russians or the Ukrainians and one has to piece together the information based on open sources. However, examinations of documents and film footage show that the Ukrainians seemed to have followed the concepts of mechanized warfare better. They used all-arms teams, maintained tactical distances, and most importantly, resorted to deep manoeuvre to make rapid gains. They used them as a rapier as they should be, and not like a battering ram.

The Lessons of the War

There had been a lot of talk about 'the demise of the tank' especially in the early days of the war, when images of shattered Russian tanks were gleefully shown across the world. That is not a true picture. The Russians had advanced over 200 kilometres deep in every sector and each of their thrust lines was invariably led by armour. The initial depth they attained could not have been possible without mechanized forces. Of course, the Ukrainian counter-offensive too was largely based on its mechanized formations.

All this does bring out a lot about the nature and composition of mechanized forces. For starters, it has been proved, that irrespective of the level of protection provided to a tank or ICV, a modern-day anti-tank weapon will be able to defeat it, and at relatively low cost. In tank design, the traditional factors of protection, firepower and mobility have reached their optimal stage. Further add-ons will be prohibitively expensive. It would also be more effective to invest in developing the nervous system of the tank—its situational awareness—rather than its mass and muscle.

A battlefield management system would be the best way of enhancing the tank's capabilities. In its simplest form, it will provide a computer screen with a digitized rolling map showing own positions and terrain features around it. On the map, the location of each friendly element—neighbouring tanks, flanking units, guns, supporting units and logistic elements—would appear on real-time basis. Information and location of the enemy could also be marked on the map, which would enhance the situational awareness tremendously. This system can be networked to surveillance and intelligence sources, air and attack helicopters and thus dramatically enhance the tank's effectiveness in today's battlefield.

Even the simple expedient of providing hand-held or catapult-launched drones and remotely-operated ground vehicles will give much needed 'over-the-horizon' capability and early warning. Drones are the game-changer and need to be introduced in all units, not merely armoured and mechanized ones, and their use incorporated in tactical and operational doctrines.

There is also a need to rethink the size of armoured and mechanized units and formations. Smaller, nimble units and formations would be more effective than large, ungainly ones. The 45-tank armoured regiment could be scaled down to 35 tanks (using three troops per squadron). Perhaps we could also consider having a greater number of independent brigades, rather than large divisions. These would be far more versatile with greater operational and strategic mobility.

The Ukraine war was the first conventional war between two conventional nations in this century—not counting the six-day Russia-Georgia war of 2008. It has surprised the world with its scale and intensity and in many ways taken warfare back to an earlier era, while preparing the ground for the future. It has shown that fighting in built-up areas will be the norm; the anti-tank weapon will only gain ascendency with time; drones and remotely operated vehicles are game-changers; and in a transparent battlefield, the focus should shift from surprise to deception. In all this, the AFV is still here to stay. The concepts of its use must evolve to make them versatile, integrated and capable of holding their own in both conventional and non-traditional battlefields.

REFERENCES

"Battle of Hostomel–Wikipedia" https://en.wikipedia.org

"Bayraktar TB2 Unmanned Aerial Combat Vehicle", https://www.militarytoday.com

"BMPT Terminator makes Combat Debut in Ukraine" – *Jane's Defence News*, 19 May 2022.

"Does the Tank have a Future?" *The Economist*, https://www.economist.com, 15 June 2022.

"Drozd-2 Active Protection System. Tanks-Military-Today" www.military-today.com

"First Battle of Kharkov", Peter Chen; World War II Database, 2007.

"Getting to Know Russian Battalion Tactical Groups", RUSI, https://rusi.org 14 April 2022.

"How many Tanks does Russia have in Ukraine?" https://www.forbes.com 15 March 2022.

"Javelin Anti-tank Missile, Symbol of Ukraine's Resistance" https://m.economictinmes.com 16 March 2022.

"NATO bolsters arms supply to Ukraine with Anti-Tank Weapons" *Al Jazeera*, 26 Feb. 2022.

"Specialist Ukraine Drone Unit picks off invading Russian forces as they Sleep" Parker, Charlie, *The Times*, 27 March 2022.

"The 90-kilometer-long journey that changed the war in Ukraine", Henry Foy, *Financial Times*, 28 September 2022.

"The Air and Missile War in Nagorno-Karabakh", https://www.csis.org, 08 December 2020.

"The Land Warfare Papers", Peter J. Vlakancic, https://www.ansa.org

"Troops and Military Vehicles enter Ukraine from Belarus" *Murphy; CNN 23 February 2022.*

"Ukraine punches through Russian lines as surprise offensive retakes land in the East."; CNBC. 11 September 2022.

"Ukraine War: Is the Tank Doomed?" BBC News, https://www.bbc.com 7 July

"Ukrainian Balakliya-Kupyansk Offensive", Mylola Bielieskov, *Eurasiona Daily Monitor*, Volume 19, Issue 133.

"Why has Russia's 64 km long Convoy near Kyiv stopped moving" www.bbc.com, 03 March 2022.

Military Balance 2021, quoted in *Kyiv Independent.*

6

THE GOD OF WAR: FIREPOWER IN THE UKRAINE WAR

"Artillery is the God of War."

—Joseph Stalin

The Opening Shots

The Russia-Ukraine war has been a war of firepower. Both sides have used it imaginatively and purposefully with good effect. A curious aspect of this war has been that the air component of firepower has been missing after the initial strikes in the initial phases. It is the ground component that has dominated. Another important aspect has been that enemy, terrain, ground, weather, and all other factors might deter, inhibit, or preclude employment of air, infantry and armour but nothing deters artillery. Artillery firepower can be delivered 24×7×365. Till now it was understood that God fights on the side with big guns. This war has proven that God fights not only on the side with big guns but also with one with rockets, missiles, and air power with longer ranges and greater lethality.

The impact of artillery can be seen through the headlines below:

"Ukraine's Artillery Might Be Winning the War With Russia."

—*Forbes*

" 'They're in hell': Hail of Russian Artillery Tests Ukrainian Morale."

—*Washington Post*

"Artillery is playing a Vital Role in Ukraine."

—*The Economist*

"One Village at a Time: The Grinding Artillery War in Ukraine."

—*The New York Times*

Some of the participants in this war who were at the receiving end of artillery felt that:

> *The war has become, as one Ukrainian soldier put it, a game of "Artillery Ping-Pong".*
>
> *"It starts with a loud whistle and you feel something fly past. Then comes the explosion, followed by the blast wave. Last is the shrapnel, which swarms through the air like flies. All you want to do is hide, not breathe, dig deeper in the ground."*
>
> *"When a person is shooting at you, you have a clear idea of how to fight back. But when a piece of metal is flying at you, you don't know where the enemy is and how to survive."*

One thing is for sure. This war has changed the way future wars will be fought. Firepower is going to have an out-of-proportion impact on the battlefield. That changes a lot of equations. The Russo-Ukrainian conflict signifies the future battlefield and the way wars are going to be fought in future.

The Russo-Ukrainian war has been fought in distinct phases with varying results for Russia, Ukraine, EU nations and NATO. While Russia and Ukraine have been prime adversaries in the conflict, the USA, EU and NATO have had a large role to play in it. The first phase was a three-pronged Russian offensive into Ukraine. This was also to decide whether or not Ukraine would survive as an independent nation. The second phase is about the territory that

Russia captured in Ukraine in the east and south (Donbas and Crimea). The third phase is the Ukrainian counter-offensive which regained large tracts of territory. Beyond this, there would be more. However, the impact of firepower in each of these phases has been distinct with different outcomes. Employment of firepower by both sides has been extensive.

When the war commenced in end-February, it was the onset of 'Rasputitsa' or the mud thaw which sets in with melting snows in that area. This is the time when the countryside becomes slushy and the terrain becomes soft. During this time, cross-country movement by vehicles or on foot is virtually impossible. Most movement remained confined to roads and tracks. Infantry and armour could not be deployed over wide frontages to conduct manoeuvres. Under these conditions, employment of firepower in the form of traditional tube artillery, rocket artillery, long-range guided missiles, Cruise missiles and hypersonic missiles was unrestricted. Strangely, the use of air power has been restricted.

Both armies have evolved based on the Soviet doctrines where firepower subordinates other forces—tanks and infantry. Firepower has always been used to punch holes in the enemy defences to enable and generate movement. In the same vein, firepower has also been used to plug holes and restrict manoeuvres by the enemy. Both sides have had similar types of fundamental artillery—guns and rockets. The difference being that Russia possesses hypersonic and cruise missiles as also modernised artillery—guns and rockets—in far greater numbers than Ukraine. In the initial stages of the war, Ukraine relied on Soviet-era guns and rockets. Recently it has been given modern artillery (M114 ULHs) and rockets (HIMARS – High Mobility Artillery Rocket System) by the USA. Both sides have used the available firepower extensively and aggressively in conjunction with other elements to achieve their respective political objectives. Firepower has been the battle-winning factor for both sides in their respective victories.

The First Phase

Prior to this war, the general thinking was that long-drawn wars were a thing of the past. It was also being propagated by military theorists that future wars would be limited and conducted surgically through multiple domains using high-technology. The first and foremost reality has been that conventional battles can and will continue to be fought. The prime constituent of any battlefield continues to be firepower through its unrestricted and premeditated violence. The scope of employment of firepower expanded vastly in the war. The realisation is also that, to realise full value and effect of firepower, it has to be integrated with other elements of the battlefield. Hence, application of integrated firepower is the order of the day. In this context, it involves integration between sensors and shooters at one level and integration between air and ground elements of firepower at another level.

Traditionally, firepower was used to neutralise an enemy or keep his firepower down. With time, artillery-based firepower progressed from a 'neutralisation and suppression' outlook to 'destruction and degradation' practices as the range and lethality of the ammunition increased exponentially. The role of firepower in suppressing enemy firepower and interdiction of the battlefield also increased with time. This aspect is not fully understood or recognised in many armies. However, during the conflict, both the Ukrainian and Russian armies have used firepower in such roles extensively. A major aspect of employment of firepower has been in its role in conventional non-contact deterrence. Utility of long-range firepower to deter adversaries from undertaking a particular course of action is an exemplar impact of this war. This new facet of warfare needs greater analysis.

The Russo-Ukrainian war has witnessed seamless employment of nuclear and conventional firepower power in a destructive and deterrent role simultaneously and interchangeably. To this end, Russia used air, hypersonic/Cruise/guided missiles, rockets, and guns extensively to deter NATO from getting directly involved in this war. While it issued a nuclear threat, it fired hypersonic missiles twice at targets near the Polish border to demonstrate its willingness to escalate and convey credibility of its intent. Simultaneously, Russia carried out multiple attacks to destroy Ukrainian military installations and targets using air, Cruise missiles, rockets and artillery across the length and breadth of the country. This has been a completely new facet of war fighting enabled by layered firepower to reach into the depths of enemy territory.

The Russian Army's initial three-pronged invasion in February and March resulted in a static battlefield for long periods. There were no major moves or manoeuvres due to the *'Rasputitsa'* factor. Moves, when attempted, were along well-known roads and tracks. There was hardly any surprise element. In this context, long-range firepower opened up the battlefield to generate strategic and battlefield manoeuvres. Firepower overcame terrain friction to enable deeper strikes. While the frontages changed only incrementally, the daily situation was rapidly changing due to orchestrated firepower strikes. It was a deep battle of a different kind. Russia has prominently employed firepower in a destructive role. Ukraine has used firepower to suppress enemy firepower and generate manoeuvres in its recent counter-offensive around Kharkiv. Though, Russia has been carrying out strategic strikes in depth as part of its eastern offensive, the effect has not been pronounced.

A striking aspect of this war has been that firepower has been used to achieve political aims in a very deliberate manner. Early in March, Mr. Putin had laid down four conditions to end the war. These were; Ukraine not to be part of NATO; Donetsk and Luhansk to be recognised as independent states; Crimea to be recognised as part of Russia; and demilitarisation of Ukraine. Firepower was applied in a planned manner to achieve each of these conditions. Russia used firepower in a deterrence role to keep Ukraine from joining NATO. An overt nuclear threat was posed to NATO to keep it on the sidelines to ensure that it does not get directly involved or actively participates in the war. This was reinforced by employment of air, hypersonic and Cruise missile strikes on targets near the Polish border. This combination of nuclear and conventional deterrence conveyed credibility and resolve of the Russian threat to escalate the situation beyond Ukraine, if warranted.

Firepower was used overwhelmingly in its traditional role which enabled rapid expansion of Russian-controlled territory in the south in areas adjoining Crimea and Donbas regions. Demilitarisation of Ukraine was carried out through systematic destruction of military assets. Air and missile strikes were carried out on Ukrainian bases especially in the west to cut off military aid flowing in and where joint training with NATO used to be carried out. Systematic destruction of Ukrainian war-waging capability was undertaken. Ammunition, fuel and logistics dumps were targeted extensively. Destruction of Ukrainian defence industry was done methodically. Lastly, Ukrainian firepower and military elements were repeatedly targeted and degraded.

A significant and noteworthy feature was that even at tactical levels, artillery was used innovatively in executing 'ambushes' by firepower and undertaking 'track and kill' operations. Firepower ambushes were carried out extensively by Ukrainian forces. As Russian forces advanced into Ukraine, ambush areas were designated along the roads. These sections of roads were kept under surveillance by drones, radars and observers. When the designated section was packed with slow-moving or halted Russian convoys, a Ukrainian gun or rocket fire unit(s) would execute a fire assault on it from a hide. Invariably the high intensity fire assault would cause extensive damage. The Ukrainian fire unit/launcher would scoot off from the hide before the Russians could deploy or retaliate. It has already emerged that the Ukrainians relied heavily on field artillery to hold off Russia's invasion. The Royal United Services Institute cites a Ukrainian military official as saying "*anti-tank missiles slowed the Russians down, but what killed them was our artillery. That was what broke their units*". When the Russians got wise to Ukrainian tactics, they deployed their drones as surveillance outposts. The moment a Ukrainian fire unit/launcher started its scoot from the hide, it was tracked by a Russian drone till its base. Then the base would be engaged conclusively by a long-range rocket/missile. Retaliatory track and kill operations warded off Ukrainian firepower ambushes and enabled Russian forces to advance to a large extent.

The Second Phase

In the ongoing second phase of the war in southern and eastern Ukraine, air power has been conspicuous by its absence and the two sides are more entrenched. In this scenario, artillery has become even more pivotal. Firepower has been the dominant force for both sides. Russian artillery was concentrated to outnumber Ukrainian artillery by a factor ranging of 57:1. Further, the Ukrainian artillery, which was largely of the Soviet era, has restricted ranges. In effect, the Russian firepower not only outnumbered Ukrainian firepower but also out-ranged it. However, to some extent, balance was restored when the USA supplied HIMARS to Ukraine.

In this phase of the war, the Russian aim has been to seize maximum territory in the Donbas area. Its overwhelming firepower has been used in a far more aggressive, and calculated manner. The *Washington Post* has reported that "*The war has seen relatively few infantry engagements or tank-on-tank battles;*

Russia, rather, is concentrating overwhelming artillery power on relatively small areas to blast its way forward in a path of grave destruction". This gives an overall idea as to how things have evolved in this phase of the war. The general pattern has been that the Russian forces operated in smaller groups unlike the large columns in the first phase. They used a sizable fleet of drones to identify and target Ukrainian positions, hitting them with artillery and air strikes. At times, Russia used cluster and thermobaric (or vacuum) ammunition also in its fire assaults. These attacks were deadly and lethal. When a particular target, zone or village was effectively levelled by firepower and ground troops, a mixture of regular Russian forces and fighters mobilized from the Russia-backed separatist territories in Donetsk and Luhansk, moved in and seized the area reduced to rubble in mopping-up operations. Russian forces also destroyed roads and buildings as they advanced, leaving few places for Ukrainian troops to take up defences. Russia captured village by village and position by position in this grinding manner. That is the reason why progress was seemingly slow and incremental.

The Third Phase

When the Ukrainians launched their own offensive in Kharkiv and Kherson, artillery made a major difference. The Ukrainians relied heavily on artillery, not only to hold off Russian forces but to generate their counter-offensive. In the initial phases of the war, the odds were completely in Russia's favour. Since Western countries gave Ukraine, some sophisticated artillery including the M777 ULH, HIMARS and the French CEASAR, which is a mounted-gun system with a high degree of mobility, some parity has been achieved. Modern artillery of Western origin redressed the balance qualitatively. It enabled Ukraine to hold out and mount some limited counter-attacks to maintain an intact front. The longer ranges and more accurate M777 ULH have been used by the Ukrainians imaginatively. When Russian artillery was in the process of getting deployed for an impending operation or about to fire, Ukrainians have fired and engaged them with the M777s in a spoiling attack mode. The longer ranges and pinpoint precision of modern Western artillery enabled the Ukrainians to strike deep and hit Russian ammunition dumps, command posts, logistic supplies and communication networks, and capitalise on the confusion to launch their own counter-offensive. Precision munitions also, to some extent, redressed the imbalance in the quantum of ammunition held by Ukraine (By some estimates, Russia had almost forty times the ammunition that was available to Ukrainian forces) The long range has been a critical component in the success of Ukrainian counter-offensives.

Even after the attacks on the Kersh Bridge, Russian retaliation largely was through firepower. Around 300 strikes were launched targeting infrastructure resources, especially energy and water, which reportedly destroyed 30 per cent of Ukraine's electricity grid. The use of long range firepower to deliver a military and political message was telling.

The Russians and Ukrainians have placed their faith in firepower to a large extent. The overall impact of firepower was massive and outsized, and its true efficacy will be known at the end of the war. In the overall context, it will not be out of place to quote Stalin, "*Artillery is the God of War.*"

Lessons for India

A thought has been expressed by a Western commentator which bears reflection in the Sino–Indian context. "*Moscow is obliterating towns with faraway artillery to minimize its losses and play to the Russian military's strengths as an artillery-focused force. Moscow is also relying on those tactics because Russian forces have been gutted by casualties and have shown an inability to fight successfully otherwise.*" We might do well to prepare and expect a similar but slightly varied approach from China. The inexperienced PLA will not risk casualties in war by resorting to infantry or tank attacks as we expect them. They will in all eventuality go hell for leather with artillery and overwhelming firepower so that they can reduce their casualties. Let us be prepared for a firepower-based battle of the Russo-Ukrainian variety but suitably adapted to high-altitude terrain and conditions.

From a wider perspective, India which faces twin adversaries in China and Pakistan has many lessons to learn from this war. The first and foremost is that the terrain conditions in which India has to most probably fight its next war will be in the Himalayas where movement will be restricted to the roads to a large extent like it happened in Ukraine. Hence the value of firepower will increase manifold. Axiomatically, the use of mechanized forces will be limited by terrain. Employment of air activity will be restricted by fickle Himalayan weather. The battles will be largely fought by infantry and artillery.

It will be beneficial to remember a major lesson from the last war in Kargil which was also in high altitude. To recount, *"The Pakistanis gained renown when their Artillery was used imaginatively and prime on the battlefield in the initial phases of OP VIJAY when they were able to heavily interdict National Highway 1A. They achieved infamy when they ran short of firepower and could not press home their initial advantage. India gained infamy initially when Artillery was inadequate in the early stages. It was only when Artillery was restored to its prime importance on the battlefield that India could gain renown."*

China also lays great emphasis on firepower and specifically on employment of rockets and missiles. It also lays a lot of emphasis on fighting wars under conditions of informatisation with using precision strike capabilities to paralyse enemy operational systems as part of their system destruction warfare. They too will have imbibed lessons from this war and will adapt it to a future conflict scenario.

The Sino-Pak-Indian nuclear environment sets the bar for conflict thresholds. The Kargil conflict with Pakistan at one end and the Sino-Indian face offs in Eastern Ladakh at the other represent the likely conflict spectrum. India must be able to operate its firepower effectively within this spectrum. It is in this context that India has to rethink on employment of firepower including air, air defence and artillery holistically. The Indian mindset needs to change. The thought that air and artillery are 'supporting' forces is no more relevant in the current and futuristic battlefield. That has been amply proven in Ukraine. India must start thinking of employing firepower in a deterrence role and be able to control the deep battle. India needs to develop its 'Reconnaissance Strike Integration' capability where its sensors and shooters are fully conjoined with a fail-safe data network. This must span air and ground elements including special forces operating deep in enemy territory. India also needs to develop deep battle concepts and be able to interdict enemy forces by control of depth communications. Very significantly, India needs to develop capacities to overcome Himalayan terrain by using long-range vectors. Fire ambushes and track-and-destroy operations will pay handsome dividends in Tibetan terrain. These concepts require a joint approach and must be developed.

It will be fair to state that firepower has dominated the Russo-Ukrainian war in a manner never seen before. That firepower includes artillery, missiles, drones, air—even nuclear weapons in the backdrop. Integrating the use of all this seems to be the name of the game. It demands new understanding and new approaches. However, one thing is clear. The imaginative and concentrated use of firepower will always bring huge dividends, and that too without the cost of precious lives.

* * *

Lt Gen P.R. Shankar, PVSM, AVSM, VSM is a former Director-General of Indian Artillery and has been closely associated with firepower and its applications. He is presently a professor at the Indian Institute of Technology, Chennai, and writes extensively on strategic affairs and technology.

REFERENCES

https://static.rusi.org/special-report-202204-operation-z-web.pdf

https://www.economist.com/europe/2022/05/02/artillery-is-playing-a-vital-role-in-ukraine

https://www.forbes.com/sites/davidaxe/2022/04/27/ukraines-artillery-might-be-winning-the-war-with-russia/?sh=423f260b3b48

https://www.gunnersshot.com/2021/10/fire-power-and-artillery-futuristic.html

https://www.gunnersshot.com/2021/10/firepower-and-artillery-futuristic.html

https://www.gunnersshot.com/2021/11/fire-power-and-artillery-futuristic.html

https://www.gunnersshot.com/2021/11/firepower-and-artillery-futuristic.html

https://www.gunnersshot.com/2021/11/firepower-and-artillery-futuristic_20.html

https://www.gunnersshot.com/2021/12/artillery-and-firepower-futuristic.html

https://www.gunnersshot.com/2021/12/artillery-and-firepower-future.html

https://www.gunnersshot.com/2022/09/published-in-ramjet-technology-can.html

https://www.newyorker.com/news/dispatch/the-fight-to-survive-russias-onslaught-in-eastern-ukraine

https://www.nytimes.com/2022/05/06/world/europe/ukraine-russia-artillery-kharkiv.html?searchResultPosition=1

https://www.washingtonpost.com/world/2022/06/03/russia-ukraine-war-news-putin-live-updates/

https://www.washingtonpost.com/world/2022/06/04/ukraine-east-artillery-war/

7

THE AIR WAR

"The Russian inability to gain control over the skies in the initial days itself, was one of their greatest shortcomings of the War."

—The Economist

The Ukraine war began with a contest of influence over Ukraine. The Western powers were trying to bring Ukraine into the European Union (EU) and NATO folds without realising that the threat it would pose to Russian security would undoubtedly provoke a violent response. When Russia massed its troops on the border, and negotiations failed, the inevitable happened. Russia invaded Ukraine on 24 February 2022, setting off the first major war in Europe after 70 years.

Despite the huge asymmetry in total air power between Russia and Ukraine, the relatively restricted use of air power by Russia is still a matter of debate. Boasting of Su-57 stealth fighters, Su-35 Flankers, how did Russia's mighty

Air Force fail to dominate Ukraine? The destruction of a significant number of Russian aircraft by Ukrainian ground-based AD weapons, effective use of unmanned platforms, destructive power of air-launched precision munitions, and the sinking of the Russian flagship 'Moskva' with two Ukrainian 'Neptune' anti-ship Cruise missiles, have brought out aspects of the air war whose final lessons will be drawn only on hindsight, but still hold great relevance.

Russia began its ground offensive with a concerted offensive into Ukraine from the north, the east, and the south. From the north, its troops moved from Belarus towards the capital, Kiev, and reached within 30 kilometres of it before they decided to withdraw. The Ukrainian resistance was possible due to high nationalist fervour and the air-to-ground, anti-tank, and anti-aircraft weapons supplied in large numbers by Western countries.

While the initial northern thrust towards Kyiv petered out, the Russian offensive in the Donbas and all along the coastline in the south did meet with a great measure of success. The Ukrainian counter-offensive did retake significant lost territory, but a large chunk of Ukraine still remains in Russian hands. Much of the reason for the land offensive not being able to make the gains they hoped for lies in the fact that the Russians never attained dominance of the air.

Russian and Ukrainian Air Power

The Russian Air Force (RuAF) is the second largest in the world with nearly 4,173 aircraft. Eight bomber squadrons operate Tu-22M3/MR, Tu-95MS, and Tu-160 bombers. 37 fighter squadrons include variants of MiG-29, MiG-31, Su-27 and over 100 Su-35 aircraft. There are 27 attack squadrons operating the Su-24, Su-25 and Su-34 variants. Ten attack-cum-reconnaissance squadrons operate Su-24s and MiG-25RB. They have only around 14 fifth-generation Sukhoi Su-57 aircraft which are still under operational evaluation. Russia operates a squadron each of A-50/A50-U aircraft and FRA Il-78/Il-78M. At any given time, Russia has around 300 modern combat aircraft normally stationed in the western and southern military districts—within range of Ukraine. They had also relocated regiments from elsewhere in Russia as part of its military build-up prior to the invasion.

Ukraine mostly has Russian and Soviet equipment and the war has seen mostly identical aircraft and systems pitted against each other. Ukraine had the world's 27th largest air force and the 7th largest in Europe. They had a significant domestic defence industry, including the original Antonov aircraft plant. The Ukrainian Air Force (UkrAF) was manned by 36,300 personnel and had 215 aircraft at the beginning of the war. As of August 2022, they were down to 175 aircraft. These included nearly 100 fighters comprising MiG-29, Su-24, Su-25, Su-27, and L-39, some of which had been recently modernized. Their aircraft had been used largely in air defence operations. Ukraine has also been using American and Turkish UAVs very effectively, both in the reconnaissance and the attack modes. They had significant AD systems including S-300 missiles with nearly 500 missiles in addition to the Western Man Portable AD Systems (MANPADS) which has been used to good effect to down Russian strike aircraft and helicopters.

One of the major Ukrainian aircraft losses of the war was the tragic destruction of the world's largest plane An-225 or 'Mriya' (The Dream). Only one of this 650-ton giant transport aircraft was ever built by the Antonov Design Bureau based at Kiev. This aircraft was destroyed in a cross-fire between Russian and Ukrainian troops in the opening week of the war, when the Russians attacked Antonov airfield at Hostomel.

Air Operations in Ukraine

Whoever controls the air generally controls the surface. Air power is an inherently strategic force. It is best used as an offensive weapon and provides deterrence and coercive power. Air power can conduct parallel operations at all levels of war, simultaneously. Precision air weapons have redefined the meaning of mass. Technology and air power are integrally and synergistically related. Air power includes not only military assets, but an aerospace industry and commercial aviation.

The Russians had a lot of preparatory time. While Russia had deployed a large number of troops and military platforms, it made limited use of its advanced air weaponry initially. Russians reportedly were conserving their assets for the eventuality of possible escalation of war involving NATO. It is not clear whether they had carried out enough Intelligence Surveillance and Reconnaissance (ISR) operations using space-based assets. NATO support to

Ukraine for ISR was phenomenal. Russia was expected to achieve air superiority, but that happened only partially and a little later in the conflict. The use of AWACS and AEW&C is not clear. Maybe they were scared that they may be shot. Fighter strikes were also limited. Air- and ground-launched Cruise missiles and ground-based multi-rocket have been used extensively.

Russia did strike military infrastructure at Ukraine's air bases and flew missions for Suppression of Enemy Air Defences (SEAD). Finally UkrAF did get grounded and thereafter Ukraine mostly concentrated on using its ground-based air defence. SEAD success is questionable as many radars and missile batteries remained intact. Some more were moved in from bases in the west which were unaffected. Initially, the main targets for Russia were the political centres of Kiev, Kharkiv, Kherson, Mariupol, and other towns which were subjected to air and missile attacks in the preparatory stages of the attacks. The Russians claimed though that they deliberately did not used air power extensively against the cities to reduce casualties.

The RuAF could fly limited sorties in the north due, but got hammered by MANPADS and lost a significant number of aircraft. Helicopter gunships were used for Counter Surface Force Operations (CSFO), and widespread video footage emerged of Russian Mi-25s being shot by a Stinger missile. Surprisingly, Russian aircraft did not use their missile warning systems or IR flares to ward of the missiles. Russian ISR and electronic intelligence components also appeared to have been spread too thin. The RuAF support focused on Close Air Support, but was limited by lack of multi-role platforms, operational exposure, and training standards. Since the area of operations was over Ukraine only, there was no air defence requirement for Russia, and no Ukrainian air strikes in Russian territory were recorded.

The widespread use of unguided munitions by Russia indicated that they were running out of PGMs or conserving what they had in case of future escalation, or a confrontation with NATO. Russia lost some of its top-of-the-line Sukhoi aircraft to attrition when employed as basic strike aircraft. The ATGM/MANPADs success by the Ukrainians reflects that just as the tank is a baggage without an active protection system (APS), so are airborne platforms viable targets without an integrated self-protection jammer. Both cannot carry out their core tasks without these layers.

Where were the Russian UAVs? They emerged only in the later stages of the war but could have been an asset especially for the protracted and persistent SEAD and interdiction missions. However, maritime air power was used quite effectively because of the availability of Crimean air bases, and the positioning of naval aviation resources there.

Notwithstanding, Zelensky has confirmed that Ukraine has suffered 'serious losses' after Russian air strikes pounded many targets, damaged radar arrays and other equipment and Ukrainian military facilities. Russian missiles hit targets in many cities, including Kharkiv, Kramatorsk, Dnipro, Mariupol, Odesa, and Zaporizhzhia. Russia continued air and missile strikes across the country to cause military and economic damage. Russia might have achieved its primary objectives but at a much higher cost than desired and through a fitful cycle of adaptation.

Cyber warfare and electronic warfare seem to have been under-utilized. Even Stinger missiles require radar input as warning of incoming threat and direction. Obviously they were been jammed. One also did not see IR flares being used against Stinger missiles. Extensive use of videos by Ukrainian civilians made effective psychological warfare. The Western world greatly supported Information Warfare through satellite communications, and internet that was kept live. It is significant that the Ukrainian internet and communication networks continued functioning—after an initial temporary outage at the beginning of the war—right throughout the war. SpaceX's Starlink satellite internet terminals have been a crucial means of communication for Ukraine's military, enabling it to fight and stay connected even as cellular phone and internet networks were destroyed in its conflict with Russia. More recently he has been asking the US Government to fund the service.

There have been air engagements, but they were few and far in between. We heard about the "Ghost of Kiev", a MiG-29 Fulcrum flying ace credited with shooting down six Russian planes in the Kyiv offensive on 24 February 2022. However this proved to be fictitious war propaganda, designed to boost morale and was not based on fact. The Russian defence ministry claimed that over 100 air defence systems and over 90 Ukrainian aircraft had been disabled or destroyed. Most UkrAF losses were on the ground. A few have been shot in the air. Most Russian aircraft losses have been by ground-based AD systems.

Many well-known top-notch Russian and Ukrainian pilots lost their lives in aerial engagements.

Russia claimed to have launched its Kinzhal (Dagger) hypersonic missile at, among other targets, a weapons depot in western Ukraine—making it the first country to ever to test this type of missile in combat. From a military point of view, using a hypersonic missile to hit a stationary target made little sense. Why use a weapon this expensive when a traditional ballistic missile could have done the job just as easily with less risk of failure? Maybe it was mostly to send a message to the West. Russia has also faced significant cases of precision-guided munitions failures.

Initially, Russian air operations were not effectively prosecuted and they did not gain full control of the skies in spite of their qualitative and quantitative superiority. Nor did they use air power effectively in support of ground operations. As the war progressed, so also the conduct of air and joint operations improved. The RuAF significantly increased the number of sorties flown in Ukraine and improved their ability to support ground operations. Russian aircraft were being committed piecemeal and often appeared in twos and threes over places such as Izyum, Rubizhne, and Popasna. However, even during the Ukrainian counter-offensive, the Russians did not use air power to effectively blunt the Ukrainian advance, perhaps due to the effectiveness of air defence systems like MANPADS provided by the West. Their inability to control the skies in spite of having such superiority of both quality and quantity, and not completely utilise the air power at their disposal, is one of the baffling aspects of the air war.

Concept of Air Denial

For long, the air strategists have been talking of the need for air superiority. With very high asymmetry of air assets between Russia and Ukraine, it was expected that the contest would be one sided. The Russian SEAD and other counter ir engagements did take place in the first two-three weeks. Both sides lost nearly 50 fighters each. The Russians lost them in the air, nearly 10 aircraft in air combat and the remaining 40 from ground air defences. The Ukrainians also lost around 10 fighters in air combat, but lost nearly 40 on the ground, hit by Russian air strikes. They later moved the remaining 50 or so fighters to safer Western airbases. What prevailed was what can be called air denial. The

Russians had grounded the Ukrainian air force for all practical purposes so that no Ukrainian aircraft other than UAVs and drones could fly. Similarly, the Ukrainians who had received over 1,000 Stinger missiles from the USA along with other air defence systems, used them to deny air space to Russian aircraft. The Russians were forced to use expensive stand-off weapons. Their large inventory of iron bombs could not be used. What was actually achieved was air denial. This served the purpose for both sides. Clearly the future of air warfare is more about denial than air superiority.

Air Power in Naval Ops

The naval war for Ukraine has received relatively little attention in the open press. There were occasional reports of Russian ships shelling the Black Sea coast. Warships from all four of Russia's geographic fleets converged on the Eastern Mediterranean and the Black Sea in late January 2022. The Russian Navy's critical tasks supporting Putin's strategic objectives included resupply of ground troops, precision fires to support military operations in littoral locations and deep within Ukraine, and maintaining sea control of the maritime passage of all concerned parties. The Russian task force in the Mediterranean continues to deter the NATO Standing Maritime Group's assurance operations by holding allied ships at risk. The Russian Navy performed adequately in the first weeks of the war. Strikes from SS-N-30 Kalibr land-attack Cruise missiles and naval gunfire, and providing resupply to Russian ground forces advancing along the Sea of Azov coast toward Mariupol. Russia lost an Alligator Class LST while pier-side in occupied Berdyansk, possibly to a Ukrainian short-range ballistic missile strike.

The Russian flagship of the Black Sea, 'Moskva' was hit by two Ukrainian 'Neptune' anti-ship Cruise missiles which caused a major fire which engulfed the ship and it had to be abandoned by the crew. Early reports suggest a brilliantly effective combination of tactics, strategy, and the exploitation of its own capabilities, combined with awareness of Russian weaknesses. The attack reportedly took place during a storm. The Ukrainians used a Bayraktar TB-2 drone to distract the Moskva. The Ukrainian Navy introduced TB-2s into service only in August 2021. It's also possible that the Ukrainians used a TB-2 to identify and target the Moskva for the Neptune battery. In naval use, they can be employed to find enemy ships and relay their positions to coastal missile batteries, as well as carry out direct attacks using their own payloads. The Moskva had a single main air defence radar, a 3P41 Volna phased array, to guide S300 missiles. The problem is, it only has a 180-degree field of vision. The 360-degree coverage is provided by MR-800 Voshkod/Top Pair 3-D long range air search radars for shorter-range SA-8 missiles. It's likely that in the storm they couldn't distinguish the sea-skimming Neptunes from the wave-tops.

Attack on Saki air base in Crimea

In August, nearly a dozen blasts rocked the Crimean airbase at Saki which has the Russian Black Sea Fleet's Naval Attack Aviation Regiment and other units. While Moscow claimed the explosions were the result of an accident, the type of blasts indicated an adversary attack. Hitting an airbase nearly 200 kilometres away from the front line was seen as a big surprise. Ukraine has got long-range weapons such as the American M142 High Mobility Artillery Rocket System (HIMARS) with a maximum operational range of 480 kilometres. HIMARS clearly outclass their Russian equivalents. It is not clear if they used these or the fighter-bombers, Tochka ballistic missiles, drones and Harpoon and Neptune anti-ship Cruise missiles with their secondary land-attack modes. The Saki base was known to have around a dozen each Su-24 bombers and Su-30 fighters. They also had some Mi-8 helicopters and the Il-76 medium-transport aircraft. At least one Su-24, several ground support vehicles and possibly one of the base's munitions dumps were reportedly destroyed. It not only indicates improved Ukrainian offensive capabilities, but questions the ability of Russia to defend vital operational assets. Earlier, the Black Sea fleet had lost the flagship cruiser Moskva. The Ukrainian drone had also bombed a Black Sea Fleet headquarters in Crimea in July. These attacks were morale boosting for the Ukrainian armed forces and the people. It has been a cause of fresh introspection for the Russian military leadership.

Western Support to Ukrainian AD Operations

The USA and its NATO allies declared that the war was a serious threat to Euro-Atlantic security and chose tough sanctions against Russia to weaken Russia's economic base and its capacity to modernize. Since Ukraine is not part of NATO, none of its members can intervene directly on its behalf because that would expand the conflict. Ukraine's request for enforcing a 'No Fly Zone' could not be acceded to. However, NATO members have been supporting the Ukrainians in many other ways like providing satellite imagery to boost Ukrainian air defence operations. NATO owns and operates more than a dozen Boeing E-3A radar planes, with about six of its long-range "eyes in the sky" craft in the air at any given time.

Many countries have supplied Stinger missiles. Some former Warsaw Pact countries have given former Soviet air defence equipment such as S 300 missiles. Poland had offered old MiG 29s, but the same was not finally allowed by NATO. NATO's Combined Air Operations Centre in north-western Germany, has been monitoring the East European airspace, and feeding Ukraine's AD units to deter aggression from Moscow. Many other forms of intelligence were provided to Kiev through individual member-states. Washington too shared intelligence with Kiev, and their information of the gaps in Russian dispositions made a major impact during the Ukrainian counter-offensive.

NATO is also carrying out surveillance over the Black Sea area. A naval carrier strike group has been positioned in the North Sea and eastern Mediterranean, with more than 140 ships at sea. US-built Patriot air and missile defence batteries with the ability to shoot down enemy aircraft or missiles have been deployed in southern Poland and Slovakia. NATO F-35 jets from Norway are shadowing or monitoring Russian intelligence aircraft that were flying off the country's northern coast. NATO is also monitoring Russian Cruise missile launches. NATO's greater eastern air presence is also acting as deterrence.

Lessons from the Air War

The air campaigns must be integrated. SEAD is a must before counter-air or interdiction. MANPADS remain very relevant. Standoff precision weapons are gaining greater significance. Air power will be increasingly used in hybrid and urban environments. Drones and UAVs are significant but also vulnerable in a contested environment.

The doctrine of air denial is now being considered as an alternative to air supremacy. It means use the airspace, and deny it to others. It is so much easier to achieve this vis-à-vis extending control and keeping control of the airspace. The combination of shoot-and-scoot mobile air defence systems like the S-300 to cover high altitude, and MANPADS to cover low altitude is lethal. Both Russia and Ukraine used this approach successfully. Ukraine denying the Russians air superiority kept them in the fight.

Big transport aircraft and even utility helicopters had serious limitations for use in Ukraine due to surface threats and flew at a very safe distance from active action. That tends to bring increased focus on unmanned air mobility and logistics. In India's context, drones will play a significant logistics role especially in the mountainous regions.

UAVs have allowed democratising air power, and made it available to all nations. UAVs have brought significant challenges in airspace at a fraction of the cost and quicker. Till now, use of air power involved very expensive exquisite platforms. Since battles are often extended and continuous, they mean more slow attrition. It is difficult to scale expansive platforms. It is cheaper to scale UAVs and autonomous aircraft.

Ukraine's use of drones, including locally available commercial ones and professionally built combat drones from the USA, UK, and Turkey, has air power lessons for all. They were very effectively used for ISR, attack, and air mobility, mostly unhindered by Russia's air defences and electronic warfare capabilities. Later, Russia adapted a new tactical approach and became more effective in detecting and shooting down TB2s. Similarly, the American Gray Eagle essentially designed for low surface-to-air threats, will be vulnerable. However Switchblades and Phoenix Ghost drones were more effective against Russian tanks.

The future of air combat is set to look different and indicates the dangers of relying solely on high-end platforms. Drones and AI is a potent combination. Losses of expensive, complex aircraft are hard to quickly replace. Losses of skilled personnel in wartime are even more difficult to cope with. Notwithstanding the increased induction of unmanned systems, the next generation advanced combat aircraft still require a highly trained human sitting in the cockpit. Losses of skilled personnel in wartime and their replacement is another area that got highlighted in the continuously extending war. When it comes to Return on Investment (RoI), a mix of surface-to-air weapons, lower-cost drones, precision-guided artillery, and Cruise missiles, makes more sense.

The conflict in Ukraine does flag some relevant initial thoughts for the armed forces of India, which are in the process of major reforms. Wars can linger. Supplies can be throttled. There is an increasing need for indigenisation. Stocking armaments is important. Just large standing armies are not enough. Hybrid war, electronic warfare and technology will come to play and concepts and force structures require a rethink.

It is emerging clearly that there is no soft power without hard power. India needs to continue to build its hard power. Nuclear deterrence continues to play. Self-sufficiency in arms manufacturing, as much as possible, is an absolute necessity. The so-called global rules-based-order is being breached by all sides. It is time that the Indian Air Force gets back to the authorized 42 fighter squadrons from the current low of 31, and the other Services modernise their inventories. We too must learn from the effectiveness of drones for a variety of roles, and use them as low-cost, high utility force-multipliers.

Conclusion

Russia is boosting air and sea military operations as it struggles to wrap up the war in Ukraine. The success of the Ukrainian air defence has, in great measure, prevented the Russians from attaining their overall military goals. Their inability to use air power optimally could be perhaps due to the fact that Russia has not fought a major war after a failed occupation of Afghanistan, and have only seen limited action in Syria. There have hardly been any dogfights, as Russia's military preferred to fire air-to-ground missiles at Ukrainian targets from Russian or Belorusian skies. They're not venturing very far or for very long into Ukrainian airspace, because the Ukrainians have been defending their airspace with great dexterity.

Drones like the Bayraktar, and even hand-held locally developed ones, have been one of Ukraine's surprise successes in fighting the invasion. Against expectations, the Turkish-supplied drones, which resemble a smaller US Predator, have taken a significant toll of Russian vehicles, flying at night and attacking with laser-guided MAM missiles also supplied by Turkey. Russia too, began using drones with greater frequency as the war progressed. Both sides developed counter-drone measures and the drones themselves were getting neutralised in large numbers.

Despite the formal annexation, the last bullet has still not been fired. The last sortie has still to be flown. While we hope that a good middle path emerges, that doesn't seem to be happening in a hurry. There will be lessons of this war that will be discussed in military academies and think-tanks for years to come.

* * *

Air Marshal Anil Chopra PVSM, AVSM, VM, VSM is a fighter pilot who Commanded a Mirage Squadron. He commanded major fighter airbases in the Western and Eastern Sectors and retired as Air Officer Personnel. He has written six books and published 650 articles and is currently Director-General, Centre for Air Power Studies, New Delhi.

REFERENCES

Andrew Higgins, Hiding in Plain Sight, a Soviet-Era Air Defense System Arrives in Ukraine, *The New York Times*, 15 April 2022, https://www.nytimes.com/2022/04/14/world/europe/ukraine-russia-nato-s300.html Accessed on 17 October 2022.

Andrew S. Bowen, Russia's War in Ukraine: Military and Intelligence Aspects, US Congressional Research Service, 14 September 2022, https://crsreports.congress.gov/product/pdf/R/R47068#:~:text=Russia's%20renewed%20invasion%20of%20neighboring,forces%20attacking%20from%20multiple%20directions. Accessed on 17 October 2022.

BBC Research Team, Ukraine: What are Himars missiles and are they changing the war? *BBC*, 30 August 2022, https://www.bbc.com/news/world-62512681 Accessed on 16 October 2022.

David Axe, The Ukrainians Hammered A Russian Air Base 120 Miles From The Front, *Forbes*, 9 August 2022, https://www.forbes.com/sites/davidaxe/2022/08/09/the-ukrainians-blew-up-a-russian-air-base-120-miles-from-the-front/?sh=561c4f0e772e Accessed on 16 October 2022.

David T. Burbach, Early lessons from the Russia-Ukraine war as a space conflict, The Atlantic Council, 30 August 2022, https://www.atlanticcouncil.org/content-series/airpower-after-ukraine/early-lessons-from-the-russia-ukraine-war-as-a-space-conflict/ Accessed on 17 October 2022.

Frederick W. Kagan, George Barros, and Kateryna Stepanenko, Russian Offensive Campaign Assessment, Institute for the Study of War, 19 March 2022, https://www.understandingwar.org/backgrounder/russian-offensive-campaign-assessment-march-19 Accessed on 17 October 2022.

Jack Guy, World's largest plane destroyed in Ukraine, *CNN*, 28 February 2022, https://edition.cnn.com/travel/article/antonov-an-225-largest-plane-destroyed-ukraine-scli-intl/index.html Accessed on 17 October 2022.

Jen Judson and Joe Gould, US Army signs deal to backfill Stingers sent to Ukraine, *Defense News*, 27 May 2022, https://www.defensenews.com/land/2022/05/27/us-army-signs-deal-to-backfill-stingers-sent-to-ukraine/ Accessed on 17 October 2022.

Laurence Peter, How Ukraine's 'Ghost of Kyiv' legendary pilot was born, *BBC*, 01 May 2022, https://www.bbc.com/news/world-europe-61285833 Accessed on 17 October 2022.

Lt Col Johnny R. Jones, "Air Power", USAF Air University, https://www.airuniversity.af.edu/Portals/

10/ASPJ/journals/Chronicles/jjones.pdf Accessed on 17 October 2022.

Maximillian K. Bremer and Kelly A. Grieco, Air denial: The dangerous illusion of decisive air superiority, Atlantic Council, 30 August 2022, https://www.atlanticcouncil.org/content-series/airpower-after-ukraine/air-denial-the-dangerous-illusion-of-decisive-air-superiority/ Accessed on 16 October 2022.

Military Aircraft Strength (2022), Global Fire Power, https://www.globalfirepower.com/aircraft-total.php Accessed on 17 October 2022.

'Multiple launches': Russia fires Kinzhal (Dagger) hypersonic missiles in Ukraine war, *WION*, 05 April 2022, https://www.wionews.com/photos/multiple-launches-russia-fires-kinzhal-dagger-hypersonic-missiles-in-ukraine-war-467136#kinzhal-hypersonic-missiles-there-have-been-multiple-launches-467121 Accessed on 17 October 2022.

N8.Читатиукраїнською, The Presence of Russian Warships in the Black Sea and the Mediterranean Sea in January 2022, *Black Sea News*, 01 February 2022, https://www.blackseanews.net/en/read/184301 Accessed on October 17, 2022.

Rep. Joe Courtney, Moskva's sinking, the rise of anti-ship cruise missiles and what that means for the US Navy, *Defense News*, 03 May 2022, https://www.defensenews.com/opinion/commentary/2022/05/03/moskvas-sinking-the-rise-of-anti-ship-cruise-missiles-and-what-that-means-for-the-us-navy/ Accessed on 17 October 2022.

Russian warship destroyed in occupied port of Berdyansk, says Ukraine, *BBC*, 24 March 2022, https://www.bbc.com/news/world-europe-60859337 Accessed on 17 October 2022.

Sebastian Roblin, An unexpected air-to-air battle is raging over Ukraine. Here's what we know about the losses on both sides, *Insider*, 6 September 2022, https://www.businessinsider.com/whats-known-about-russian-and-ukraine-losses-in-aerial-combat-2022-9?IR=T Accessed on 17 October 2022.

Sneha Swaminathan, SpaceX wants Pentagon to foot bills for Starlink satellite services in Ukraine, *WION*, 15 October 2022, https://www.wionews.com/world/spacex-to-no-longer-pay-for-crucial-satellite-services-in-ukraine-requests-pentagon-to-cover-cost-525264 Accessed on 17 October 2022.

Ukrainian Air Force (2022), World Directory of Modern Military Aircraft (2022), 18 August 2022, https://www.wdmma.org/ukrainian-air-force.php Accessed on 17 October 2022.

8

THE WAR AT SEA

"The long-term strategic aims of the war will be decided in the Sea."

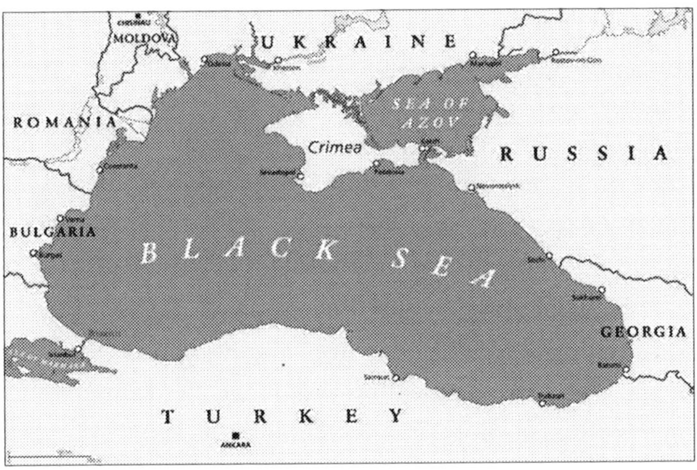

When Russia attacked Ukraine on 24 February 2022, most (including this writer) expected a short, brief conflict. However, the war has continued with numerous twists and turns, in the battles of Kyiv, Kharkiv, the Donbas and the Ukrainian counter-offensive changing the course of the conflict. Most of the attention has been focused on the land battles (which have been covered in detail in the earlier chapters) but the effective utilization of air and naval power has also influenced the course of the conflict. There have been no widespread naval actions, but maritime security and control of the Black Sea and the Sea of Azov—along with the Baltics and North Atlantic, form a major rationale and unseen arena of the war.

This chapter will focus on the maritime dimension of the conflict highlighting:

- The conflict at sea.
- Sea Control and Sea Denial.
- Global implications.
- The nuclear dimension.

The Conflict at Sea

The genesis of this conflict lies in President Putin's dream of making Russia a great power again and his concern at Russia's shrinking sphere of influence in its neighborhood. The Black Sea is important to Russia as it is its only access to the warmer waters of the Mediterranean and the shortest approach to the Red Sea and the Indian Ocean. This conflict actually began with the annexation of the Crimean Peninsula by Russia in 2014. In the maritime domain, this included not only the town and port of Sevastopol but also most of the Ukrainian naval fleet that was berthed there. Subsequently, Russia did return a few ships but it had effectively neutralized the Ukrainian navy.

On 25th November 2018, a Ukrainian tug and two gunboats, while transiting through the Kerch Strait from the Black Sea to the Sea of Azov, enroute to the Ukrainian ports of Mariupol and Berdyansk were fired upon and rammed by Russian ships and aircraft and the vessels were detained. The obvious reason for this provocative action was Russia's intention to choke Ukraine economically and subdue it politically. The Kerch Strait had become a bone of contention between the two countries when Russia constructed the 19-kilometer-long bridge connecting Crimea and Russia across the Kerch Strait as the height of the bridge precludes large vessels from transiting under it, thus affecting the movement of Ukrainian trade. The bridge was a major project for President Putin in his effort to consolidate Russian control of the Black Sea as it provided road connectivity from the Russian mainland to the Crimean Peninsula. Russia's intention has been to establish a land route connecting its mainland to Crimea since the present access via the sea or over the bridge is vulnerable, as the recent attack on it clearly demonstrated. The lack of land connectivity also highlights the vulnerability of the Russian naval presence at Sevastopol.

The movement of Russian naval ships towards the Black Sea began prior to the outbreak of the conflict, with units from its other fleets amassing in the Mediterranean. On 8th February 2022, the Russian Ministry of Defense announced that six ships of the Baltic and Northern Fleets were passing the Bosporus to participate in naval drills in the Black Sea. The Black Sea Fleet then went on to carry out naval exercises with its 30 or so ships in the Black Sea, which also included live-fire drills from 13-19 February. By the time Russian forces commenced their action on land, they had already established sea control around Ukraine. The Russian Navy had also closed the Kerch Strait thus establishing complete control of the Sea of Azov, and had deployed its ships off Odessa and other Ukrainian ports.

While not officially announcing one, the Russian Navy had also virtually affected a *de-facto* blockade over the entire Black Sea and the Sea of Azov in contravention of the UN Convention on the Law of the Sea (UNCLOS). This led to widespread indignation as merchant ships from various nationalities found themselves restricted in their movements. The Black Sea is the only maritime outlet for Ukrainian trade from Odessa in its south-west directly into the Black Sea, and primarily through Mariupol in its the east via the Sea of Azov and the Kerch Strait. Thereafter, this passes through the narrow Strait of Bosporus which runs through Turkey and onwards into the eastern Mediterranean and to different parts of the world. The Russian intention was to establish complete control on south eastern Ukraine, consolidate its position in Crimea and establish complete sea control on the Black Sea, thereby crippling the Ukrainian economy. Notices to Mariners (NOTAMS) were issued to warn merchant vessels which were prevented from entering the Black Sea. A number of foreign merchant ships were also attacked, including an Estonian freighter. This was a dangerous move since Estonia is a member of NATO and could have led to an unintended escalation.

The Black Sea washes the shores of six other countries including Russia, and includes three NATO members—Turkey, Bulgaria and Romania. Of these Turkey has become a critical factor in the conflict since it controls the Bosporus, the only link from the Black Sea to the waters beyond. Before the start of the conflict Turkey invoked the Montreux Convention of 1936 which allows it to deny access to warships through the Bosporus. This effectively checked the Russian navy's intention to augment its Black Sea fleet and led to tensions arising in the eastern Mediterranean which witnessed an enhanced Russian naval presence comprising Slava-class cruisers, Udaloy-class destroyers, two frigates, at least one Buyan-M-class corvette and two Kilo class SSKs. NATO had deployed three carrier task Forces led by the USS *Harry S Truman,* the French Navy's *Charles de Gaulle* and the Italian Navy's *Cavour.*

The denial of the Bosporus notwithstanding, by 24 February 2022, the Russian navy had a formidable presence in the Black Sea comprising the Slava-class cruiser Moskva which was the flagship of the Black Sea Fleet, two Admiral Grigorovich-class frigates, three Buyan-M-class corvettes and a Kilo class diesel-electric submarine (SSK), all of which were armed with the Kalibr family of cruise missiles. In addition, at least ten amphibious landing craft were also present in the Black Sea. Hence the Russian presence in the Black Sea was overwhelmingly superior to the Ukrainian Navy's, 'mosquito fleet' of small vessels for near-shore operations to primarily protect Ukraine's territorial waters and shorelines. This coastal defence force was established after Russia had reappropriated the Ukrainian Navy's vessels in Sevastopol during its annexation of Crimea in 2014. Till then, the Russian navy had in fact, leased a part of the Sevastopol port from Ukraine to base its Black Sea Fleet. To add to Ukraine's woes, the initial gains seemingly made by Russia on the maritime front led to the Ukrainian Navy scuttling its own flagship and its only frigate, the Krivak III class 'HETMAN SAHAIDACHNY', alongside its pier, lest it fall into Russian hands. Soon after that, Russia made an amphibious landing to take control of Mariupol which was important to prevent any Ukrainian interference in the Sea of Azov, virtually making it a 'Russian lake'. The amphibious assault coupled with the land attack from Donbas eventually led to the isolation and eventual capture of Mariupol.

The Russian Navy also supported this effort by firing a large number of Kalibr land attack missiles from seawards at targets well inland as well as along the coast. With the blockading of the Sea of Azov and effective neutralization of the Ukrainian navy, Russia was able to intensify its assault on Mariupol including large scale bombardment of the city from seawards.

Despite these setbacks and virtually no naval forces to speak of, Ukraine managed to offer some resistance even in the initial stages of the war. The exchange of words between the defiant Ukrainian sailors on Snake Island and the Russian missile cruiser Moskva became the defining element of Ukrainian resistance in the early days of war. Snake Island, which is called ZmiinyOstriv in Ukraine is a barren 46 acres of land located 180 miles from Crimea and seemingly, of little significance to Russia. However, strategically, its importance lies in its ability to control the movement of shipping from Odessa and South Ukraine to the Black Sea. That is the reason it was targeted by the Russians at the very beginning of the conflict. Ukraine was equally determined to prevent Russia from establishing its stranglehold on the island and continued to disrupt Russian efforts to consolidate its position. By mid-May, Ukraine had effectively neutralized the Russian presence on Snake Island and also destroyed some of the Russian assets there. This enabled Ukraine to prevent the Russians from carrying out their planned amphibious operation to capture Odessa. Had Odessa been captured, the last vestige of Ukrainian maritime resistance would have also ended.

The second significant loss for Russia was the sinking of its 12400 tonne heavily armed Black Sea Fleet flagship MOSKVA. On 13 April, two Ukrainian 'Neptune' cruise missiles successfully struck the ship and while Russia tried towing it back to harbour, it sank *enroute* because of the damage it had sustained. This was a remarkable success as it was the largest Russian ship sunk since World War 2, and more than the loss of the ship, it was the loss of face and the inherent weaknesses in the Russian Navy which stood exposed. Ukraine also sank the Russian Alligator class amphibious ship SARATOV in Berdyansk. It also used the Turkish supplied Bayraktar TB-2 drones to attack various targets including the Headquarters of the Black Sea Fleet, though with limited results. The inability of the Russians to achieve their naval objective of swiftly neutralizing Ukrainian resistance, crippling its economy and taking full control of the Black Sea and the Ukrainian ports, despite its overwhelming naval superiority would be worth analyzing once the war is over.

Sea Control and Sea Denial

Both these classic concepts of sea power have been on display during this conflict. The Indian Maritime Doctrine defines sea control as a condition where one is able to use a defined sea area, for a defined period of time, for one's own purposes and at the same time deny its use to the adversary. Sea denial, on the other hand, is a concept of denying the adversary the use of a sea area for a certain period of time. While large blue water navies like the Russian navy are structured for sea control, sea denial is the preferred strategy for smaller navies. Ideally, submarines are considered the ideal platforms for sea denial but in this conflict the Ukrainian Navy did not have a submarine capability.

The MOSKVA

The preponderance of Russian naval forces in the region and the successful blockading of the Sea of Azov enabled Russia to exercise substantive sea control north of the Kerch Strait. However, despite its dominance in the Black Sea, Russia was not able to establish absolute sea control. The sinking of the MOSKVA was testimony to that. For the Ukrainian Navy, the options for sea denial were restricted to shore-based missile capability, small patrol craft and to some extent mine warfare, which is a very potent and low-cost option. The use of drones added one more dimension. The successful missile attack on the Moskva, despite its considerable area air-defense capability reflected poorly on the combat readiness of the Russian Fleet and highlighted the vulnerability of large heavily armed platforms of the 1980s in an agile contemporary maritime battlespace. Coupled with the neutralization of the Russian area air defense capability by Ukrainian missile strikes in Snake Island, the Russian fleet exhibited a certain degree of hesitation when deploying in areas where adequate area air defense was unavailable. This restricted much of its movement to within shore-based air defense range and the much-vaunted occupation of Odessa could not happen.

Global Implications

This global crisis has emanated from the Russian blockade of the Black Sea which prevented Ukrainian grain and commodities from being shipped to various parts of the world. Food security, energy security, inflation, disruption of global supply chains, shortage of commodities, rising prices of raw materials and the possibility of a global recession are some of the visible fall-outs. The United Nations has also flagged a possible food crisis in the developing economies as a major concern with far reaching global consequences. Despite Russia agreeing to let grain shipments exit Ukrainian ports from 22 August, the increase in prices due to enhanced insurance rates for shipping and the need to transit from more distant alternate ports, increased the overall costs and contributed significantly to the inflationary pressures being felt across world.

From a geostrategic perspective, this conflict has the potential to spill over into Russia's neighborhood across its other borders as well. While President Putin blamed NATO for instigating Ukraine, and his fears of NATO coming to Russia's doorstep, his actions has led Sweden and Finland to seek NATO membership. In effect therefore, President Putin's attempt to drive a wedge within NATO not only backfired, but it also created two more possible military 'adversaries' for Russia in its northwest while further hemming in Russia in the North Sea and the Baltic, thus limiting its access to the Atlantic Ocean. It has a naval enclave in Kaliningrad which remains Russian sovereign territory between Lithuania and Poland (both NATO members), and more than 400 miles from the Russian mainland. It is the only Russian port in the Baltic which does not freeze in winter. The Baltic Sea Fleet is also based here and it is defended by nuclear missile installations. In the event of a stand-off with NATO or Europe in the Baltic Sea, its Baltic Fleet could therefore find its room for maneuverability and deployment severely curtailed and continuously monitored. NATO's. This conflict and its likely effect on future Russia-Europe relations is leading all Baltic Sea navies to augment their military capabilities with a focus on their undersea warfare capability.

President Putin has clearly stated that NATO's direct intervention has the potential to spark the Third World War. Hence there is an apprehension that even an unintended maritime incident between Russian naval ships and NATO forces either in the Black Sea or in the Mediterranean and the Baltic Sea, could lead to NATO invoking Article 5 and thereby trigger a violent backlash from Russia in this uncertain and tenuous environment.

The Nuclear Dimension

President Putin has also not hesitated in brandishing his nuclear card. The recent sighting of Russia's newest nuclear submarine, BELGOROD at sea, probably armed with the Poseidon nuclear torpedo, as recently as 27 September 2022 is a worrying development. The Poseidon is meant to be a game changing underwater nuclear torpedo and has been described by the US Navy as an 'Intercontinental Nuclear-Powered Nuclear-Armed Autonomous Torpedo'. A US Congressional Service Report of April 2022 suggests that this torpedo is still undergoing trials and is unlikely to be fully operationalized before 2027. However, concerns still remain that this deployment could be Russia's first step on the nuclear escalatory ladder.

There is also a view that this is the beginning of a new Cold war in Europe and the most serious crisis since the Cuban Missile Crisis of 1962. Both Russia and NATO have a formidable nuclear capability between them and the repercussion of a first strike could lead to a devastating retaliatory attack. However, the presence of nuclear powered and nuclear armed ballistic missile submarines (SSBN) on both sides, which had ensured that the earlier Cold War that 'raged' for over four and a half decades remained 'cold' despite numerous provocations, are likely to serve as an effective deterrent this time too.

However, there is a possibility of President Putin, perhaps detonating a 'tactical' nuclear device over the Black Sea where it would not cause much material damage and therefore may not trigger a retaliatory response, but will still be a statement of intent and a likely precursor to another strike on an actual target. Nuclear sabre rattling is not unusual when megalomanic leaders feel insecure about their perceived invincibility. India is familiar with this rhetoric emanating frequently from our western neighbour.

The focus of this conflict has been on land but the maritime dimension has been a significant factor in shaping the course of the conflict. Control of the Black Sea and the consequent economic ruin of Ukraine was one of the principal reasons for the annexation of Crimea in 2014 and this conflict eight years later. Any further escalation, or the entry of NATO into the war could inevitably shift the focus into the maritime domain with far-reaching global consequences.

The prevailing uncertainty makes it difficult to predict the ultimate outcome of this conflict. Various likely scenarios have been analyzed in another chapter. Will Russia be able to take full control of the Black Sea, either by annexing Ukraine or strangulating it economically and militarily; will the conflict spill over across Russian borders into other regions; will Putin play the nuclear card; will NATO come into play? Any of these scenarios are possible, and, the maritime domain will have a significant kinetic and non-kinetic role in shaping the final outcome.

* * *

Commodore Anil Jai Singh is a seasoned submariner and Anti-Submarine Warfare specialist from the erstwhile Soviet Union who has commanded four submarines and a Fleet ship. He has also served as the Indian Naval Adviser at the Indian High Commission in the United Kingdom.

He writes and speaks on maritime affairs extensively in India and abroad. He has also been a part of Track 1.5 expert groups of the EAS, BIMSTEC and other forums on maritime security. He is presently a Senior Vice President of a large European MNC in India and the Vice President of the Indian Maritime Foundation

REFERENCES

Brad Lenden, *CNN*, 24 July 2022. https://edition.cnn.com/2022/07/23/europe/russia-belgorod-submarine-nuclear-torpedo-intl-hnk-ml/index.htm

Cdr Daniel Mazhruff, USN. https://www.defensenews.com/naval/2021/08/09/after-2014-decimation-ukrainian-navy-rebuilds-to-fend-off-russia/

Cynthia J Parmley, Raul "Pete" Pedrozo. Russia's Illegal Restriction of Navigation in the Black Sea. 27 April 2021. https://www.lawfareblog.com/russias-illegal-restriction-navigation-black-sea

https://www.iiss.org/publications/strategic-comments/2018/the-kerch-strait-incident

https://www.mfa.gov.tr/implementation-of-the-montreux-convention.en.mfa

https://www.navalnews.com/naval-news/2022/10/new-images-reveal-russias-missing-submarine-belgorod-in-arctic/

Indian Maritime Doctrine 2009. https://www.indiannavy.nic.in/sites/default/files/Indian-Maritime-Doctrine-2009-Updated-12Feb16.pdf

James Bosbotnis. The role of naval forces in Russia's war against Ukraine and its implications. 25 March 2022. https://behorizon.org/the-role-of-naval-forces-in-russias-war-against-ukraine-and-its-implications/

Radio Free Europe, 08 February 2022. https://www.rferl.org/a/russia-warships-black-sea-ukraine/31692995.html

9

THE NUCLEAR SHADOWS

"If its territorial integrity is threatened, Russia will use all means at its disposal. This is not a bluff. Russia has various means of destruction, some more modern than NATO countries."

—Vladimir Putin

The Nuclear Threat

On the morning of 24 February 2022, over 100,000 Russian troops amassed on three sides of Ukraine, crossed the border and started what Russia called a 'Special Military Operation' and the West, a full-scale invasion of Ukraine. It was the first major war in Europe after 70 years, and what increased the stakes was the nuclear shadow that now hovered over the continent and across much of the world.

When Putin readied for the invasion of Ukraine, amongst his final actions was an exercise of Russia's nuclear forces which tested the readiness of its nuclear arsenal and the delivery systems of ships, submarines, aircraft, and missiles that would carry them across the globe. Ostensibly it would have also checked the communication systems to ready the weapons for launch and the codes to activate the actual launch. Coming as it did, just a month before the invasion of Ukraine and accompanied by much publicized photos of Putin himself watching the exercises, it was a clear statement of how far he was willing to go in pursuit of his eventual aims.

The nuclear threat came up repeatedly during the war, mainly voiced by Foreign Minister Sergei Lavrov, who warned that "World War III will be a nuclear war"—a thinly-veiled warning that should external forces enter the conflict, it could resort to nuclear means. The bombast cannot be completely discounted as an idle threat. When the West did launch the most powerful weapon in its arsenal—sanctions—Russia went ballistic (pardon the pun). It compared the crippling sanctions to a nuclear strike on its economy and placed its nuclear forces in a state of 'Special Readiness Alert'. On 1 June, Russia again flexed its nuclear muscles by conducting another exercise comprising over a 100 vehicles including the launch of Yars, a thermonuclear intercontinental ballistic missile. The message seemed to have gone home. The USA cancelled the test firing of its Minuteman III ICBM to 'avoid raising tensions', but Russia's nuclear posturing had just begun.

As the war progressed, and Russia found itself facing unexpected reverses, the nuclear shadow lengthened, rather than reduced. The loss of hard-captured territory was not only a setback, it was also a huge loss of face for the Russian military and evoked calls from hard-liners, notably the Chechen warlord, Ramzan Kadyrov, who urged the use of 'a low yield nuclear weapon' to stem the flow of military reverses.

The point was made. Russian could use weapons of mass destruction, if the situation so demanded. Soviet and Russian commanders routinely play the scenario of using tactical nuclear weapons for immediate battlefield gains and it is ingrained in their doctrines. For many, a tactical nuclear device is just another weapon in their arsenal and feel they could get away with its use, without a climb up the escalatory ladder.

That itself is unlikely, because the use of a nuclear device, no matter how small, will lead to a rapid escalation. It would be the crossing of a red line that could not be condoned. Even if low-yield nuclear weapons are not used, there are other weapons of mass destruction that can be employed. The Russians are suspected to have used chemical weapons in Grozny to suppress the Chechen uprising and against Syrian rebels in support of their ally, Assad. Using them in Ukraine will be a different proposition all together, but it cannot be entirely discounted. More so, since they seem to be building up the ground for it by claiming that biological and chemical facilities were found in places like Mariupol. They have also accused Ukraine of using a 'radiological device'—a bomb laced with radioactive material (which Ukraine denies using). Perhaps that could be in preparation of a 'leak' at a later juncture, or even the use of a 'false flag operation' to use a radioactive device against own troops and use the incident as a justification for their own use of nuclear weapons later.

The 'referendum' conducted in the Donetsk, Luhansk, Kherson and Zaporizhzhia regions and their subsequent amalgamation into Russian territory has raised the escalatory ladder by quite a few rungs. When Putin announced that the regions had become part of Russia and *de facto* Russian territory, he also vowed 'full protection' for them with all means at their disposal, including nuclear weapons. As per Russia's nuclear doctrine, nuclear weapons can be used in three contingencies:

- if similar weapons are used against Russia;
- if Russia faces an existentialist threat;
- or by an attack on its own territory.

So, an attack on the soil of the newly-amalgamated territory, or even military reverses there, could be used to justify the use of nuclear weapons by Russia. When Russia faced reverses on the battlefield, it ramped up its nuclear belligerence. Not only did it discount the use of tactical nuclear weapons on the battlefield, it also threatened to use strategic weapons to defend their territories. In another ominous warning, Putin said that NATO's entry into the war would lead to World War III, which could be a nuclear war.

All this could be part of his grand "Escalate to de-escalate strategy" in which he would raise the levels, forcing the other to back down to his demands. Yes, there is a possibility of Russia using nuclear weapons, especially if the chips are down. A major battlefield reverse which threatens Putin's own position may provoke him to use a nuclear warhead. With that the line would be crossed. Any nuclear warhead, no matter how small a yield, will lead to a rapid escalation. It will bring NATO into the war, and then, with the knowledge that Russia could never win against the combined forces of NATO, it may just lead Putin to exercise the 'Samson Option' and unleash his nuclear arsenal, not only on Ukraine, but also its NATO allies, irrespective of the consequences. It is the last scenario which is the most unpredictable and hence the one for which the world must be most-prepared.

Russian Capabilities

Putin has the wherewithal to call his bluff. Russia is the world's largest nuclear power with 5,977 nuclear warheads, which includes 1,458 strategic warheads which are deployed and ready to fire. These have been deployed in the complete array of delivery means including intercontinental ballistic missiles, submarines and strategic bombers and can reach virtually anywhere in the world.

In comparison, the USA holds 5,428 nuclear weapons of which 1,389 are operationally deployed on a similar array of delivery means. NATO, in totality holds 5,943, (the bulk with the USA, with France accounting for 290 and UK for 225). However, the numbers don't really matter. Even the use of a single weapon, or maybe the escalation of up to a dozen or so, would be enough to change the world completely, and get the nuclear genie out of the bottle that it has been locked in since 1945.

In is in terms of tactical nuclear weapons that Russia has a clear edge. It holds almost 2,000 warheads of different yields and capabilities which can be fired from Kalibr SS-N-30 ship-launched missiles, or the shorter range Iskandar M missile (SS-26 'Stone') which can hit targets 400-500 kilometres away, sufficient for the tactical battlefield. Incidentally, Russia moved 200 of these mobile launchers to the Ukrainian border just before the start of hostilities. They can even be fired from conventional artillery guns like the 155 mm Malka self-propelled guns or the more deadly 2S7, 203 millimetre gun (also called the Soviet Atomic Cannon) which can fire up to four nuclear tipped warheads across the battlefield.

It is significant that there was some control on the deployment of tactical nuclear weapons till around 2019. Then, the USA, following Trump's policies, withdrew from the Intermediate Nuclear Forces Treaty, which regulated the move and deployment of ground launched nuclear weapons with ranges up to 500-5,500 kilometres. Hence, even the treaty restrictions, which could have been leveraged to a small extent, cannot be applied now.

Should the situation escalate dramatically, Russia has a massive complement of 286 ICBMs, which can carry up to 958 warheads and hit even the US mainland. Its recently developed RS-28 Sarmat ICBMs can fly at over seven times the speed of sound, penetrate anti-missile defences, and deliver 15 nuclear warheads 35,000 kilometres away. Its ability to strike as far as mainland USA gives it a deterrence that will hold NATO's hand considerably. It is significant that Russia has already used Kinzhal hypersonic missiles to destroy ammunition and supply dumps in Lyiv, where Western aid was collected and distributed, in a veiled threat that it could use these weapons (with deadlier warheads) should the need arise.

It is significant that at the height of the nuclear tensions, both Russia and NATO held their nuclear preparedness exercises in October 2022. The Russian exercise called 'Grom', which roughly translates to 'Thunder', is held every year around this time and involves missile launches, and deployment of strategic nuclear assets. This exercise was one of the largest since the break-up of the Soviet Union and involved land, ground and sea-based nuclear weapons. It had also conducted simulated launches of nuclear weapons in the Kaliningrad enclave of the Baltics in May which included launches of Iskandar M ballistic missiles. NATO too conducted its annual nuclear exercise called 'STEADFAST NOON' which included 14 countries, and involved flying of strategic bombers all the way from the USA. Significantly, the exercise was not cancelled, but held a good 1,000 kilometres away from Russia to avoid aggravating tensions. The testing of nuclear capabilities was again subtle nuclear posturing.

Probability of the Use of Nuclear Weapons

Will Russia use these capabilities? And if it does, what can be the NATO response?

Even at this juncture, the likelihood of the use of nuclear weapons seems unlikely. They have reportedly used 'Vacuum Bombs', a thermobaric munitions, whose destructive power is just short of a nuclear device (minus the radioactivity) in the initial days of the war in Ukraine. There are speculations that they could resort to a limited nuclear strike, maybe detonating a tactical nuclear device with a low yield of .2 of .3 kilotons or so, to attain immediate battlefield success. But would they do it?

It thus seems that perhaps the nuclear posturing is part of the 'escalate to de-escalate' strategy, in which Putin has raised the stakes counting on the West to back down. However, should he resort to a nuclear strike what could be the response? Ukraine has no weapons of its own and the only countries that could retaliate in kind are the UK, France, and the USA. Would they risk a strike which can invite a nuclear attack by Russia's impressive arsenal of hypersonic missiles which have the capability to penetrate defences and hit targets which are a continent away?

By using nuclear weapons, Putin would be crossing the 'thin red line' that will invariably bring NATO and the full weight of the USA into the conflict. NATO could enter the conflict on the grounds that the impact of nuclear weapons transcends borders and affects NATO countries bordering Ukraine, leaving them free to respond using Article 5 of the NATO charter that states an attack on one will be considered an attack on all. The USA has promised that it would react to a Russian nuclear attack "with all means available at our disposal" and even indicated that they could use strategic nuclear weapons in response. In all probability, the initial NATO response will be a conventional one. Its very entry into the war will tilt the scales irrevocably and leave Russia with no chance against its combined might.

Which again raises the fear. If Putin is faced with defeat, will he unleash his arsenal of nuclear weapons, irrespective of the retaliation that would follow? By doing so, it would lead to a global holocaust and a scenario that one fears the most.

The Threat to Nuclear Reactors

At the time of the break-up of the Soviet Union, Ukraine held the world's third largest nuclear arsenal; an estimated 1,900 strategic warheads, 176 ICBMs and 44 strategic bombers, almost one third of the Soviet arsenal. When the USSR disintegrated and Ukraine became an independent nation, it willingly surrendered its nuclear weapons in 1994 in exchange for economic aid and security assurances through the Budapest Memorandum of Security Assurances of 1994 signed by the USA, Russia, and the UK. Most of the weapons were transferred to Russia for the paltry sum of one billion dollars. Others were dismantled and their cores used as nuclear fuel for their reactors. It is quite significant that both Russia and the USA had offered security guarantees to Ukraine—guarantees which neither have kept in this war.

Today, there is a distinct sense of regret in Ukraine that it voluntarily handed over its nuclear assets in return for mere promises. Had they held on to them, it would have been the deterrent that may have prevented the Russian invasion.

Though Ukraine does not hold weapons, it still has one of the largest nuclear power programs in the world. Its five nuclear power plants generate over a third of its electricity, and now these plants themselves are at risk of a nuclear accident. Ukraine is no stranger to nuclear accidents. The catastrophic radioactive leak of the Chernobyl plant in 1986 claimed over 4,000 lives over a period of time and led to an environmental residual radioactivity that lingers on even today. When advancing Russian forces took over the now defunct Chernobyl nuclear plant, a plant still encased in a steel and cement dome, the mere movement of tanks and heavy vehicles increased the radioactivity levels in the area. Zaporizhzhia, the largest nuclear power plant in Europe, was hit by an artillery shell which set a building ablaze, but fortunately did not affect the reactors. Russia has its sights on all five of Ukraine's nuclear reactors and should military action initiate a leak in any of them, it could lead to a radioactive leak that can engulf all of Europe and reach as far as the east coast of the USA.

It is Zaporizhzhia that is the greatest threat. The nuclear plant there is the largest in Europe, and its six reactors generate 5,700 megawatts of electrical power that supplies one-fifth of Ukraine's electricity. The plant was taken over by Russian forces on 03 March during their initial advance, and since then run by the Russian agency, Rosatom, though it continued to be staffed by Ukrainian workers. This plant came under heavy fire when the Ukrainians launched their counter-offensive in the south in August. During the fighting the plant, which is strategically located on the Kakhovha Reservoir on the South bank of the Dnieper River came under artillery and small arms fire. The firing set a training facility ablaze, damaged the radiation sensors and shells landed dangerously close to the nuclear storage facilities. Predictably, both sides blamed each other, and though local fires were put out before they could cause much damage, the dangers of a nuclear accident are rife. In fact, locals around the area were issued with iodine pills (which provide some measure of protection to the thyroid, in case of radioactive exposure), as anticipatory protection in case of a radioactive leak. The protective domes around the reactors have been reinforced after the Chernobyl disaster, and are strong enough to withstand the impact of a stray shell, but it is not enough. A strike on one of the critical components like the cooling system could lead to a dangerous overheating of the plant which can cause the nuclear reactors to erupt—a danger which the IAEA called a "potential catastrophe".

In mid-August, Russia shut off the electrical grid for the first time in the plant's 40-year-old history. This was done to disconnect it from the Ukrainian electricity grid and connect it to the Russian grid. What it implied was that Russia was effectively shutting off Ukraine from its own electrical supply and diverting it to Russia in a flagrant energy theft. The act was a potentially dangerous one, since the shutting off of electric supply could disable the safety mechanisms and could cause the reactors to overheat dangerously and perhaps even blow up. (In fact, even the Chernobyl disaster was caused by the electrical power being shut off temporarily.) Should such a contingency arise in any of Ukraine's five power plants, it could give rise to a potential radiation disaster, which could sweep across Europe and engulf it in lethal radiation much worse than that seen at Chernobyl.

Nuclear Proliferation

A large number of people in Ukraine feel that giving up nuclear weapons in 1994 was a mistake. The ongoing war would never have happened if Ukraine possessed nuclear weapons. This has sent a wrong signal to other nations. Iran, Saudi Arabia, South Africa, perhaps even Syria and Turkey amongst others, may decide to seek nuclear weapons as a guarantor of security. Iran especially, which is now just six to seven months away from developing a nuclear weapon, will be loathe to re-enter a nuclear deal which will require it to abandon its nuclear program (especially after being betrayed by Trump earlier). It could go ahead with developing its own nuclear weapons as a hedge against a future attack by the USA or any other adversary. This could set off a nuclear race in the Middle East with Saudi Arabia and Israel following suit. Of course, Pakistan and North Korea will be similarly emboldened. So, nuclear proliferation, which the world tried so hard to contain over the past few decades, will be back.

Nowhere is the threat of the nuclear shadow as large as it is looming over Europe. Only two other nations there, the UK and France, possess nuclear weapons, but most come under the US nuclear umbrella. The USA has deployed around 100 B 61–3 and 4 nuclear gravity bombs of variable yield, ranging from .3 KT to 170 KT. These are deployed in six airbases in five nations (Belgium, Germany, The Netherlands, Turkey, and Italy (two)). These weapons are complemented by France and the UK's arsenal and it is likely that the USA would now deploy more nuclear weapons as more European nations seek their nuclear umbrella. This would prompt Putin to upgrade his own nuclear arsenal and also arm his allies. Russia intends to transfer Iskander-M missiles which carry both conventional and nuclear warheads to Belarus and begin upgrading Belarusian Su-25 fighters to carry nuclear weapons. The nuclear arms race and the Cold War are back in Europe.

With the attention focusing on Europe, China has been momentarily forgotten. It is the third largest possessor of nuclear weapons in the world. Its stockpile of 350 nuclear weapons is likely to increase to around 500-600 by the end of this decade. It possesses the entire triad of delivery means to drop them on any target in the world. Its impressive array of missiles can hit any corner of the globe, including mainland USA. Significantly, China is not party to any arms reduction treaty (which both Russia and the USA abide by) and thus is free to develop its arsenal unchecked.

India too is the possessor of over 150 nuclear weapons with the complete triad of delivery means—aircraft, submarines and missiles. With both China and Pakistan possessing nuclear arms, perhaps we should be grateful to the far-sighted decision of Prime Minister Vajpayee to develop our nuclear arsenal. The Ukraine war has shown that a nation, unable to defend itself, can be threatened by larger powers. India's nuclear arsenal is a weapon of deterrence, which in itself is a harbinger of national security.

Conclusion

The longer the war continues, the greater is the threat of the use of nuclear weapons. The rhetoric itself has upped the ante considerably and as President Joe Biden pointed out, "The world is closer to a nuclear Armageddon than at any time since the Cuban crisis of 1962" Yet, it is ironic that he should make this statement. The Cuban crisis came about when the Soviet Union began moving missiles towards Cuba where they would pose a threat to the US mainland. The USA was prepared to use nuclear weapons to ensure that the threat was removed. Even now, this war has been caused by the threat that Russia sees to its security by Ukraine joining NATO and the likelihood of missiles and offensive weaponry being deployed at its doorstep, an unacceptable threat to its own security.

The escalation of the war has made the use of nuclear weapons a distinct reality. There would be no dividing line. If nuclear weapons, in any form are used, it will escalate dangerously out of control and there would be no distinction between tactical or strategic weapons, or even geographical areas. So far, the nuclear genie has remained bottled up since the two dark days of 06 and 09 August 1945. Now it seems dangerously close to escaping.

REFERENCES

"Chernobyl Accident 1986–World Nuclear Association", https://world-nuclear.org, 9 September 2022.

"Fact Sheet–US nuclear weapons in Europe", Centre for Arms Control and Non-Proliferation.

"Kadyrov says Russia should use Low-yield Nuclear Weapon", Reuters, https://www.reuters.com, 01 October 2022.

"NATO and Russia hold Exercises of Nuclear Forces as Tensions over Ukraine remain high," Barbara Starr, *CNN Politics*, 16 October 2022.

"NATO entry could lead to World War III: Russia," *Times Global, The Times of India*, 14 October 2022.

"Nuclear Armageddon risk worst since 1962", *Times Global, Times of India*, 8 October 2022.

"Number of nuclear weapons Worldwide, 2022," *Statista*, https://www.statista.com, 5 August 2022.

"Putin leads sweeping Nuclear exercises as Tensions soar", *Reuters*, 19 February 2022.

"Putin's Threats: How many Nuclear weapons does Russia have?" https://www.bbc.com, 07 October 2022.

"Russia's Grom Strategic Nuclear Exercise," https://www.lisi.org

"Russia's Lavrov: Do not underestimate threat of Nuclear War," *Reuters*, 25 April 2022.

"Russia's Nuclear Weapons: Doctrine, Forces and Modernization", https://sgp.fas.org, 21 April 2022.

"The Eurobomb"–C. Raja Mohan, *The Indian Express,* 27 September 2022.

"Ukraine once claimed 3rd largest Nuclear Arsenal in the World", https://www.republicworld.com, 24 February 2022.

"Ukraine War: Could Russia use Tactical Nuclear Weapons? *BBC*," https://www.bbc.com, 25 September 2022.

"Why the Zaporizhzhia Nuclear Power Plant Matters?" https://www.wilsoncenter.org, 19 September 2022.

"Why Ukraine gave up Nuclear Weapons and what that means?" https://www.npr.org, 21 February 2022.

10

Russia, NATO and the Ukrainian Conflict

"Not an inch of NATO's present military jurisdiction will spread in an eastern direction. Not one inch."

—US Secretary of State, James Baker to Mikhail Gorbachev, 1990

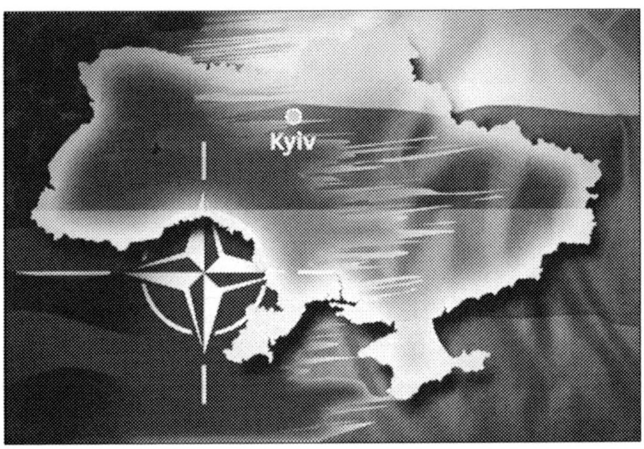

Introduction

Leon Trotsky famously said, "You may not be interested in war but war is interested in you". The world is confronted precisely with this, as the most dangerous international conflict of the 21st century erupts. A conflict that has affected virtually every other nation due to globalisation and interdependencies.

Russia did start the war and is responsible for it. Why did it do so? Why did it risk becoming an international pariah and sacrificed its economic goals with this action? At the heart of it all is Putin's vision to recreate Russia in the mould of the former Soviet Union, and ensure its security. The root to the war was Ukraine's decision to join NATO, an action that would directly impinge Russian security.

Ukraine's joining of NATO would have brought the alliance right to Russia's borders, and enable its missiles to strike Moscow in minutes. As Putin himself put it, "Don't they see? We have no place further we can go now. It is not a situation that we can accept." He was right. NATO had expanded 1,000 kilometres eastwards since the USSR imploded, in spite of US Secretary of State, James Baker's guarantee to President Gorbachev in Moscow in 1990 that there would be no extension of NATO's jurisdiction, "not one inch to the East."

When the USSR broke up and Russia took over the mantle, Boris Yeltsin proposed that NATO be dissolved since the threat was no more. He even suggested a pan-European peace force, which would include Russia. Yet, Russia was ignored as NATO marched inexorably eastwards, inching closer towards Russia. Dr. Henry Kissinger himself warned that the expansion of NATO would be a red line for Russia, a direct threat to its security, which would force it to respond. His warnings, and that of many strategic thinkers were ignored and the red line was crossed when NATO proposed to allow Ukraine to join the alliance.

Russia has always been vulnerable to invasion from Europe. Napoleonic France, Imperial Germany and Nazi Germany swept through Eastern Europe to wreak havoc on Russian or Soviet territory for much of the last century. An expansion of NATO, virtually to Russia's doorstep, thus increased Russian vulnerabilities, and their insecurities of invasion from the West. When Ukraine pressed ahead to get NATO membership and even enshrined it in their constitution, it touched upon the same Russian insecurities and fears.

The Russian response, as they say, is history.

Ukraine and NATO

The North Atlantic Treaty Organization (NATO) was formed in 1949 by 12 founding members, including the USA, UK, Canada and France. Its members agreed to help one another if they came under armed attack. The original aim was to counter Russian expansion in Europe after World War. It has been expanded a number of times, the first additions being Greece and Turkey in

1952. In May 1955, West Germany joined NATO, and Spain followed in 1982.

In 1990, the Soviet Union and NATO reached an agreement that a reunified Germany would join NATO under West Germany's pre-existing membership, although restrictions were agreed to on the deployment of NATO troops on former East German territory. Following the Soviet Union's collapse in 1991, many of its former Eastern European allies joined NATO. Poland, Hungary, and the Czech Republic became NATO members in 1999. NATO then formalized the process of joining the organization with "Membership Action Plans", which aided the accession of seven Central and Eastern European countries: Bulgaria, Estonia, Latvia, Lithuania, Romania, Slovakia, and Slovenia. Albania and Croatia joined in April 2009. The most recent member-states to join NATO were Montenegro on 5 June 2017 and North Macedonia on 27 March 2020. Ukraine proposed joining it initially in 2008, but both the German Chancellor, Angela Merkel, and the French President, Nicolas Sarkozy, opposed it because they feared it would infuriate Russia. It was only in 2019, when Zelensky took over as President, that Ukraine's process of seeking entry into NATO was galvanised.

The process of membership is long. It can take a year to apply and become a member, and all member-states must agree that a new country can join. Ukraine felt that by becoming a member it would stand to benefit from the protection of the alliance, especially Article 5 of the NATO charter, which states that "an armed attack against one shall be considered an attack against them all."

However, Ukraine's membership was denied. However, the process continued, Russia insisted that it be given written guarantees that it would never be allowed to join NATO—guarantees that could not be provided, as it would imply a Russia veto on future NATO membership. As negotiations between the USA, Russia, NATO and Ukraine failed, Europe plunged into war.

The root of Ukraine joining NATO goes back to NATO's Bucharest Summit in April 2008, when it was announced that Ukraine and Georgia "will become members". Russian leaders responded immediately with outrage, characterising this decision as an existential threat to Russia. President Putin "flew into a rage" and warned that "if Ukraine joins NATO, it will do so without Crimea and the eastern regions. It will simply fall apart."

The USA ignored this red line, however, and pushed forward to make Ukraine a Western bulwark on Russia's border. In December 2017, the Trump administration decided to sell Kyiv "defensive weapons" but these weapons looked 'offensive' to Moscow. Other NATO countries got in on the act, shipping weapons to Ukraine, training its armed forces and allowing it to participate in joint air and naval exercises. In July 2021, Ukraine and America co-hosted a major naval exercise in the Black Sea region involving navies from 32 countries. Operation Sea Breeze almost provoked Russia to fire at a British naval destroyer that deliberately entered what Russia considers its territorial waters.

In November 2021, Russian President Vladimir Putin stated that an expansion of NATO's presence in Ukraine, especially the deployment of any long-range missiles capable of striking Russian cities or missile defence systems similar to those in Romania and Poland, would be a "red line" issue for Russia. President Putin asked US President Joe Biden for legal guarantees that NATO wouldn't expand eastwards or put "weapons systems that threaten us in close vicinity to Russian territory". NATO Secretary-General Jens Stoltenberg replied that "It's only Ukraine and 30 NATO allies that decide when Ukraine is ready to join NATO; Russia has no veto, Russia has no say."

Russia found this evolving situation intolerable and began mobilising its army on Ukraine's border to signal its resolve to Washington. Talks began between Russia, Ukraine, NATO and even the USA, all of which were inconclusive. Russia demanded a written guarantee that Ukraine would never become a part of NATO and that the alliance remove the military assets it had deployed in Eastern Europe since 1997. The subsequent negotiations failed, and a month later President Putin launched an invasion of Ukraine to eliminate the threat he saw from NATO.

NATO's Response to the Ukrainian Conflict

Even though the membership of NATO was the root cause of the conflict, NATO did little to halt it. Perhaps Putin's warning that if NATO got involved it would have "consequences that you have never faced in your history"—a indirect threat to use nuclear weapons. Putin said he would regard direct NATO intervention as a threat to Russia. For that reason, President Joe Biden and other Western leaders stopped short of sending their own troops and even refused to impose a no-fly zone over the airspace of western Ukraine, since it would increase the possibilities of a confrontation, and could widen the conflict into a regional war or even a third World War.

Although NATO has not intervened directly, a flood of Western arms and equipment have flowed into Ukraine, largely coordinated through NATO. Western nations have relaxed the limits on heavy weapons. Even Germany, which for historical reasons, has steered clear of any intervention in foreign wars, voted overwhelmingly to send Ukraine heavy weapons. The USA itself has sent $ 60 billion to Ukraine, an amount that exceeds the $ 40 billion that the USA spent each year on its own 20-year war in Afghanistan.

President Biden also invoked the World War II–era Lend-Lease Act to speed up the transfer of weapons from the USA's military stockpile. That legislation authorized the lending of military equipment to foreign countries "whose defence the President deems vital to the defence of the United States".

NATO has also built up its forces in battalion-size "battle groups" along the alliance's eastern flank in Estonia, Latvia, Lithuania and Poland. The alliance has sent planes and ships to NATO territory in Eastern and SE Europe, and there's a multinational brigade in Romania. Plus, in one of the most significant moves in recent times, NATO has pledged to increase its rapid reaction force from 40,000 to a whopping 300,000 troops as part of its "response of the era of strategic competition". Mr Stoltenberg said several NATO battle groups in Eastern Europe would be bolstered to "brigade level", tactical units of several thousand troops, which was intended to send a clear message of deterrence to Russia.

The USA now has approximately 100,000 forces in the European theatre, and four new enhanced forward presence battalions led by European nations have been deployed in Bulgaria, Hungary, Romania, and Slovakia. However, are the current NATO forward forces postured to meet a Russian attack against the alliance arising outside the context of Ukraine?

The USA has provided Ukraine with anti-aircraft weapons, though, which can be used to shoot down aircraft and Cruise missiles. The alliance is likely also providing help in ways it isn't talking about. There is no doubt that US and NATO satellites provide information and advance warning of Russian actions, and use their communication networks to track, identify, and kill senior military personnel. However, is it enough? Materiel aid will help, but cannot stave Russia away indefinitely. For that, NATO needs to intervene directly, which it is loathe to do. In many ways, this situation suits them. At low cost, they are weakening Russia, without being directly engaged in the war themselves. Perhaps it merely intends to fight Russia till the last Ukrainian.

Although Putin started the war in the hope of weakening NATO, he has actually strengthened the alliance. Russia's attack on Ukraine has unified the alliance like never before. It has also led to Finland and Sweden starting the process of joining the alliance, which will take it to 32 members. Both countries were neutral for many years, but their joining will bring NATO dangerously close to Russia's north western flank and increase its vulnerabilities in the Baltics and Russian enclave of Kaliningrad there. With the acceptance of Finland, its 1,340-km border will become NATO's longest boundary with Russia, more than doubling the length of Europe's front line. Russian vulnerabilities have thus increased, and rather than keep the alliance away, it had crept up closer to Russia's doors.

Will NATO Intervene?

What role should NATO play in an armed conflict which does not involve a member-state directly but cannot be ignored because of the role it has played in bringing about the conflict. What kind of response can it take as the conflict escalates?

Officially member-states still honour Article 5; "that each member will consider an attack on the other as an attack on itself." So, should any of the neighbouring states—Poland, Rumania or even Finland, be inadvertently be hit by a missile or so, it could lead to direct NATO involvement.

Should Russia resort to the use of nuclear weapons, even a low-yield tactical one,—it would again lead to a NATO involvement, more so since nuclear weapons have no boundaries and can affect even neighbouring countries. The question bothering NATO planners is what would be the response in a situation like that? Putin has stated unequivocally that any entry of NATO into the war would lead to World War III and could lead to a use of even strategic nuclear weapons. That may hold their response. Should NATO enter, Putin knows he would not be able win over its combined might, and that could increase 'Russia's existentialist threat' and justify its use of nuclear weapons.

NATO would ideally prefer to continue the battle and provide arms and aid to Ukraine to weaken Russia on their behalf. As the war progresses, the dangers of NATO being sucked into the conflict increases, and with that, it could easily spiral out of control into a regional or even global confrontation.

In any case, NATO has already expanded eastwards and, with the membership of Finland and Sweden, increased the long-term threat to Russia. Europe will face a fundamentally changed security environment now. The larger issue remains how Russia will view this expansion. Will its growing insecurity provoke it to react even more irrationally?

With NATO's eastward expansion, its members together have nearly four times more military personnel than Russia and also many more tanks, warplanes, and artillery. The desire to humiliate President Putin and reinforce US global military dominance is also short-sighted and dangerous. It risks escalating, expanding, and prolonging the war in Ukraine and make it more difficult for Putin to back down. It was a mistake to incorporate the former Warsaw Pact countries into NATO after the end of the Cold War, as many leading analysts and policymakers argued at the time, and it ultimately served to reinforce Russia's sense of isolation and encirclement. Even Henry Kissinger had warned that isolating Russia will merely increase the threat, and not alleviate it.

However, the principal challenge for NATO is that 'it remains in the shadow of the USA.' There is no doubt that NATO follows the US lead willingly, and many in Europe, especially Germany and France, proposed having a European security alliance that would focus on European security and not get sucked into American wars. Yet, the resurgence of the Russian threat means that the nations will come together under the US and NATO banner once again to counter the threat, and perhaps US influence in European security will become stronger than at any time after World War II.

Conclusion

Even as NATO expands to counter the threat posed by Russia, it must remember that this war is a result of just that. After the removal of the Soviet threat, there was a golden chance for lasting peace in Europe, but the USA threw it all away. Rather than embracing a defeated rival, Washington repeatedly humiliated it by expanding a vast military alliance up to Russia's borders and even into the former Soviet Union. This provocation led to the war, and its dreadful consequences.

At the end of it all, it would be wise to remember that the long-term threat to world peace is not Russia, but China. NATO was slowly moving towards the Indo-Pacific, into the area which it perceived as 'the emerging threat'. It has now become more inward looking and Europe-centric again, which could have grave consequences for world peace, should China decide to flex its own muscles in the Indo-Pacific. It is significant that NATO unveiled its 'New Strategic Concept' in June 2022, which for the first time addressed the security challenges posed by China,—and a possible China-Russia collusion, in the wake of this war.

As NATO plays on the sidelines of the Ukraine war, and gradually building up its own strength, perhaps it is waiting for a sufficient weakening of Russia before it plays its own hand, and perhaps initiates military action—perhaps through the imposition of a no-fly zone, the flying in of humanitarian aid, or even military action. It would be wise to remember that this war has been provoked by NATO expansion. A further escalation of the conflict through direct NATO intervention could well prove catastrophic and could suck in all of Europe, and the rest of the world. As Clausewitz stated; " war has unexpected outcomes."

* * *

Maj Gen Jagatbir Singh, VSM, is a distinguished officer who has commanded an Armoured Division. He is a renowned writer and military analyst who is closely associated with the USI and writes extensively on contemporary issues.

REFERENCES

"Global Catastrophe warns Vladimir Putin, if NATO clashes," https://www.livemint.com

"How the Ukraine Crisis ends," Henry Kissinger.

"Military Assistance to Ukraine since the Russian Invasion," https://commonslibrary.parliament.uk

"NATO and Russia: A view from Moscow," S. Rogov, https://www.cairn.info, 2009.

"NATO expansion and Russia", *The Indian Express*, https://indianexpress.com, 20 May 2022.

"NATO once Feared a Putin Victory. Not it worries over his defeat," https://indianexpress.com 8 October 2022.

"NATO Summit: New weapons pledged to Ukraine," https://www.voanews.com 30 June 2022.

"NATO's Response to Russia's Invasion of Ukraine," https://www.nato.int

"Sweden and Finland journey from Neutral to NATO," *BBC News*, https://www/bbc.com, 28 June 2022.

"Timeline of NATO expansion since 1949", *ABC News*, https://abcnews.go.com, 9 May 2022.

"Ukraine's entry to NATO can lead to World War III," https://www.hindustantimes.com

11

THE XI-PUTIN TANGO

"The friendship between Russia and China has no limits. There are no forbidden areas of cooperation in this relationship."

—Joint Statement after meeting of Xi and Putin in Beijing, February 2022

The Putin-Xi Meeting

It seems no coincidence that just before Vladimir Putin launched his invasion of Ukraine, he met the Chinese Premier, Xi Jinping, at the beginning of the Winter Olympic Games in Beijing. It was the 38th personal meeting between the two leaders and had more than just symbolic value. It was the bonding of two similar powers in an alliance "which is superior to the political and military alliances of the Cold War; in a friendship that has no limits". A fortnight after the meeting (and conveniently, just after the Olympic Games had ended) Putin launched his invasion of Ukraine.

Although the details will never emerge, it seems very likely that Putin would have shared his plans for the invasion of Ukraine in closed-door meetings with Xi. He would have got the tacit go-ahead for the venture, and also indications of China's support for an action which was bound to ostracize Russia by the rest of the world. Even as the war unfolded, though China made the usual sounds for peace, it did not criticize Russia's actions in any way. They abstained from all United Nations resolutions against it (as did India), and even toed the Russian line, criticizing the USA and the Western powers for not considering "Russia's legitimate security concerns" in the westward expansion of NATO.

Perhaps the only thing that would have surprised China was that the war has gone on so long. Like many, they would have shared the view that Russia would attain its military objectives in a week or so, as they did in Georgia. After that, Western interest would wane and it would be back to business as usual. The undue extension of the war and the inability of Russia to attain its military goals have diluted Chinese support a bit. After all, China has more to gain from its economic ties with the USA and the West and would not like to be seen as overtly supporting Russia, and should Russia be seen as appearing to lose, they would distance themselves from it. Though China has suffered economically from the war, as has every country, in many ways it has been to their benefit.

The war helped divert attention from China at a time when much of the world was closing rank against Chinese belligerence and the dangers of its rise were becoming clearer. The USA and even NATO were seeing China as a 'major threat' to the world and slowly veering towards the Indo-Pacific to counter it. With Russia now taking over as Enemy Number One, the focus has shifted back towards Europe and the world has been distracted from its major threat. In many ways, this could embolden China to re-assert itself in the region, especially in Taiwan, the China Sea, and Ladakh. Also, both Russia and China were feeling a sense of isolation. Their growing closeness could lead them to join rank for the creation of a new Russia-China axis, perhaps supplemented with other nations such as Iran, North Korea, and Pakistan.

China-Russia Ties

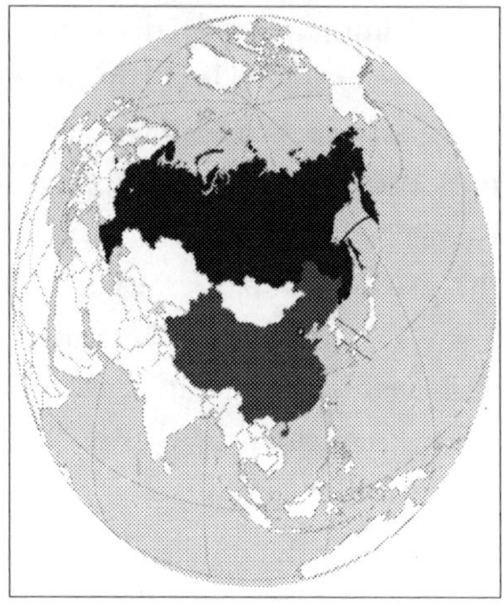

Although Russia and Chinese are ideologically linked, their ties have been bitter-sweet. Sino-Soviet relations hit a high in the Mao-Stalin era, but collapsed soon thereafter and remained frosty for most of the Cold War Era. The two sides fought a bitter seven-month long border war in 1969, and mutual mistrust forced Russia to position 27 divisions along the 2,700-long Siberian border it shares with China. One of the signs of their growing closeness was the fact that Russia pulled out troops from its Siberian border for the offensive in the West.

After the Soviet Union imploded in the 'Nineties and Russia faced economic and internal chaos, Putin turned to China in 2001 and there was an upsurge of economic and strategic ties. The two signed the Treaty of Good Neighbourliness and Friendly Cooperation, which was extended in 2022. The political convergence developed after Russia's annexation of Crimea in 2014. Faced with a sharp downturn of ties with the USA and the EU, Putin turned increasingly towards China. This period also marked the rise of Xi Jinping and with it, China's increased belligerence. As the world pushback began in the form of trade embargoes, criticism of human rights in both Russia and China, and condemnation of actions in Crimea and Xinjiang, the two leaders, who shared the same autocratic views for themselves and their nations, became drawn closer to each together.

It is the personal chemistry and ideological outlook of the two leaders (both *de facto* rulers for life of their respective countries) that has shaped the trajectory of Sino-Russia ties. Xi considers Putin as "my closest friend" and would not like to see Russia defeated which could lead to Putin's fall. Both also share the world view of the USA as a strategic adversary trying to curb the rise of both Russia and China. Though Russia and China are not formal allies, or even natural ones, this strategic convergence will bring them closer. In the long run, the two nations will be drawn even closer in an axis very akin to the

Germany-Japan axis of 1940. There is so much commonality. Russia is playing the role of a nationalistic Germany seeking to establish its lost influence in Europe, and China is trying to protect its economic and strategic interests in the Indo-Pacific, as Japan did, with similarly hyper nationalistic views. This axis and their joint actions could engulf the world from the Atlantic to the Pacific in much the same manner as Germany and Japan had done in the dangerous days of 1941.

Economic Linkages

Russia and China have developed a strong economic and strategic convergence. Economically they share an annual trade of $ 147 billion but the equation is heavily skewed in China's favour. China accounts for 18 per cent of Russia's exports while Russia provides just 2 per cent of China's trade. Economically too, Russia's GDP of $ 1.7 trillion is dwarfed by the Chinese GDP of over $ 19 trillion. Russia would thus be expected to be the very junior partner in the relationship.

Russian trade has actually increased after the war. Russian shipments of oil, gas, and grain to China have increased. Russia has turned increasingly to China while it itself is one of the prime providers of gas and oil to energy-starved China. In fact, Russian exports to China increased by a whopping 30 per cent after the war. Russia was more than willing to provide gas and wheat to China at sharply reduced rates to make up for its losses elsewhere.

Both sides also share a similar vision of expanding their domains. Russia seeks dominance in Europe, and China in the Indo-Pacific, and both support each other's claims—be it in Ukraine or in Taiwan. Russia has extended into arenas such as Syria and the Middle East, and is inching towards the Central Asian Republics and Afghanistan. China's projections are more subtle, and it uses its BRI projects to get footholds in Sri Lanka, Pakistan, and East Africa, which can later be developed into bases. This could see a convergence of interests in Central Asia, Eastern Europe, and Africa. Plus, global warming is helping open up the Arctic Route, and with this, the shipping route between Europe and Asia will be reduced by almost 12 days, reducing the geographical distance between China and Russia. This could lead to greater economic and political convergence and enable the two sides to cooperate even more strongly.

With the invasion of Ukraine, Russia has distanced itself, perhaps irrevocably, from the USA and much of Western Europe and will turn even closer to China, perhaps even accepting the role of junior partner in the relationship, to counter the alienation it faces from Europe. Russia is economically dependent on Europe and vice versa. Nearly 27 per cent of Russia's exports go to the European Union accounting for over $ 188 billion of trade. Should this lessen because of sanctions, Russia needs other markets like China and India to make up the shortfall.

Chinese support will enable Russia to ride over Western sanctions. Although the USA and its allies have proposed a set of sanctions that will hurt, Russia seems to have sought economic alternatives in China. Russia has already made up for the losses incurred by the blocking of Nord Stream 2, the gas pipeline that was to funnel Russian gas to Germany and Europe by going ahead with the Power of Siberia gas pipeline which will supply gas to China for the next 30 years, and offset the losses in Europe. With China not coming on board, Western sanctions will no longer have the same effect (not that sanctions have much effect, anyway) and Russia would be able to bypass them.

Both sides have also started the process of moving away from the US dollar (which in a way, is not such a bad thing). Russia now deals extensively in Euros or roubles, and China in its Renminbi. Both sides are also working on the SPES financial transfer systems to counter the US-led SWIFT banking system (which Russia was cut off from as part of the sanctions). Perhaps China is developing an economic hedge in case the West decides to impose similar sanctions on it at a future juncture.

While China will prop up Russia, it will only do so up to a point. It is dependent on the USA and Europe for its own economy and would not want to alienate itself from the West. It would thus continue to play the waiting game and watch the war unfold, without committing itself overtly to Russia. In fact, with the Russian military reverses in Kherson and Kharkiv, China seemed to distance itself from it. During the meeting of Putin and Xi at the SCO meeting in Samarkand, Xi expressed "questions and concerns' about the war. Should the war not go Russia's way, China will quickly withdraw support, and not risk its relationship with the West for an unequal ally.

The Strategic Convergence

The Russian invasion of Ukraine has actually strengthened China's strategic posture considerably. With increased Chinese belligerence and also its role in the global COVID pandemic, the USA and the West were gradually veering towards the Indo-Pacific as the area of greatest strategic importance and China as the greatest threat. The USA had formed a slew of alliances—QUAD and AUKUS—and even NATO was aligning its strategic interests towards the east. Then came Putin's invasion and once again, everything was calibrated back towards Europe which became the arena of war.

The shift in focus gave China time to recalibrate its own strategy, as it formed alliances with the smaller countries of the region. The balance of power was shifting away from China which has been now corrected. As the West moved to counter China, it wooed Russia. If Russia had joined the European and US camp (or more importantly, had it been admitted into it) the balance of power would have been squarely against China. Instead, it is Russia that is isolated now, and as it turns closer towards China, the triangulation of power has shifted China's way. It has an ally that can engage the West in Europe, leaving it free for its own actions in the Indo-Pacific.

With the USA and Western nations pre-occupied in Europe, China could decide to up the ante in Taiwan and the China Sea, or even Ladakh. Like Putin, Xi could decide to 'reunify' his country and launch an invasion to decide the issue. He could be emboldened by the fact that the West has not intervened directly in Ukraine. Although the USA is treaty-bound to defend Taiwan, unlike Ukraine, which is not a formal member of NATO, he may bank on the fact that a certain degree of war-weariness has set in, and the USA may be loathe entering a war so far from their shores for the nebulous ideology of democracy. Like Putin, he would be banking on the fact that his military is strong enough to attain its military aims and perhaps even defeat an outside force that comes into the area.

It is significant that both sides support the other in their claims. China has repeatedly stated that "Russia's security concerns should be respected" and Putin has blamed "provocations by the USA and its satellites in the Taiwan Straits" for rising tensions there. With the re-election of Xi Jinping as President for an unprecedented third term, one that paves the way for him to become

President for life, the commonalities in their actions will increase. It is significant that in his address Xi stressed on the "re-unification of Taiwan with the mainland", something that is almost an article of faith. Even more ominously, China stressed that it "would not renounce the use of force" to attain it, and warned outside powers not to intervene. He shares this trait with Putin, a willingness to use force to redress perceived 'historical wrongs',—that has forebodings for the future. With Xi as the undisputed ruler, Chinese focus on Taiwan will definitely increase. Much will depend on the manner in which the war pans out. If Russia gets away with the invasion of Ukraine, and takes over the area it has captured as 'historically Russian', China will feel it can do the same with Taiwan, Ladakh, and the China Sea. But if Western response is steadfast, and the Ukrainians succeed in pushing the Russians back, or even make the campaign exorbitantly expensive, China could hold its hand.

Already, tempers are rising in Taiwan, especially after the visit of US Secretary of State Nancy Pelosi to the island. It provoked a fierce response, including amphibious exercises in which PLAN ships and aircraft came dangerously close to Taiwan's shores. It is also significant that around the same time Russian and Chinese armies exercised together and in a joint show of force sent strategic bombers close to the Japanese mainland where the QUAD heads of state were meeting in Tokyo. Also, Russia and China participated in the Vostok-2022 war games in the Far East which saw over 50,000 personnel, 150 aircraft, and over 5,000 pieces of military hardware. Coming against the backdrop of the Ukraine war, it was a clear, though subtle, signal.

The war in Ukraine has merely hastened the strategic and economic convergence between China and Russia. In many ways, the relationship will be based on how the war unfolds. If Putin achieves his political and military aims, China would be emboldened. Should the war go badly, China would quickly distance itself from Russia and focus on enhancing economic ties with the West. It would not risk its own international standing for a losing cause and the friendship "without limits" may soon have limits on it.

REFERENCES

"3 Ways China and Russia are Forging Closer ties", *Economic Times*, https://www.cnn.com, 15 September 2022.

"China asked Russia to delay Ukraine War until after Olympics", *The New York Times*, https://www.nytimes.com, 02 March 2022.

"China extends Threatening Military Exercises around Taiwan", https://thediplomat.com, 9 August 2022

"China-Russia Trade rose 29 in January–July," https://www.globaltimes.com 07 August 2022.

"Hands off Taiwan, Xi warns World, only China will decide on Reunification", *Times Global, The Times of India*, 17 October 2022.

"India, China abstains in UN vote on Russia's 'illegal referendum', https://www.tbsnews.net, 01 October 2022.

"Melting Ice could open Arctic Sea Route", https://www.newscientist.com, 20 June 2022.

"Power of Siberia 2 Pipeline puts Pressure on Europe", https://www.pipeline-journal.net 15 February 2022.

"Putin Arrives in Beijing for Winter Olympics" Reuters, https://www.reuters.com, 04 February 2022.

"Putin, Xi meet in Samarkand: China is Russia's Senior Partner," https://warsawinstitute.org 28 September 2022.

"The Sino-Soviet Border Conflict, 1969", https://nsarchive2.gwu.edu

"What Xi Jinping as President means for China and the World", https://indianexpress.com 16 October 2022.

"Xi has 'Questions and Concerns' over Ukraine," https://www.reuters.com 15 September 2022.

"Xi praises 'Best Friend' Putin, during Russia visit", *Financial Times*, https://www.ft.com 19 September 2022.

"Xi-Putin Olympics Meeting Stresses 'no-limits' in China Russia Ties," https://news.cgtn.com, 05 February 2022.

12

Gas, Grain and Sanctions: The Economic Weapons of War

"When two elephants fight, it is the grass that get trampled."

—Kenyan Proverb

In the winter of 1941, the Germans had advanced to within 30 kilometres of Moscow. (Around the same distance as the Russians were from Kyiv in the early days of the war). As some of the German generals described it later, "On a clear day, we could see the spires of the Kremlin." Though the threat to the heart of the Soviet Union was dire, the Germans were at the end of their tether too. They had set out on the invasion expecting to be home by Christmas, and were not clothed or equipped for the brutal Siberian cold. The Soviets waited for the Germans to over-extend themselves, and then launched a counter-attack with fresh divisions newly inducted from the Siberian border, which halted the Germans at the gates of Moscow and delivered a crippling blow.

Marshal Winter had come to the rescue of the Soviets. Winter has always played a crucial role on any campaign in Russia (Napoleon would vouch for it). The winter of 2022 too will play a major role, as the Russians unleash another ace up their sleeve—energy. Russian gas and oil, which provides 40 per cent of Europe's energy requirements; heats up homes, lights up streetlights, keeps factories running and powers their economies, is the weapon used by the Russians to end the war on their terms.

The use of energy is nothing new. The USA has fought in arenas across the world to maintain its energy supplies from the Middle East. India and China will go to great lengths to ensure their energy security. After all, it is oil and gas that keep the engines of the economy running and in this war too, as in all others, economics has been a major weapon. The USA used sanctions to punish Russia, hoping to cripple its economy that funded the war. Russia responded by blockading Ukrainian wheat and grain in its ports, causing a global food scarcity. When it disrupted the flow of gas to Europe, it brought in a long cold winter and the threat of recession in the major economies of the world. Even as the land war continued, the economic war raged in the background to eventually determine the direction it would take.

Sanctions and their Impact

As Russia prepared for its invasion of Ukraine, and the Western allies mulled over their response, their most explicit threat was "sanctions, as never before". Russia, in any case, was already under heavy sanctions after its annexation of Crimea in 2014. Individuals and businesses in Crimea and Eastern Ukraine were sanctioned and Russia was dropped from the select group of G-8 (which went back to being G-7, thereafter). Those sanctions were pinpricks and had little effect on Russia's economy, which continued to surge ahead on its oil and gas revenues. The sanctions that followed in the wake of its invasion in 22 February 22 were more widespread and designed to squeeze the entire economy.

For starters, Russia was barred from the international financial messaging system—SWIFT (Society for Worldwide International Financial Telecommunications)—which would make it impossible for Russian banks to conduct international financial transactions. Russian assets held in US and Western banks were also frozen, in effect blocking Putin from most of the

$ 640 billion in foreign reserves that he had built up as a war chest for the invasion.

However, the biggest targets were the revenues from Russian oil and gas imports. Russian oil imports were banned; refined oil products were banned and Russian coal was banned from the USA and Western nations. Of course, none of the sanctions had a United Nations mandate, but implicitly, nations dealing with Russia would also come under US sanctions. No immediate sanctions were applied on the existing flow of Russian gas which Europe was desperately dependent upon, but Germany froze the plan to open Nord Stream 2, the 1,234-kilometre-long undersea pipeline running from Russia to Germany that would double the gas funnelled in to Europe to 110 billion cubic metres annually. The pipeline had been completed in September 2021 and was all set to enter service, but its certification was halted by German Chancellor Olaf Scholz following the Russian invasion. Russia had invested over $ 2.1 billion in the project and the move would hurt but halting the gas would hurt Germany and Europe more than it hurt Russia.

The sanctions also targeted over 1,000 Russian individuals and businesses, especially oligarchs who were close to Putin, like Roman Abramovich, the owner of the Chelsea football club. Putin and his foreign minister, Sergei Lavrov, were also targeted. Russian flights were banned from US, Canadian, EU, and UK air space and over 1,000 foreign companies ranging from Starbucks to General Motors to Prada wound up operations in Russia, pulling out vital foreign investment and shutting down almost 200,000 jobs. Other sanctions ranged on the ridiculous, like the banning of Russian players from Wimbledon and the imposition of exorbitant taxes on Russian vodka.

It was thought that the sanctions would effectively collapse the Russian economy and its ability to fund the war machine. Yes, in the early days there were long lines outside banks and ATMs as people made a run for their money, expecting the worst. Inflation racked up to 22 per cent in the first month and the rouble collapsed to its lowest level since the breakup of the Soviet Union but after an initial contraction, the Russian economy rebounded. The GDP which was expected to shrink by 11 per cent contracted to just a manageable 3.7 per cent in the year. The sanctions could not have effect because most independent-minded nations, India and China included, continued to import

Russian oil and grain at knockdown prices and with payments in rupees and Yuan. Rightly, most countries put national interest above a war that was engineered by the West. In the era of globalization, major Russian industries like automotives and aviation took a hit with the unavailability of critical components like chips for semi-conductors. Russia responded by barring the export of titanium (of which it is the world's largest exporter) which is essential for making aircraft bodies, thus impacting the world aviation industry. Yes, the long war has taken a toll on the Russian economy which pumped in $ 1 billion a day to sustain it, but overall, the Russian economy seems to have weathered the worst of the sanctions and it were Western economies that felt the heat more.

The Weaponization of Energy

On 02 September 2022, the G-7 added another slew of sanctions to punish Russia for its war. This time they also decided to impose a price cap, initially at $ 60 per barrel, on Russian oil and oil products. This would allow the flow of Russian oil into the global market, but only at prices below the cap. It was a ridiculous proposal, one designed to ensure that much-needed Russian oil would be available to global markets but deny its revenues to Russia.

It was actually a ham-handed proposal since implementing it would be difficult. The only way to enforce it was to block tankers carrying Russian oil. The USA, EU, and UK had already blocked Russian tankers from entering their ports. Tankers carrying Russian oil purchased above the cap price would be denied entry into ports for 120 days thereafter. Nor would insurance be provided, something that could be managed since over 90 per cent of insurance companies are Western.

However, this cap failed to consider the needs of nations desperately requiring oil. India itself had purchased Russian oil at discounts of $ 15-20 per barrel to shore up its reserves, and would continue doing so. Russia had more than made up its shortfall of energy sales to Europe by sending more oil and coal to India and China on much sweetened terms. Joe Biden's move faced its first major hurdle when Putin got Saudi Arabia to side with them to cut OPEC oil production by 2 million barrels per day, a move that sent prices spiralling and put the already stressed oil market in a tizzy. The move also severely damaged Saudi-US relations, which Joe Biden had been trying hard to repair and brought out that in this war, the coalition of "with us or against us" would not hold good.

Around the same time, in October 2022, Putin also made a proposal to Turkey's Premier, Erdogan, to make the strategically-located Turkey into an 'energy hub' from where Russian gas and oil would flow to Europe and Asia. This would veer Turkey away from NATO and towards Russia and China. Energy was not only determining the direction of the war; it was also reshaping the global geopolitics.

Russia counter-attacked violently to the G-7 decision to impose a price cap on its oil. That same day, it halted the flow of gas into Europe by shutting down the Nord Stream I gas pipeline. The European Union gets 40 per cent of its gas from Russia which gives the Russian economy $ 850 million daily. Cheap and abundant Russian gas heats the homes and powers industries all across Europe. If this gas is shut off, a long cold winter beckoned, with cold homes, darkened street lights, and closed factories. The additional expenditure on energy, coupled with loss of production, could send all of Europe into recession.

The Nord Stream I gas pipeline, a 1,200-kilometre-long pipeline running under the Baltic Sea from St. Petersburg to north-eastern Germany has been funnelling 170 million cubic metres of cheap and abundant gas every day since 2011 to all of Europe. Russia reduced the flow by almost 75 per cent in June and then shut it down in August on the grounds that it needed repairs and maintenance. They stated that Western sanctions had caused "absolute commotion" in the maintenance of the gas delivery system forcing them to shut down the pipeline, "as long as sanctions are in place." The irony and implicit threat of the statement was lost on no one.

The cutting off of gas to Europe and the looming energy shortages caused absolute chaos. Gas prices surged by over 30 per cent, inflation galloped and households faced an unprecedented rise in energy bills that would force millions into fuel poverty. Germany, UK, and the EU were forced to provide energy crisis relief packages to help citizens overcome the impact of surging energy prices. Germany, one of the nations most affected, announced an energy allowance of 300 Euros per family—a move that would cost $ 65 billion. The

UK dished out around $ 60 billion for the same. In a bid to save energy, the illumination of iconic landmarks like the Eiffel Tower and the Brandenburg Gate were switched off, along with street lights. The shortage of gas forced factories to reduce working hours and thus their output. Europe's economy relies heavily on steel, chemicals, car makers and heavy industry, all of which require massive amounts of energy to keep running. These factories could come to a halt and the energy crisis could send Europe—all most of the world—into recession.

Worse was to follow. In September, a series of underwater explosions rocked both the Nord Stream I and Nord Stream II gas pipelines, which created leaks. Later investigations revealed almost 50-metre gaps punched into them with explosives. The pipelines were not functioning, but gas was stored in them and methane bubbles, some of them a kilometre wide in diameter, came up to the surface. Methane is one of the major contributors to global warming, and the quantity of methane released is estimated to be equivalent to half of Denmark's annual emissions. The leaks implied that Europe could expect no more gas for quite some time to come and braced for an even colder winter.

It was clearly a case of sabotage, but by whom? Russia accused the USA of engineering the blasts to boost the sales of their own LPG to Europe (which would be shipped in containers from the USA and cost thrice as much). The USA accused Russia of the blasts. Why would Russia want to damage its own pipelines on which they had invested so much, and that too since they had already blocked gas supply? Whatever the reason, the blasts heightened the energy insecurity in Europe and raised the price of gas by over 30 per cent, something that Russia used to its advantage.

In any case, Russia was also preparing to offset the losses caused by the denial of gas sales to Europe by increasing the gas flows to Asia and other parts of the world. During the meeting of Putin and Xi, just before the Beijing Olympics, they had announced with great fanfare the Power of Siberia 2 gas pipeline—a 1,700-kilometre-long pipeline that would funnel 50 billion cubic metres of gas into China every year after 2024. Other such pipelines, including one to India, are also under consideration as Russia seeks to diversify from Europe.

If Russia was subtly blocking energy flows to Europe in retaliation for its support to Ukraine, it was actively destroying Ukraine's own energy infrastructure. Ukraine had been hit by strikes since the start of the war, which intensified after the attack on Russia's Kerch Bridge in October. In retaliation, Russia launched a series of missile and drone attacks that targeted power and water infrastructure across Ukraine. The deliberate targeting destroyed a third of its power stations, caused massive outages and left entire cities without electricity, forcing them to curtail power use to just 7 a.m. to 11 a.m. daily. In any case, Ukraine had lost one fifth of its electrical supply when Russia took over the Zaporizhzhia Nuclear Power Plant and transferred its electrical supply to the Russian grid. With winter approaching, the situation would worsen, and 'Marshal Winter' would help Putin in his "escalate-to-de-escalate" strategy, that would put pressure to end the war on his terms.

The winter will determine the staying power of Europe and Ukraine. Should it prove unbearable,-public support for the war will dwindle and even governments may not be able to sustain the effort for another year or so. Already the West is divided into two camps "The Peace Camp" and "The Justice Camp". Almost two-thirds of them fall in the Peace Camp which wants the war to end even at the cost of concessions to Russia. The Justice Camp believes that Russia must be punished for its aggression, while a smaller hard-line minority felt that only Russia's defeat would bring lasting peace. How the European nations manage the winter, and whether Ukraine could sustain it for another campaigning season will determine its eventual outcome.

Food Insecurity

Russia and Ukraine provide 27 per cent of the world's market for wheat, 16 per cent of corn, 23 per cent of barley, and a whopping 53 per cent of sunflower oil. With disruption of supplies from the two major producers, food shortages will hit the world, striking nations as far as Ethiopia, Mexico, and Bangladesh. Global prices rocketed, raising inflation worldwide. The world supply chains were just recovering from the COVID-19 pandemic when it was hit by this whammy.

Ukraine's bumper crop had been harvested and stored in warehouses when the Russian tanks rolled in. The war damaged prime farmland which lay in the war zone, and the planting of the next crop was severely curtailed. Even worse, the grain held in the warehouses could not be exported due to the Russian blockade of the ports. The Black Sea ports of Odesa, Mariupol, Melitopol, and Kherson accounted for 95 per cent of Ukraine's grain exports and were either in Russian hands, or blocked by Russian ships. Nor could the grain be taken out of the country by rail. Ukraine still has the Soviet-era broad gauge railway lines, while its Western neighbours hold medium gauge lines. This would thus involve trans-shipment and reloading of trains at the border, an expensive and time-consuming process. The difference in the gauge of the railway lines had even disrupted German logistics during their invasion of the Soviet Union. Their own medium gauge railway lines, engines, and rolling stock could not be used on the Soviet broad gauge lines forcing them to send their supplies ahead by road or air, a factor that contributed to their ultimate defeat.

Over 20 million tons of Ukrainian wheat and corn were stranded in the port of Odesa, with the fear that they could be hit by rockets and missiles, or simply deteriorate if stored for too long. Eventually in August a deal was brokered by Turkey in which Russia would permit cargo ships to leave the port, (after Ukraine de-mined them, thus also opening them up for a probable Russian assault at a later juncture). On 16 August, the first ship MV BRAVE COMMANDER left Odesa heading for Ethiopia, with much-needed grain in its holds. Over 300 ships followed in the next two months, carrying around 9 million tons of much-needed grain that helped ease the global food shortages considerably. Then in November Russia walked out of the deal after what it claimed were drone attacks on Russian ships in Odesa. With Russia not renewing the deal, the spectre of global food scarcity looms once again. Putin knows the impact the war has on food security across the world and the longer it continues, the worse would the worldwide economic situation. The war has already raised the Food Price Index by around 30 per cent and the shortages that it has created puts over 450 million people at a risk of food insecurity.

India could fill the gap to some extent, and in April, Prime Minister Modi stated that "India can feed the world if the WTO allows it". Just a month later, India banned all wheat exports to control rising domestic prices, in effect diluting our commitment. Yet, in the past year, India more than doubled the quantity of wheat exported (compared to the corresponding period of the previous year) exporting over 43.5 tons of wheat to help offset some of the losses caused by the war. India could emerge as a major food supplier to the world, and perhaps use this crisis to its advantage.

The Economic Effect of the War

The world was just recovering from the disastrous COVID pandemic which plummeted economic growth and ruptured global supply chains. The global recovery will now be much longer after the war.

Already the predictions for 2023 are bleak. Global growth is expected to drop from 4.5 per cent to just 3 per cent, and a major threat of recession looms over most economies. With the shortages of fuel and grain, prices have risen, leading to world-wide inflation in the region of 9 per cent which will reduce the standards of living and push millions into poverty. The war has also disrupted global supply chains for commodities ranging from semi-conductor chips to toilet paper. Russia is a major supplier of base metals like palladium, neon, and platinum that are essential for microchip production. It is also the major exporter of birch wood, the main ingredient in pulp used for toilet paper. One million tons of pulp vanished from European markets leading to acute shortages of toilet paper. The impact that energy and grain will have on the world has been covered in detail.

There are also going to be indirect and long-term repercussions caused by the sweeping sanctions regime put in place by the Western world. The sanctions have hit Russia hard, but their economy has managed to weather the worst of it. The blowback from the sanctions have hit other nations more. The current set of anti-Russia economic sanctions strike at the heart of the international capitalist order based on trust in open global trade and business. By imposing such widespread sanctions, it implies that assets can be taken away by a foreign power if it so desires.

Most countries hold foreign exchange reserves that represent the earnings of a country from the goods and services exported by it to other countries. Most reserves are held in dollars; it is the universally acceptable currency. What has happened now is that if the dollar issuing country so desires, such reserves can be just taken away. The USA has done it with Afghanistan and now again with Russia.

This is surely going to be a cause of concern to any non-Western country with relatively large forex reserves (e.g., China, India, Saudi Arabia, Brazil, Indonesia) that may at some point of time happen to be on the wrong side of the USA. It would lead to a lessening of the confidence in the dollar as a reserve currency. Eventually, it will lead to a weakening of the dollar's historically dominant status in the world economy.

The action on SWIFT is equally significant. SWIFT (Society for Worldwide Interbank Financial Telecommunications) is a financial messaging protocol that enables secure and quick worldwide money transfers to happen. Over time, it has evolved as a widely acceptable facility that has become the *de facto* industry standard. Over 11,000 financial institutions in 200 countries use it, and that's why it matters. It's almost essential for enabling international money transactions. Complying with an American-led directive, the "independent" SWIFT overnight cut off Russian banks from its network, barring their banking links with the rest of the world. As a result, today SWIFT is no longer "worldwide" in scope.

This opens up room for parallel systems to fill the gap. Russia and China have begun developing their own systems for dealing in Yuan and Roubles which can by-pass SWIFT. India has the technical capabilities, having put in place far more complex domestic systems like RTGS/NEFT and the UPI. While SWIFT has the first mover advantage, it is likely that sooner or later an alternative with acceptability in the non-Western world may emerge.

The economies of both the combatants, Ukraine and Russia, are going to be hard hit. Russia is spending over $ 1 billion a day for its operation, and would have already burned over $ 250 billion, not counting the losses they have incurred by sanctions. Sanctions too will take their toll in the long run. Nevertheless, being a large country with immense natural resources, Russia may be able to tide over the sanctions regime. Demand and supply will ensure that sanctions or no sanctions, commodities and resources will find their way to where there is a requirement (Iran is a classic example).

Ukraine has been the worst sufferer. Its economy has contracted by over a third and it will take $ 600 billion just to rebuild the country and its destroyed infrastructure. The human cost is of course, incalculable, and it does not take into consideration the fact that it has lost over a fifth of its territory—its richest and most fertile areas. Should they be cut off from the sea, their economic development will be stunted for ever. For Europe, the impact will vary. Their long-term economic interests still lie in stronger economic linkages with Russia. However, short-term compulsions are forcing them to snap these linkages, and also contribute financially to the NATO war effort. Europe is heavily reliant on Russian gas and receives over 40 per cent of it from Russia. The breaking of this natural linkage will affect the economy of Russia and Europe alike, and be detrimental to both. European countries will also be spending a lot more on arms, at the expense of development and welfare. Even a normally pacifist Germany (which had invested heavily in building a relationship with Russia) has declared that it will spend an additional $ 100 billion on armaments. Similarly, other EU countries are also raising their military spending with similar trade-offs. Europeans also have to bear the burden of the refugee influx caused by the displacement of populations due to the conflict.

The USA will be a gainer from the conflict in the short term, at the expense of European countries. In Europe, it has created a huge demand for its weapons industry. The US government has already committed $ 60 billion military assistance to Ukraine and is flooding the war zone with modern weapons. It suits them to prolong the war, and thus weaken Russia, while re-establishing themselves in Europe all over again. It has also created a market for its own gas and oil, so what if it would now cost European nations thrice as much.

However, the longer-term economic fallout for the USA may be less rosy. The weaponizing of private sector entities may eventually threaten their trans-national credibility. The arbitrary seizure of another country's dollar reserves may hasten the decline of the dollar as a universally acceptable currency. The present defining of Russia as the "enemy" also means a dilution of focus on China. In reviving Cold War hostilities with gusto, the USA has lost sight of its main adversary. This might cost it in the years to come in ways yet to be foreseen.

China stands to benefit from the new US focus on Russia as enemy number one. In case the USA decides to relax some of the trade and technology restrictions on China (which seems possible) it will leave China better off compared to the pre-war situation. With its sizable domestic economy, manufacturing capabilities, close relationship to Russia, and potential weakening of the US-dominated global financial order, China is well placed to emerge stronger once the conflict is over. India too has advantages in that its historical relationship with Russia, and present strategic utility to the USA. may enable it to ride out the storm relatively unscathed, despite pressures from the West.

For the rest of the developing world in Africa, Asia and South America, in the short term, there will be hard times. They will have to put up with shortages of food, essential commodities and tackle domestic inflation. The spectre of economic distress like in Sri Lanka may stare some vulnerable countries in the face. The Kenyan proverb "*When two elephants fight, it is the grass that gets trampled,*" more or less reflects the state of the world today!

REFERENCES

"As Europe falls into Recession, Russia climbs out", *The Economist*, 13 October 2022.

"Catastrophe: UK Households face Fuel Poverty as Energy Bills Jump, " Paul Sandle, *The Indian Express*, 9 September 2022.

"Europe faces Winter Chill as Russia halts Gas Flows", Surojit Gupta, *The Times of India*, 11 September 2022.

"Gas Leaks in Russian Pipelines Stoke Sabotage Fears", *The New York Times* in *The Indian Express*, 27 September 2022.

"Kremlin: Gas Cut-off to Stay till Sanctions are in Place," *The Indian Express*, 13 September 2022.

"Moscow says Power of Siberia 2 pipeline to China will replace Nord Stream 2", https://euronews.com, 15 September 2022.

"Nord Stream 2- Wikipedia, https://en.wikipediain.org

"Nord Stream I: How Russia is cutting off Gas Supply to Europe," *BBC News*, 29 September 2022.

"Now Toilet Paper Supply at Risk", *Times Global, Times of India*, 13 October 2022.

"Oil Cap Plans will open New Front in Russia-West Conflict", https://carnegieendowment.org

"Operation Typhoon: The Battle for Moscow," https://www.historyextra.com

"Putin proposes Gas Hub in Turkey", *The Indian Express*, 13 October 2022.

"Putin threatens to halt Supply as EU plans to Cap Russia Gas Price", *Times Global, Times of India*, 8 September 2022.

"Ripple effect from Russia-Ukraine War Test Global Economies", Beth Stackpole, MIT Sloan School; https://mitsloan.mit.edu

"Russia destroys Power and Water Infra across Ukraine", *Times Global, The Times of India*, 18 October 2022.

"Russia sends more Energy to Asia, as Europe cuts back", *Times Global, The Times of India*. 07 September 2022.

"Saudi Arabia: OPEC + oil production cut 'Purely Economic' https://www.dw.com 13 October 2022.

"Ukraine War: Deal to end Grain Blockade by Turkey", *BBC*, 02 August 2022.

"Ukraine War: Indian wheat export double of Last Year," Harikishan Sharma, *Indian Express*, 16 October 2022.

"Ukraine War: More than 60 percent of Putin's war-chest Frozen," *BBC News*, 5 April 2022.

"Ukrainian Grain Export helps Curb Global Food Inflation," https://www.livemint.com 7 September 2022.

"Under unprecedented Sanctions, how the Russian Economy is Faring?" *The Economist*, 02 April 2022.

"War in Ukraine impacting Global Trade and World's Poorest", https://www.weforum.org, 26 April 2022.

"War in Ukraine is Reverberating across World Regions," https://www.imf.org 15 March 2022.

"War in Ukraine will Cripple Global Food Markets", *The Economist*, 12 March 2022.

"What are the Sanctions on Russia and are they Hurting", *BBC News*, https://www.bbc.com, 30 September 2022.

"Why Pipeline Leak is a Clear and Present Danger", *Times Global, Times of India*, 28 September 2022.

US Saudi Spar over decision to cut Oil Production", https://www.washingtonpost.com, 13 October 2022.

13

A Western Perception of the War

"War? Here in Europe? It is not possible."

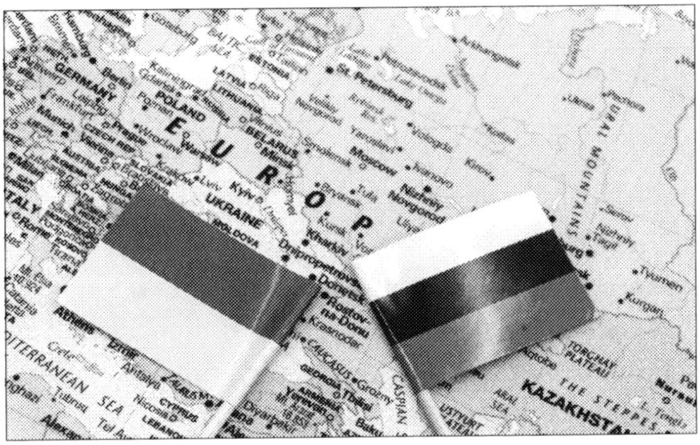

The war in Ukraine came as a surprise to many in Europe but it should have been expected. For several weeks, if not months, the news and social media were abuzz with the escalating tensions in the area. Many people thought that the Russian war gaming on Ukraine's borders was simply a show of strength rather than preparations for a full-blown war but anyone with a deeper understanding of the history and politics of the region could see the warning signs. Right from the beginning, both sides used the media to push their agendas to their people and the world. As 2021 comes to a close, tensions increased further and stories from Ukraine and Russia began to dominate the news. There was also increased political posturing by the governments of Europe and the USA in preparation for what was to come. Then on 24 February, the inevitable happened and Russian troops crossed the border into Ukraine.

The governments and Press across Europe continued pushing their sides of the narrative, reinforcing their own agendas, fears and positions to shape public opinion in support of their actions or inactions. As in any conflict, each side uses the facts that fit their story rather than giving a full and balanced account. History is littered with examples of how governments use propaganda to influence populations and of how their people blindly follow blindly with a herd instinct and fall in line with the political narrative. This conflict was no different than any other in this respect.

Across the United Kingdom (where I live) and Europe, Ukrainian flags began appearing on social media as profile pictures. Stories from the region, whether real or manufactured, began to feature in the news, in papers and all social media platforms. More and more Ukrainian flags began to be flown from public buildings, shops and homes in a groundswell of public sympathy and support. Very few people were taking the time to think about what was really happening; they simply followed what was being reported. The pressure on everyone, driven by the underlying anti-Russian sentiment to tow the official party line was palpable.

Stories were published with a clear bias one way or the other. Of particular note were the stories regarding the 'world's position' on the conflict. How could certain countries, India included, not join with those who were imposing sanctions on Russia for this obvious act of aggression? The feeling on the street was disbelief that these countries were not standing up to what was clearly an illegal act of war. Unaware of how joined up the world has become and how interdependent many things are, people were becoming more polarised in their views and opinions.

The media in Europe told the story of how Ukraine had been guaranteed sovereignty by Russia for the destruction of their nuclear arsenal. The Budapest Memorandum, signed by Russia, the United Kingdom and the USA prohibited any of the document signatories from threatening or using military force or economic coercion against Ukraine, Belarus and Kazakhstan. In conjunction with other agreements this resulted in these three countries giving up their nuclear arsenals. Clearly, Russia had breached this agreement and their invasion of Ukraine was therefore unlawful. Other aspects, including how NATO had promised never to expand after the breakup of the Soviet Union in 1991, but still moved 1,000 kilometres eastwards thereafter, rarely emerged.

There were stories of Russian atrocities on the civilian population of Ukraine, images of Russian weapons hitting hospitals, schools and buildings used by the local population. The media was full of images of Ukrainian refugees fleeing the conflict into neighbouring countries and campaigns were set up across Europe asking local families to provide rooms and support for Ukrainian refugees. The picture that appeared to be emerging was that it was the well-meaning public that were helping the fleeing refugees by taking families into their homes at their own cost while the governments provided the arms.

Support for Ukraine began to flow into the country as well in the form of both humanitarian supplies and weapons. Ukrainian soldiers began to receive training both inside and outside Ukraine and the Russian advances slowed. The threat of nuclear conflict also raised its ugly head as Russia warned the Western powers to keep away. In fact, as the war progressed and the possibility of a nuclear conflict became larger, the fears increased. An earlier generation had spoken of the fears they had of a nuclear holocaust, and how they had prepared themselves for it by making bunkers and shelters. Those fears resurfaced once again.

Daily reports illustrated the progress, or lack of progress, of the Russian advance, the brave fighting of the Ukrainian armed forces. Ukrainian farmers were shown towing Russian military equipment away from the battlefield. News footage showed Ukrainian soldiers using Western weapon systems with great success against the Russian war machine. The success of the Ukrainian counter-offensives in Kherson and Kharkiv was met with great jubilation and widely reported, but the discerning observer noted that the news quickly vanished—an indicator that perhaps the initial successes were not being followed up.

It was not just the nuclear fears that got the war closer to all of Europe. The energy war perpetuated by Putin got the war virtually into the homes of all Europeans. When the supply of gas was abruptly switched off in September, the prices of energy almost doubled, raising the costs of everything, from rents to transport to heating, and food. The rampant price rise was due not just to the cessation of gas supplies. Energy companies and providers also took advantage of it to raise the costs exorbitantly and make huge profits. As the calls to reduce energy usage increased, and street lights began shutting off, and central heating stopped, the realisation of a long, cold winter hit us.

The fact that the war was touching each one of us, perhaps divided most of the population into two camps—those who wanted an early end to the war, and a negotiated peace (even if it meant agreeing to Russia's terms) and those who insisted that the war should continue till victory and till 'justice' was delivered. As the winter progressed, the 'peace camp' definitely grew larger and more vocal.

This propaganda war was in truth equally being waged on the other side but only one side was visible in Europe. The Russian agenda was clearly being pushed by the media favourable to Russia. The corruption of the 'Fascist' Ukrainian government that the Russians sought to oust, and atrocities undertaken by the Ukrainians was widely promulgated on the 'other side'. To get a more balanced understanding of the conflict I did follow the Russian version of the conflict as best I could in news stories and social media. It did give me a very different perspective, counterbalancing the stories from the West, but again the Russian account was a very biased one, and it was difficult to get any sense of balance.

It is also interesting to note how a conflict such as this is taken advantage of. There has been significant news coverage of how effective Western weapons have been against the Russian war machine. Very effective advertising on a global scale for Western arms manufacturers! As arms sales form a large part of government revenues you can see why, despite the obvious need for secrecy on actual performance, stories of this nature are all over social media providing defence equipment manufacturers with a significant advertising platform.

The global economy and reliance on global supply chains has highlighted how a conflict can affect virtually every economy in today's connected world. It is almost impossible to use sanctions as a weapon today because of the dependence of countries on each other. Russia is a key supplier of many raw materials including titanium. Sanctions placed on Russia have had far-reaching effects across the globe and not necessarily where expected. For example, the aviation industry, struggling with the effects of COVID, has now been hit by a huge reduction in the supply of Titanium and the consequential issues this has raised are causing real problems throughout the industry. In this instance, sanctions are probably more damaging to the aviation industry outside Russia and its allies than to Russia itself.

Russia is also a major supplier of gas to the rest of the world. Europe imports just under half of its gas supplies from Russia, with Germany and Italy being the largest importers of Russian gas in Europe. These countries have effectively been rendered impotent in this crisis through the threat of constricted energy supplies and the effect that this would have on their economies. Europe is dependent on Russian gas supplies and as such Russia could turn off their economies if it decided to stop the flow of energy into Europe. The moral high ground so often put forward as a reason for European countries to act and defend the oppressed had clearly been superseded by economic drivers.

There is an interesting historic parallel to the Ukraine conflict of today but with the protagonists reversed. If we wind the clock back to October 1962, the USA were in the same position as Russia was prior to its invasion of Ukraine. In 1962, it was the fear of Russian missiles being based in Communist Cuba, uncomfortably close to the USA, that sparked the Cuban Missile Crisis. The Americans instituted a naval blockade of Cuba to prevent the delivery of these missiles and for a while the world was very close to a nuclear conflict. Fortunately, a way out was found that allowed both sides to save face and tensions de-escalated. Returning to today, Russia has been concerned about the encroachment of NATO on its borders and had issued warnings to Ukraine not to seek its membership. This warning, not overly publicised in the West, was ignored by both NATO and the Ukraine. The threat of NATO missiles on Ukrainian soil is potentially a key reason for the invasion of Ukraine by Russia. So, was NATO and the Ukraine partially to blame for this conflict? Put in this context, Putin had a very valid reason to invade Ukraine but one that had little exposure in the Western media.

Conflict in the modern age is still driven by the perceptions of what is right and wrong. These perceptions are manufactured via governments, people in power and the media who serve one side of the conflict or the other. Today, the advent of social media provides the ability to deliver targeted messaging into the homes of specific demographic groups globally and is truly worrying. Besides the actual conflict between Russia and Ukraine (and *ipso facto* the USA and NATO), a war of perception is playing out across Europe and much of the world. Perhaps, even when the war ends, the fault lines between Russia and the rest of Europe and the USA will have widened to the point beyond repair in the short term. The long-term impact of the war will ensure that tensions remain, and will shape Europe and the world for years to come.

* * *

Jason Hall is a widely travelled writer, photographer, historian and artist, based in London. He has over 35 years' experience in the defence industry. A keen watcher of the war, he has followed the conflict as it unfolded. These views are based on his personal observation of the war and its coverage.

14

THE GLOBAL IMPACT: A NEW WORLD ORDER

"The tragedy of the war in the heart of Europe will hit all of the world."

—Pope Francis

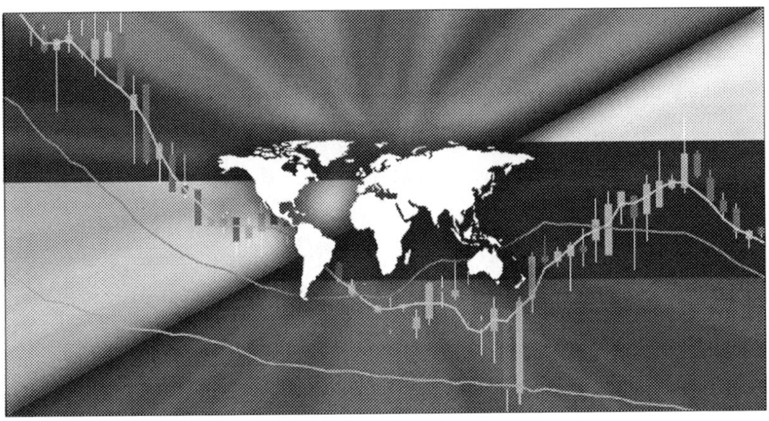

The invasion of Ukraine by Russia was certainly not unexpected. Right after the breakup of the Soviet Union, various assurances were given to Russia by the Western world, which were diluted systematically over a period of time. The likelihood of conflict between the two countries emerged as a distinct prospect as the two countries became more and more disenchanted with each other. The USA had been warning about the impending Russian invasion of Ukraine for months before the actual invasion. However, it was never anticipated that the war between the two would be so long drawn.

Before understanding the impact of the ongoing conflict, it is essential to understand as to why Russia invaded Ukraine and why the war has not progressed as expected by both the parties. Ukraine was expecting direct military help from the Western world, which did not materialise, while Russia expected a quick victory with no resistance. War, clearly, has returned to Europe and it does not help that the opening to this dark tunnel is nowhere in sight.

With certain vested interests probably wanting the conflict to continue, this war is goes on. It has seen the fiercest battles in Europe since the Second World War, and seen offensives and counter-offensives from both sides. Its impact has spread beyond Europe and across the world and, it in the long term it could shape a New World Order.

Economic Impact

The war compounded the effects of the COVID-19 pandemic which had derailed supply chains and economic growth in most parts of the world. Just as some countries were carving out plans for post-pandemic economic revival, Russia and Ukraine went to war, introducing new challenges to these plans and the economic wisdom that had designed them. The economic impact of the war has been covered in an earlier chapter. The war has precipitated a cost-of-living crisis everywhere: global inflation has skyrocketed, and the IMF has slashed global growth projections to 3.2 per cent, a far cry from the expected 6.1 per cent last year, and it is likely that Europe and the world will slip into a major recession due to the energy and food crisis caused by the war.

The use of energy and grain as a weapon has created shortages across the world, with precarious economies such as Turkey, Egypt, and Sri Lanka slipping into hyperinflation. Russia, the world's largest exporter of natural gas, second largest exporter of oil, and the third largest producer of coal; has simply switched off the energy tap in retaliation for sanctions, which brings in a very cold winter in most of Europe. More dangerously, the war in Ukraine has caused a world food crisis in nations as far off as Egypt, Ethiopia, and Sri Lanka. Even if energy and food supply resumes, it will take many years for the supply to stabilise, while food insecurity will impact half a billion people across the world.

Diminishing US Supremacy

The war severely dented the status of the USA, as the conflict followed the disastrous American withdrawal from Afghanistan. After the initial setbacks, when the Russians almost reached Kyiv and captured Kharkiv, Zelensky, the Ukrainian President, requested the USA for a No-Fly Zone over Ukraine. The fact that the USA did not do enough to help has helped reinforce the image that it is an unreliable ally. Although, US intelligence proved its reach by correctly forecasting the Russian invasion, it could not correctly assess the direction of major Russian thrusts, which came from north and south. Barring, intelligence, materiel, and moral support, the USA has kept out of the fray so far.

The US attempts to economically cripple the Russian economy were also not completely successful. Even its allies in the Europe were not on the same page about cutting energy imports from Russia. The US attempts to bring down the energy prices by persuading OPEC to boost production fell on deaf ears. The leaders of Saudi Arabia and the UAE even refused to take calls from the US President. America has tried to take the leadership position in the battle against Russia, but its influence seems to be waning, both in Europe and elsewhere. As America shifts its gaze to the vast blues of the Indo-Pacific and faces the ascendant Chinese dragon, its legitimacy is being increasingly challenged and the effects of the disastrous policies of President Trump are increasingly coming to the fore.

However, it will be premature to sound the death-knell of American power, notwithstanding how prescient it may appear at the moment. The USA has not only bolstered its aid to Ukraine, but has used the conflict to test its new weapon systems by providing them to Ukraine and training its troops to operate them. This has stymied the Russian advance after its initial success and at the moment the USA seems to have been successful in trapping Russia in the Ukrainian quagmire. The USA also helped in cyber-attacks on Russia and used its monopoly over the big technology to use social media for concerted information warfare against Russia. This led to public opinion across the globe moving away from Russia. This also brought thousands of mercenaries, mainly from Europe, to augment the Ukrainian forces. Russian actions have also galvanised NATO, but whether, the USA can use this crisis to regain its pole position in the world order remains to be seen.

Weakening of Russian Influence

Despite initial Russian successes, the war has exposed the chinks in the Russian armour. It was widely expected that Russia would attain its war aims in a week or so, which they have been unable to do in spite of months of conflict. Notwithstanding the rhetoric, the continuing war does not bode well for Russia. The Western sanctions have not had the effect that was expected, and after an initial shock, the Russian economy has managed to steer safe. However, the Russian economy contracted by 4 per cent and starved Russia of MNCs and foreign investment. Many Russian enterprises are bleeding after the exit of component suppliers in the aftermath of the sanctions.

Geopolitically, the war has kick-started the enlargement of the European Union, a process that had been stalled since 2013. The EU had been sitting on the bids of Moldova, Georgia, and Ukraine; but the war compelled it to accelerate the application stage of Ukraine's membership. Similarly, Russia's invasion has set in motion the very forces it had resisted: the eastward expansion of the NATO. The Russian offensive has actually pushed even Sweden, which had maintained its neutrality for centuries, and Finland, which was under treaty obligations, not to join any military bloc, to apply for NATO membership. Russia's legitimate concerns of having a cordon of non-interference in its near-abroad are now a pipe-dream. Russia's annexation of Georgia, Crimea, and now Ukraine have unsettled its Nordic neighbours and though Russia has sent no signals of its intention to attack them, Finland and Sweden will soon be part of NATO, bringing the alliance even closer to their shores. NATO member-states have now overwhelmingly inclined to increase their military budget and defence spending. In a way, the conflict has made NATO relevant again at a time when the alliance was weakening.

The conflict has not only pushed Ukraine into the European Union, but has also hardened the stance of East European countries against Russia. Almost all the CIS countries, which have traditionally been under Russian influence, have exhibited neutrality in this conflict and are drifting away from Russia. Kazakhstan refused to contribute troops for Russian aggression and has even halted all arms exports for one year. During the Caspian summit in June 2022 in Turkmenistan's capital, Ashgabad, Putin was the only visiting head of state who was not greeted with bread and salt. It is only Belarus, amongst all the former Soviet states, that has allied with Russia in its invasion, but as the war progresses, even their support seems to be dwindling.

Moreover, Russia's image has taken a beating from which it will take years to recover. The hope of amalgamating it with the Western world against the main threat—China—has dwindled, and instead it has become public enemy number 1. Its army too has lost its sheen. Russian military was perceived as the second most powerful force on the planet after the USA. However, its inability to attain their military objectives, and the immense casualties suffered, have exposed serious weaknesses in the once mighty military force. Their losses in the war have weakened it considerably, and left it vulnerable in the future.

European Dissonance

Europe is looking at a winter of discontent. Large areas of Europe are facing drought with rivers drying up, and a cold winter approaching. Public dissatisfaction over war-induced hardships is gnawing at the unity, and high costs of living, job crisis, and losses to trade and businesses are exposing schisms in European society. Although most Europeans are sympathetic to the Ukrainians cause, they are divided into those seeking a quick cessation of the war against those who want to see Russia defeated. The war is precipitating what may soon become the largest refugee crisis and certain countries—Poland, Romania, and Hungary—have accepted disproportionately more refugees than the others; public acceptance in these countries for Ukrainian refugees is slowly but certainly disappearing.

Despite accelerating the application process, it is unlikely that the road to EU membership will be smooth for Ukraine. The bureaucratic-bound process demands stringent conditions, including implementation of reforms that Ukraine will be unable to meet. The enlargement of the NATO too, may be counter-productive and will further alienate the current generation of Russians, sowing seeds for a more revanchist leader after Putin. It may serve no end, except probably to militarise Europe. This would consign the EU's agenda for peace and cooperation to play second fiddle to NATO's geopolitics.

The conflict has reversed the growing chasm across the Atlantic between the USA and its European allies, but NATO itself has been divided into two factions, Anglo-American and Franco-German. Germany, which has a 30-year-long robust trade relationship with Russia, faces a conundrum regarding its ties with Moscow, especially, its energy requirements, more than half of which comes from Russia. France has also supported a negotiated settlement to end the war in which Russia should not be humiliated, something which has drawn support from the Italian Prime Minister as well. The rift between the two factions is out in the open. The USA and UK are in favour of Ukraine prolonging the war, as their economies are not much affected by it as are many East European countries, who want Russia to be weakened considerably. On the other hand, France Germany and Italy do not believe that Ukraine has the combat capabilities to win the war. More significantly, their economies are extremely dependent on trade with Russia.

The war has destroyed any chance that Europe had of emerging as a powerful political entity not tied to the apron strings of the USA. It has brought into the open their differences and enhanced their dependence on the USA for their security.

China's Eminence

The long-drawn war and the Western opposition have drawn Russia closer to China to create a countervailing force to Western domination. The invasion of Ukraine was a part of Russia's efforts to reposition itself in global affairs and, irrespective of its losses and isolation in the war, a strategic partnership with China could change many equations.

Like elsewhere, America's loss of face is a point scored by Beijing. Analysts have extensively analysed the complex dynamics of a Russia-China marriage of convenience to synergise their capabilities against their common enemy. Both have found a common voice on NATO's eastward expansion and Taiwan. Not surprisingly, Beijing has thrown its diplomatic weight behind Moscow, illustrated by its repeated abstentions from UN resolutions condemning Russia. After Russia was banished from SWIFT, Chinese banks were quick to incorporate the MIR, the Russian alternative to the global financial messaging system. China has gone ahead to remove trade barriers on Russian wheat and energy exports. There is a mutuality in Sino-Russian ties, with China proving to be Moscow's economic and trade cushion, and Russia its security and energy guarantor. It is likely, though, that this relationship of convenience will witness China in the saddle and Russia slipping swiftly into Beijing's geostrategic orbit.

The USA appears to be focusing on countering China and Russia via Europe using the European Union and NATO to counter them. However, the European Union's engagement with China still continues. How the Russia-China partnership will impact Chinese engagement in Europe is yet to be seen. The USA had planned to confront China economically to retain its pole position in a unipolar world; how the Russian war plays out will impact US plans. During the entire gamut of the Cold War, the US strategy was to keep China and Russia apart, but they are now extremely close since the Sino-Soviet split in the 'Sixties, and, from all signs, are drawing still closer.

The conflict has not only diverted Western attention from China towards Russia, allowing China to pursue its own agenda unobtrusively. Fortunately, Russia's failure to achieve a quick success has deterred China from pursuing a similar agenda against Taiwan, but has increased its aggressive posture. Some analysts believe that the huge military aid pledged by the USA to Ukraine is intended to keep Russia entangled in a long unwinnable war, which by extension, could entangle China as well. The danger of this policy is that Russia and China (perhaps with Iran and North Korea) could well form an axis against the USA and the Western world which could divide the world irrevocably and even set the stage for a future global confrontation.

Hedging in Asia

The response of Asian states has been very interesting and a pointer to new emerging power equations. Most of them are hedging their bets and are unwilling to take sides. Many of them have withstood US pressure and are importing cheaper Russian oil and trading in local currencies. Both Japan and South Korea, which have close security ties with the USA and perceive themselves as part of a global alliance of democratic forces have condemned the Russian invasion of Ukraine. Japan has territorial disputes with both China and Russia while having a flourishing trade with both of them. Japan, after stopping its imports of Russian crude, resumed its purchase of Russian oil in July 2022.

The ASEAN has been fairly divided and has taken a fairly weak stance on the Russia-Ukraine war. Russia remains the major arms supplier and a significant trade partner for the region. At the same time, Ukraine remains a major supplier of raw materials to ASEAN countries and, consequently, the war will impact the region's post-COVID recovery. Barring Vietnam and Laos, which abstained, all the other countries of the region voted in favour of the first UN resolution. However, on the resolution to remove Russia from the UNHRC, almost all the countries abstained, with only the Philippines and Timor Leste voting in favour. Singapore, with a strong military and its own vulnerabilities, has been the most vociferous in its opposition to Russia. Malaysia, Indonesia, and Thailand have been relatively cautious in their public statements.

Most dramatic shifts in Asia have been seen in West Asia, a region that has traditionally toed the US line. Syria, a Russian ally, has overtly supported Russia, while other countries of the region have been reluctant to criticise Russia. Immediately after the war, however, the rulers of major oil-producing nations, namely, Saudi Arabia and the UAE declined to speak with President Biden. In a major embarrassment for the USA, the two leaders subsequently, took calls from the Russian President. The US requests to them to increase oil production to compensate for Russian oil have fallen on deaf ears. As a result of the war, West Asia is now far more geopolitically fragmented. Iraq is moving away from Iran, whereas Qatar has moved away from Saudi Arabia and the UAE is pursuing a more independent foreign policy. Turkey has emerged as a big factor in the region. Not only has it the military muscle to back its allies, it controls the traffic in and out of the Black Sea from where it is playing a major role in reviving the export of food grains from Ukraine. Many of the Arab countries are extremely dependent on Ukraine for their food security.

Though Iran is not directly affected by the conflict, it will emerge as a major game-changer in the future. In spite of Joe Biden's efforts to revive the Iran nuclear deal, Iran is still smarting from Trump's insult of scrapping the deal and would not trust the USA any longer. It is far more inclined towards Russia and China—and perhaps should the two come together in a anti-USA bloc—would be a willing partner. Similarly, Saudi Arabia, would be willing to hold its cards and then, depending on the flow of the war, choose sides. In either case, it speaks of an erosion of US influence to the benefit of both Russia and China.

In South Asia, the Russia-Ukraine crisis has had wide reverberations. The then PM of Pakistan, Imran Khan, arrived Moscow on an official visit on the day when Russia invaded Ukraine. (An act which he feels contributed to his subsequent ouster). Pakistan's economy has been deeply impacted by the war. Rising oil prices and shortages of wheat could impact its floundering economy by a full percentage point and increase hardships. Similarly, Bangladesh is also deeply impacted by the Russia-Ukraine conflict. Russia has been an important market for readymade garments from Bangladesh, while being a major source of wheat and millet supplies. Decreasing exports and a rising import bill, coupled with a disruption of supply lines due to the war and sanctions, have impacted its just recovering economy. Wisely, it has not overtly taken sides.

Implications for India

India is treading a delicate diplomatic balance in the Russia-Ukraine war. It has withstood US, European Union, and their allies' pressure to take a firm stand against Russia. India had been abstaining from voting on all UN resolutions on Russia till 24 August, when it voted against Russia for the first time in the UNSC when it, along with other UNSC members (China abstained and Russia opposed), invited Zelensky to address the UN body. Minister of External Affairs Dr. S. Jaishankar has been categorical in distancing India from the Russian-Ukraine conflict. India has been acting in its best strategic and economic interests, as it always should, pursuing its 'Strategic Autonomy', exhorting talks and negotiations to end the war and limiting itself to expressing concern on the humanitarian crisis unfolding. India has not issued any statements supporting or opposing the Russian invasion, nor has it supported any sanctions against Russia. India needs to have access to cheap energy, which Russia is providing to India, and that too at concessional rates and procured in favourable currency. Russia is the major arms supplier of India with 60 per cent of Indian weaponry being of Russian origin. The complex geopolitics of India's neighbourhood dictates that India maintains its friendship and influence with Russia. Russian influence in Afghanistan and Iran and India's interests in both these states require a closer relationship with Moscow.

In trying to remain neutral, India has maintained its healthy ties with Ukraine. It has ensured evacuation of its citizens from active war zones in Ukraine and has offered humanitarian aid to Ukraine. India has been affected by both rising oil prices and shortage of edible oil, which were primarily sourced through the Black Sea. More significantly, Russia's growing dependence on China and its 'Greater Eurasian Partnership' and 'No limit Friendship' are a matter of serious concern for India. More so, since India-China ties are frosty, to say the least.

India should not become a frontline state in a new Cold War between 'Democracies' and 'Authoritarian regimes of Eurasia' that is unfolding. Our interests lie in neutrality without being directly aligned to any bloc. India is already a member of the China-led Shanghai Cooperation Organisation (SCO), the Russia led RIC, Russia India China Forum, BRICS, as well as QUAD. Our long-term threat is from China, and yet, that can be best countered by having ties with all. The Russia-Ukraine conflict challenges Indian diplomacy, though we have staved off the pressure from Western nations quite well, and continued on the middle path that best suits our national interests.

Conclusion

The Russia-Ukraine conflict has redrawn fault-lines and unravelled schisms in domestic and international politics. It has mowed down years of calm and complacency in the EU and handed out a reality-check to NATO and the USA. War has revisited Europe after 70 years and the promise of European stability and unity has been shaken at its foundations. In many ways, perhaps, the war has brought the Cold War back to Europe and much of the world.

The war will also test the US position in the world order. Already shaky, it has tried to provide leadership and even succeeded in bringing in some measure of European and Western unity. The longer the war extends, the weaker the unity will become, as nations pursue their own self-interests, and perhaps could even go back to business-as-usual with Russia.

China, of course, could be one of the unlikely beneficiaries of this war. The theatre has shifted back to Europe after a brief re-focus towards the Indo-Pacific, leaving it free to pursue its own agenda there. With Russia leaning towards it, as a junior partner, in fact, it has succeeded in creating a power bloc that easily counters that of their perceived common enemy—the USA.

The war has also provided some sobering lessons for Russia. Putin is fast realising that his hopes of ensuring security to Russia and take it back to the position and authority of the erstwhile USSR, has rebounded. They may succeed in redrawing the map of Europe, but what they gain will definitely not be commensurate with the long-term loss of prestige and global image.

The war has affected global geopolitical and economic equations far more than is widely realised. The long-term impacts of shifting power equations could well shape a New World Order.

—Alok Bansal & Nidhi Bahuguna

* * *

Captain Alok Bansal served in the Indian Navy for 32 years, He is the Director, India Foundation, and also Secretary-General of Asian Eurasian Human Rights Forum. He has been the Executive Director of the National Maritime Foundation and worked with CLAWS and IDSA. He has authored and edited a range of books, articles, and research papers.

REFERENCES

"'No-Limits-Friendship' between China and Russia" *CNBC*, https://www.cnbc.com, 16 September 2022.

"Finland, Sweden propose to join NATO together in United Front", https://www.reuters.com

"How War in Ukraine is Reverberating across World Regions?" https://www.inf.org, 15 March 2022.

"India offers nuanced response to Changing Tides of War", *Frontline*, https://frontline.thehindu.com, 14 October 2022.

"Russia and Ukraine Conflict: Economic Implications," https://home.kpmg.com

"Russian Collateral Damage," https://carnegieendowment.org

"The Longer-term Impact of the Ukraine Conflict", https://csis.org

"The Paradox of Russia-China Relationship," https://carnegieendowment.org, 18 August 2022.

"The Ukraine War: A Resilience Test for the EU," https://www.institutmontaigne.org, 15 September 2022.

"Ukraine War Impact on the US Dollar, a Challenge for America", https://frontline.thehindu.com, 11 October 2022.

"Ukraine War: How has it changed Europe?" https://www.euronews.com, 24 August 2022.

"Ukraine War's Rising Cost on daily Russian lives," *Al Jazeera*, https://aljazeera.com, 17 March 2022.

"Ukrainian War: What is the Impact on the World Today?" https://www.rescue.org, 23 August 2022.

"What does the Ukraine Crisis mean for the US?" https://www.eiv.com, 12 April 2022.

"What is in our Interest: India and the Ukraine War," https://carnegieendowment.org, 25 April 2022.

"Why Ukraine wants a 'No-Fly-Zone'; why is NATO Reluctant?" https://indianexpress.com, 20 March 2022.

15

THE IMPACT AND LESSONS FOR INDIA

"The India Way, especially from now on, would be that of a shaper or a decider, than merely an abstainer."

—S. Jaishankar, External Affairs Minister

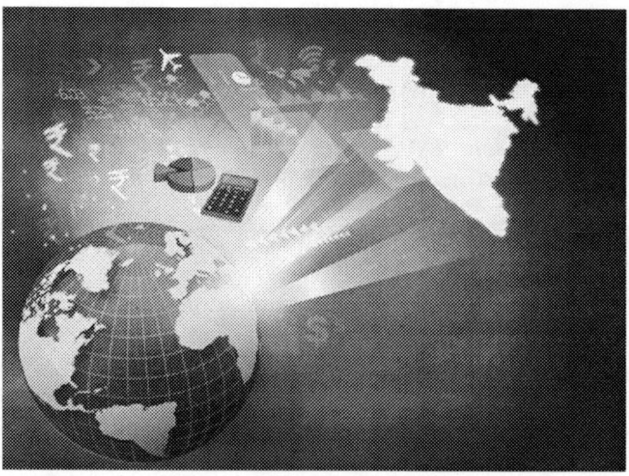

The Ukraine Conflict is a watershed of many sorts. It began as an attempted surgical occupation of Ukrainian cities by the VSRF—a Russian acronym for its Armed Forces—the world's fifth largest. It then dissolved into a series of grinding infantry—tank assaults and massive artillery duels. Ukrainian military resurgence (domestic resilience and ingenuity propelled by the support of more than fifty nations from across the globe) and some artful deception thereafter, enabled a dramatically successful counter offensive through Kharkiv, and also significant gains in the South which regained vital territory in a matter of days. By way of retaliation, Russia declared an annexation of occupied territories, partial military mobilisation and in order to sap national will—

brutal strikes on Ukrainian cities, population centres, power, energy and water supply grids with missiles and drones. Yet, on balance thus far, the conflict has been a saga of Ukrainian successes and Russian failures. Even as the conflict waxes and wanes—*the only certainty with regard to outcomes seems to be that Ukraine will not lose and that Russia is unlikely to win.*

Nine months of warfighting, however, have thrown up some valuable lessons in statecraft and warfighting. Some of these lessons are for immediate implementation, others could impact the Indian military in the longer term.

Ten key issues have been highlighted in the article.

The conflict has breached the long-standing norm against territorial conquest. The conversation has expanded from the 'democracy vs autocracy' debate to one that is now transfixed more broadly on expansionism, respect for international borders and exclusive hemispheres of great powers. The instrument of force has returned to the centre of the power calculus. Given the strategic uncertainties around India, the surest guarantor for peace in the coming decades will be a modern, joint, calibrated, technologically enabled, ready, instrument of force: each word indicative of deep military capacities that could take decades to create. Comprehensive and wide-angled resourcing of the military/defence apparatus is just as critical. Even though Russia and Putin have invested greatly in the more glamorous defence—industrial complex and strategic—military capacities viz, Strategic Rocket Forces, Ballistic Missile Submarines, Strategic Bombers, they seem to have neglected the fundamentals of combat—facets like realistic troop training, large scale formation exercises and orchestration of forces, combined arms manoeuvre, integration, leadership, combat ethos, organisational cohesion, logistics, et all. The overall combat readiness seems to have suffered leading to the dramatic unravelling (some might even say mauling) of the Russian military in Ukraine. *Crafting a war winning instrument in the highest state of readiness, should be a strategic priority and a key lesson for Indian statecraft to internalise.*

The conflict has accelerated major realignments in the global strategic landscape. The conflict has exacerbated the divide in the international order, and also given a harsh reminder that nuclear weapons continue to be a vital component in the strategic toolkit of nations. The re-assertion of a US led

West against Russian aggression, had brought about a greater sense of unity in Europe—which has surprised many by its resolve to navigate a winter of discontent and economic slowdown. Sanctions have also impacted the Russian economy and caused more than a thousand companies to close down and led to over a million, young, productive, Russians fleeing their own country. The sanctions on Russia have had such a debilitating effect, that it has had to turn to Iran and North Korea for combat wherewithal. NATO too, is deploying forward, enhancing weapon stocks, ramping up military grade production and building cutting edge capacities in defence. For the first time in the history of the European Union, President Ursula von der Leyen has committed to spending on defence from the EU budget. NATO supply lines providing aid to Ukraine have been impressive. Such western resolve may also have calming consequences on Chinese assertiveness. In a dual containment strategy; a Europe led containment of Russia and a US led containment of China, (out competing China is the new buzzword in American strategic lexicon) could well be in the making. It may also be useful to reflect on the fact that if a confrontation with Russia could be so cataclysmic, what would be the fallout of a possible confrontation with China—a country with a far larger economy and military might? The latter throws up some critical challenges and opportunities for India. *We may like to think through our prospective role as a critical balancer in the Indo-Pacific, to include the conception of imaginative pathways (of hard and soft power) to constrict and constrain China.*

Many paradigms regarding the 'character of war' have been upended and some myths shattered, most notable amongst them being that all-out war is a thing of the past and that modern conflict will be sharp and swift. The abiding lesson from the conflict for militaries worldwide, is to focus on wide spectrum preparedness, arduous slogs and long haul industrial and logistics sustainment. Comprehensive techno-strategic competitiveness, grey zone proficiencies, traditional warfighting, industrial era prowess, digital combat and nuclear capacities are all equally salient. We have to embrace all six domains equally. We must adopt emerging, disruptive, technologies. The nation that dominates the commanding heights of technology will be the strategic leader in the global pecking order. In India, there are a plethora of dual use technologies, ranging from chips to space to AI to IoT, that need to be developed and pursued. *Equally, even as the Indian military pursues technological sophistry to include digitisation, it must not be at the cost of neglecting the fundamental tenets of combat—that is the central lesson from Ukraine.* We will need to review our industrial capacities (manufacturing and surge) and military inventories for prolonged conflict, in terms of equipment, munitions and spares. We will need to upgrade existing combat platforms in terms of digital capacities: micro-electronics, active protection systems, situational awareness, star link type terminals, jammers, creation of data pipelines, big data, robotics and Internet of Things. *Priority to digital capacities over legacy platforms must get reflected in our defence budgets of the future.*

Nuclear capabilities are the ultimate guarantor of national security. The fact that Russia boasts of the world's largest nuclear arsenal (4,447 warheads) has been a significant factor in US and NATO planning and decision making. We, in India, need to understand the modern nuclear paradigm, and re-examine some of our doctrines—viz, that theatre/tactical nuclear weapons, do not matter. The Chinese nuclear posture is growing in size, precision and sophistication—it has a strategic nuclear force and a theatre (tactical) nuclear force and can strike counter value and counter force targets in India. The Chinese FOBS (Fractional Orbital Bombardment System) has introduced the possibility of an additional hypersonic, nuclear vector through space. The Chinese nuclear doctrine is based on ambiguity while the Indian system is based on transparency. The doctrine of nuclear ambiguity has several virtues. *It may be wise, to re-visit our nuclear posture, focus on modernisation of our nuclear triad, and refine processes and systems so that our nuclear deterrence holds its own in moments of grave crises.*

Precision strikes/long range fires merit deeper analysis. Precision strikes has been the dominant theme through the conflict. The game changing role of the HIMARs (critically during the Ukrainian counter offensives in targeting Russian reserves, headquarters, ammunition dumps, bridging systems and logistics in depth) or even the targeting of critical Ukrainian infrastructure by the Russians has demonstrated the importance of pin-point strikes in modern combat. Precision fire systems are the future. In India, our ordnance factories are geared to produce conventional munitions with little capacity to manufacture smart and precise munitions of the future. The critical role of long-range fires is also instructive. Ukrainian inability to secure its depth areas through air and missile defences and also respond to Russian long-range strikes in kind (on Russian cities and infrastructure) impacted its capabilities, especially in the early days of the war. The ability of HARM missiles integrated with Ukrainian MiG-29 platforms to disable Russian radars has been significant. The role of the Javelin in neutralising Russian tanks with precision has also raised questions about the efficacy of the tank. The Indian military needs to evaluate the entire challenge of precision weaponry and upgrade its capacities. In the light of Chinese long range strike capacities encapsulated by their Rocket Force, we will also need to re-visit the mechanics of our operational posture/ deployment along our Northern Borders—the need to fight distributed and dispersed to thwart the might of the PLA's Rocket Force is a challenge that we need to address. Do we have such a plan? What options does the Indian military have to offer to its political masters in in terms of long-range retaliatory strikes? These *critical posers merit deep thinking and the development of a sophisticated eco-system of precision and long range strike, is the need of the hour.*

The underwhelming performance of Russian airpower despite an overwhelming superiority in numbers across aircraft types, the absence of SEAD and DEAD and the broader inability of the Russian Air Force to establish air supremacy, merits deeper understanding and analysis, especially since our own IAF operates a largely Russian origin fleet with similar operational concepts. Was the underwhelming performance of the Russian Air Force due to ineptitude or on account of the changes in the nature of air wars? Perhaps, a bit of both. The Ukraine conflict has shown that the battlespace has shifted quite dramatically from the 'close kinetic' to 'beyond visual range (BVR)'. It has also underlined the fact that increased capacities in space, air and intelligence challenge the ability of conventional air forces to operate with relative freedom. The significant contribution of unmanned systems like the Bayraktar and Switchblade drones also needs to be acknowledged. In recognition of the role of Drones and UCAVs, the US INDO—PACOM is in the process of re-organising/re-structuring and embracing hybrid sea fleets (manned and unmanned). The US Air Force is taking similar steps to arrive at a hybrid force structure—a mixed array of manned and unmanned systems. We may consider revisiting the aerospace domain and find solutions within the Indian operational framework.

The role of chips and micro-electronics in the conflict has been emphasised like never before. It turns out that the formidable Russian military machine has come a relative cropper on account of a severe deficit in indigenous chips and allied micro-electronics. As many as 27 Russian military systems (from tactical radios to kill chains to high end missiles) and 450 micro components used by the Russian military in the Ukraine conflict have been subjected to Western sanctions; the resultant squeeze has led to declining levels of Russian combat effectiveness on the battlefield. Sanctions have emerged as a strategic asset in the toolkit of nations to neutralise adversary combat prowess. The lesson for the future is more than apparent—*self-sufficiency in micro-electronics will undergird the strategic autonomy of nations.* We in India will need, therefore, to work with renewed diligence and vigour to indigenise our capacities in micro -electronics and chips—and here, we have a long road to travel.

HR/Combat Culture/Leadership. *A glaring deficit in the Russian campaign, perhaps, has been the visible lack of generalship—the lack of imagination, creativity, critical thinking and the inability to speak truth to power—which came up at all levels.* Poor NCO leadership, an absence of trust and a feeble ethos led to lack of cohesion and reflected on Russian combat capacity. The lack of jointmanship was evident in the poor coordination between various thrust lines in the opening phase of the campaign. It has also led to glaring deficits in combined arms manoeuvre as also naval and air capacities being under leveraged / going unexploited. In spite of its qualitative and quantitative advantage, the Russian combat machine performed sub-optimally, that there is something grossly amiss with the manpower in the Russian military. The Indian military will do well to analyse this vital aspect of war fighting.

We need to re-think our relationships and re-visit the metrics of our strategic autonomy. Indian dependence on Russian equipment, logistics and spares especially, when much of that equipment is not sophisticated enough for the modern battlefield is a cause of great concern. We need to diversify our military inventories and consider the choices for Indian geopolitics as the Sino-Russian embrace deepens. With regard to our partnership with the USA, we need neither American blood nor treasure. What we need is access to American technology. Existing frameworks like the 2+2, the QUAD and the DTTI need to be exploited to provide access to American technological prowess and enable us to develop our own capabilities in emerging technologies.

Private sector competencies in terms of capacity aggrandisement and warfighting should be exploited. From Elon Musk's Starlink Terminals to the deployment of Microsoft Cyber Threat Identification Centres to the Javelins and HIMARs churned out by Raytheon/Lockheed Martin, the defining narrative is that, no single institution, least of all Defence PSUs, can deliver all the needs of the modern battlefield. *The expertise of the Private Sector must be exploited to provide the critical edge in military capabilities.* The lesson for India is obvious—unless we embrace and encourage private sector competencies with greater ambition, vigour and scale, our defence industry will continue to lag behind.

There are three other issues that arose in the conflict: the **failure of deterrence**, the power of **asymmetric balancing** and the utility of **enabling narratives/IW**. These have been covered in the earlier chapters in detail. A few elaborations, relevant to India, may be pertinent.

While there are some that view the Ukraine conflict as a Western provocation (on account of NATO's eastward expansion), there was a gross failure of Western deterrence. What weaknesses did the West radiate that got Russia to think (however mistakenly) that it was powerful enough for its instrument of force to prevail? Why did Western deterrence fail? We must dissect the causes and not repeat the same in the Chinese context. Viewing events through the adversary lens may be useful. In this regard this comment of Gary Killingworth, an Australian commentator on strategic affairs could be prescient, "China perceives India to be an ambitious, over confident, yet militarily powerful neighbour with whom it may eventually have to have a day of reckoning." Yet, China consistently denies that New Delhi is a potential rival, driven by the shrewd calculation that acknowledging India as an adversary would elevate its importance undeservedly and undermine China's position in Asia. India must therefore do all that it can to strengthen its integrated deterrence—by itself and in concert with partners—to prevent conflict.

Ukraine's heroic military response should also assure us that smart, asymmetric, balancing of Chinese power is possible. If China with a similar defence budgetary differential with USA as India's is with China, is causing great displacement anxiety in Pentagon, there is no reason as to why India should not cause equal discomfiture in Beijing. If we develop other facets like integration, civil-military fusion, technological innovation, doctrinal re-evaluation, developing imaginative operational concepts—asymmetric balancing of China is well-nigh possible.

Developing a narrative and leveraging information platforms to supplement the war effort (IW) is essential to win the war of perception. Ethnic Indians are global leaders in software engineering and information technology—we must mobilise such talent in service of the Indian state. In this regard we also need to develop capacities which will enable dominance of the electro-magnetic spectrum, because such leverage provides the foundational basis for information dominance. Our structures and capacities are weak in this regard—we will need to strengthen them significantly.

Conclusion

We have evaluated some of the scenarios of likely end-states earlier in the book, but here are a few additional thoughts. It is unlikely that the West will give the Ukrainians sufficient weaponry to allow them to take the fight to the Russians. It they do so, the Ukrainians could well re-take territory under Russian occupation to include Crimea, and that will take the war to a new dimension.

It is thus likely that the US led West, will carefully calibrate its military assistance to Ukraine—to ensure a Russian defeat while skilfully avoiding a Russian military humiliation—anything that could lead to escalation and ignite a direct Russia—US/NATO clash or even the use of tactical nukes.

There are other scenarios as well: a disintegration of the Russian military on the battlefield, as a consequence of regime change in Moscow, even a palace coup.

What is more likely however, is that the war terminates in an armistice and not necessarily in permanent peace. Ukraine could be given membership of the EU and NATO as also a substantive Western dole to re-construct the Ukrainian economy. **So, larger considerations quite de-linked from territorial ones, may provide the basis for conflict termination.**

* * *

Lt Gen Raj Shukla, PVSM, YSM, SM (Retd) has had a distinguished career in the Indian Army of over forty years. He retired as the General Officer Commanding in Chief, of the Army Training Command. He has also served as Director General Perspective Planning and as the Commandant of the Indian Army's prestigious Think Tank—the Army War College. He is presently a Member of the Union Public Service Commission. A prolific writer and speaker, he has authored numerous articles and publications, as also spoken widely on a range of contemporary strategic-military issues.

REFERENCES

"86 percent of Indian Military Equipment of Russian Origin," https://indianexpress.com, 22 Jul 2022.

"Biden's National Security Strategy Flags China as Top Threat," https://www.hindustantimes.com, 12 Oct 2022.

"How do India's choices in the Ukraine Crisis affect its Foreign Policy," https://www.orfonline.org, 24 Mar 2022.

"India can play big role to End Ukraine War," *Tribune India*, https://tribuneindia.com, 17 Oct 2022.

"India offers Nuanced Response," Frontline, https://frontline.thehindu.com, 14 Oct 2022.

"India's Military Dependence on Russia," https://www.institutemontaigne.org, 05 Jul 2022.

"NATO declares China as Security Challenge," https://www.aljazeera.com, 30 Jun 2022.

"Russia-Ukraine War: What all affected in India," https://www.businessworld.in, 18 Jun 2022.

"Russia-Ukraine War: What Impact can it have on India," https://www.businesstoday.in, 20 Mar 2022.

"Semi-conductor Crisis an opportunity for India," https://www.financialexpress.com, 10 Aug 2022.

"The Reason why there is a Global Semi-Conductor Shortage," https://glginsights.com

"The Ukraine Crisis has Impacted India," *The Statesman*, https://www.thestatesman.com

"What are China's Cyber Capabilities and Intentions," https://carnegieendowment.org, 01 April 2019.

CONCLUSION

It has been a year and the Russia-Ukraine War rages without any sign of an early conflict termination. With the success of the southern offensive and the re-capture of Kherson, the Ukrainians have had major success in both the South and the East. As the Russians try to hold on to the areas they claim as their own, they have consolidated themselves around the line of the Oskil River in the East and the Dnieper in the South, it is very likely that the front lines will stabilise around these lines, at least during the winter.

The pause which the winter brings could open the door for negotiations. After all the Ukrainians are in a better bargaining position now, and there will be pressure by Western allies to enter into talks. But with Putin maintaining that the captured territories are 'Russian' and Zelensky insisting that all occupied areas—including the Crimea—must be vacated before commencement of talks, there seems to be little common ground. A little pressure—subtly applied on both sides, by Europe, China, India, and other nations could help in bring the war to some kind of a conclusion—even if just a temporary reprieve. One solution that may be acceptable to both sides is that Russia moves back to its pre-February 22 boundaries, but is allowed to retain Crimea. Ukraine could be given European Union membership to formalise its alignment with the west, but in deference to Russia's legitimate security concerns, would not be given entry into NATO and formal guarantees of that would be provided to Russia.

This in a way, would address the immediate concerns of the two sides and give a measure of victory to both. The moot point remains of the immense havoc and destruction caused to Ukraine—estimated to be around $600 Billion. Who would recompense that? In the post-conflict scenario, a massive aid program, on the lines of the Marshal Plan that rejuvenated Germany after World War II, may have to be implemented to enable Ukraine to rebuild its shattered cities and infrastructure and get back to its feet.

Though a permanent and lasting peace is desirable, as of now, it does not seem to be on the horizon. The Ukrainian offensive has perhaps reached its culmination point and it is not clear if they have the capabilities to cross the river lines and dislodge the strongly entrenched Russians on the other side. There are also fears that the Russians may be drawing them deeper into a trap. With winter, large scale offensive movement will not be possible and that may freeze the front for a while.

As has been brought out earlier in the book, there are four ways in which the war could end; by a Ukrainian victory, a Russian victory, a stalemate, or the escalation into a broader war that draws NATO and other nations within it. As of now, it seems that a stalemate is the most likely situation. Like the Germany-Soviet Union war of 1941, this war could go on interminably, and continue into the next year or so. After all, the war between Russian sponsored separatists and Ukrainian forces in the Donbas, which began in 2014, went on for eight years and has still not ended. This present Russia-Ukraine war could become a wider manifestation of that, and extend interminably in a 'no-war-no-peace' scenario, punctuated by occasional cease fires and periods of violence.

It is still unclear as to how the war would end, but one thing is clear. With this the world has changed irrevocably. The war in Europe has deflected attention from China and its actions in Taiwan, Ladakh and the China Seas. Chinese actions may just intensify there, more so with the elevation of Xi Jinping as President for a third-term. It is also very likely that Russia would turn closer towards China. Both, in any case, see the US as a common enemy and share common threats and aspirations. That embrace would make Russia the much junior partner in the relationship, but would help counter its global isolation. Perhaps Iran, North Korea could also become part of the axis—which could signal the alignment of New World Order—one with China and its allies; the other with USA, the Western countries and their own allies.

How does India fit into the overall matrix? India has adopted a very nuanced stance in this conflict, based solely on national interest—exactly the way it should be. While maintaining close ties with Russia, and equally balanced support to Ukraine, our lines of communication with both are open. Also, the personal chemistry between Prime Minister Modi and the leaders of both countries is strong. This makes us ideally placed to be the 'honest broker' for some kind of truce. Should we be able to work that out, India's global standing will rise tremendously and it could cement its position as one of the poles of the emerging order.

Russia had begun the war hoping to assert itself in Europe and take on the mantle of the former Soviet Union as one of the global superpowers. It seems to have failed in that gamble. The war has weakened it, economically and militarily, and diminished its stature. Regaining that will be well-nigh impossible. Just like the invasion of Afghanistan weakened the Soviet Union irrevocably and led to its ultimate demise, this war has weakened Russia significantly and put paid to any hopes of it rising as a global power.

But one cannot help but compare the war with the events of World War II. That war too dragged on interminably from one campaigning season to the next. The War too, did not culminate with its end, but set off a chain of events leading to the Cold War, and proxy wars fought by the two superpowers in Korea, Vietnam and Afghanistan. This war could have similar consequences. Even when it ends, it could set into motion a chain of events, not just in Europe but across the world. It will have cascading effects, with an impact that will extend decades. So even when the war ends, it would not be the concluding chapter, but the start of the next.

INDEX